About Island Press

Since 1984, the nonprofit organization Island Press has been stimulating, shaping, and communicating ideas that are essential for solving environmental problems worldwide. With more than 800 titles in print and some 40 new releases each year, we are the nation's leading publisher on environmental issues. We identify innovative thinkers and emerging trends in the environmental field. We work with world-renowned experts and authors to develop cross-disciplinary solutions to environmental challenges.

Island Press designs and executes educational campaigns in conjunction with our authors to communicate their critical messages in print, in person, and online using the latest technologies, innovative programs, and the media. Our goal is to reach targeted audiences—scientists, policymakers, environmental advocates, urban planners, the media, and concerned citizens—with information that can be used to create the framework for long-term ecological health and human well-being.

Island Press gratefully acknowledges major support of our work by The Agua Fund, The Andrew W. Mellon Foundation, Betsy & Jesse Fink Foundation, The Bobolink Foundation, The Curtis and Edith Munson Foundation, Forrest C. and Frances H. Lattner Foundation, G.O. Forward Fund of the Saint Paul Foundation, Gordon and Betty Moore Foundation, The Kresge Foundation, The Margaret A. Cargill Foundation, The Overbrook Foundation, The S.D. Bechtel, Jr. Foundation, The Summit Charitable Foundation, Inc., V. Kann Rasmussen Foundation, The Wallace Alexander Gerbode Foundation, and other generous supporters.

The opinions expressed in this book are those of the author(s) and do not necessarily reflect the views of our supporters.

ECOLOGY
AND RELIGION

Foundations of Contemporary Environmental Studies
Series Editor, Peter Crane

Global Environmental Governance
James Gustave Speth and Peter M. Haas

Ecology and Ecosystem Conservation
Oswald J. Schmitz

Markets and the Environment
Nathaniel O. Keohane and Sheila M. Olmstead

Water Resources
Shimon Anisfeld

Coastal Governance
Richard Burroughs

ECOLOGY AND RELIGION

John Grim and Mary Evelyn Tucker

ISLANDPRESS

Washington | Covelo | London

ISLAND PRESS is a trademark of Island Press/The Center for Resource
Economics.

Library of Congress Cataloging-in-Publication Data

Grim, John.
    Ecology and religion / John Grim and Mary Evelyn Tucker.
      pages cm.—(Foundations of contemporary environmental studies)
    Includes bibliographical references and index.
    ISBN-13: 978-1-59726-707-6 (cloth : alk. paper)
    ISBN-10: 1-59726-707-4 (cloth : alk. paper)
    ISBN-13: 978-1-59726-708-3 (pbk. : alk. paper)
    ISBN-10: 1-59726-708-2 (pbk. : alk. paper) 1. Ecology—Religious aspects.
2. Ecology—Moral and ethical aspects. I. Tucker, Mary Evelyn. II. Title.
    BL65.E36G75 2013
    201'.77—dc23
                                                              2013010485
Printed on recycled, acid-free paper ∞

Manufactured in the United States of America

10 9 8 7 6 5 4 3 2

Keywords: religious ecology, environmental ethics, the Earth Charter, interreligious
dialogue, Christianity, Confucianism, Indigenous traditions, Hinduism, cosmology,
Ecumenical Patriarch Bartholomew

Contents

Acknowledgments

We take great pleasure in acknowledging the following people who read all or parts of the manuscript and offered advice and recommendations. We thank Brian Thomas Swimme for his unflagging encouragement, insights about organization, and the exchange of friendship over many decades. We are grateful to Lucy Wilson, Loyola Marymount University professor of English, who gave us careful readings and detailed editorial advice. Donald St. John, emeritus professor at Moravian College, offered invaluable comments on the entire manuscript. Leslie Sponsel from the University of Hawaii, who has done important work in spiritual ecology, was unstinting in his support and insightful in his suggestions.

We also thank our colleagues for their readings of various chapters: Donald Worster, Willis Jenkins, John Chryssavgis, David Haberman, Christopher Key Chapple, Harry Blair, Warren Abrahamson, Dan Spencer, Elizabeth Allison, Sam Mickey, Frederique Helmiere, Nancy Wright, Paul Draghi, and Ken Hiltner.

Many thanks to our Forum on Religion and Ecology team, Elizabeth McAnally, Christy Riley, and Russ Powell, for their steady support during the writing of this book. We express special gratitude to Matthew Riley, who gave excellent feedback on each chapter and the glossary. He offered his scholarly acuity generously, even after the birth of his daughter, Maia. It is our great pleasure to acknowledge the remarkable work of Tara Trapani, our forum administrative assistant and project director for *Journey of the Universe*. We are indebted to Tara for her attention to detail and organizational skills, especially in preparing this manuscript for publication.

We would also like to thank the editors of the Harvard volumes, along with Heather Eaton and James Miller and the Canadian Forum on Religion and Ecology, for their support of this work. In addition, our gratitude goes to our many conversation partners in these efforts at the outset some 20 years ago: Steven Rockefeller, Tu Weiming, Seyyed Hossein Nasr, Larry Sullivan, Donald Swearer, John Cobb, John Berthrong, Rick Clugston, Paul Waldau, Kimberley Patton, Duncan Williams, Ken Kraft, Norman Girardot, Chris Chapple, David Haberman, Vasu Narayanan, Hava Tirosh-Samuelson, Dieter Hessel, Rosemary Ruether, Fred Denny, Richard Foltz, Sallie McFague, Larry Rasmussen, and Tom Collins. We are grateful to so many scholars and activists who have helped to create this growing academic field over the years and engaged the forces of religion and ecology. Their efforts are evident in the research, teaching, and outreach shared at the annual lunch of the American Academy of Religion.

Our dean at the Yale School of Forestry and Environmental Studies, Sir Peter Crane, is a source of collegial support and continuing inspiration. Our former dean, Gus Speth, helped establish the religion and ecology master's program at Yale and invited us to do this book in the series he initiated at Island Press. Emily Davis, our editor at Island Press, has been remarkably patient throughout this process and gave helpful advice about the manuscript. Sharis Simonian has done a superb job with production of the book.

We have been supported in this work in religion and ecology by several foundations, to which we are most grateful: Germeshausen, Kendeda, V. Kann Rassmussen, Engelhard, and Kalliopeia. Susan O'Connor, Reverend Albert Neilson, Marianne and Jim Welch, Barbara Sargent, Barbara Cushing, Diane Ives, Margaret Brennan, Miriam MacGillis, Julianne Warren, Terry Tempest Williams, Kathleen Dean Moore, Nancy Wright, and Kimie and Tatsuhiko Watanabe have understood why religion, ethics, and spirituality matter in environmental issues. Their steady companionship has meant so much to us.

It is a special joy to thank our friends and long-term fellow travelers in the field of religion and ecology, Nancy and Dick Klavans and Marty and Wendy Kaplan. Without them this work would not have gone forward at Harvard, Berkeley, and Yale. Our gratitude knows no bounds.

We were pleased to use earlier versions of the manuscript with a class of students at Yale in the spring semester 2013 and at Princeton in the fall semester 2012. Their comments were perceptive and much appreciated. This book is dedicated to our students at Yale and beyond who have inspired us with their remarkable competence and boundless idealism. May they help promote the flourishing of the Earth community for future generations.

Introduction

Our Journey into Religion
and Ecology

A shared sensibility regarding our planetary future is spreading around the globe—from native peoples seeing their homelands altered by climate change to megacity dwellers in Asia suffering from the pollution of air, water, and soil. We are facing a critical moment in Earth's history as our overextended human presence is affecting every region of land and water. Our explosion from two billion to seven billion people in the last hundred years is exacting a toll on ecosystems and species.[1] Rapid industrialization, heightened consumerism, and unrestrained technologies are causing environmental degradation on an enormous scale. Indeed, not only are we altering the climate and radically undermining life, but we are also triggering a mass extinction of species.[2] What will future generations say of this diminished legacy of life? What can world religions contribute?

This book arises from our long journeys of experiencing and studying world religions, first in the Western Abrahamic traditions, then in Asian and Indigenous contexts. These journeys over many decades have involved an appreciation of the remarkable diversity of religions around the planet and their engagements with the rhythms and seasons of the natural world. Even when the forces of modernity have diminished human connections with nature, they persist in local festivals, in rites of passage, in parables and stories, and in subsistence knowledge related to food and healing practices. Amid the challenges of modernity and the growing environmental crises, the ecological dimensions of religions are becoming clearer. Scientists and policymakers, along with religious practitioners and scholars, recognize that religions have shaped views of nature for millennia. Simultaneously, religions themselves have been formed by their interactions with landscapes and the life therein. This is what we will explore as *religious ecologies*. Within religious traditions, narratives of the origin and unfolding of the universe are transmitted as *religious cosmologies*. Now both religious ecologies and religious cosmologies are being reexamined and reformulated alongside scientific understandings of nature and the universe.

Our personal stories as historians of religion illustrate the continual effort to understand cultural perspectives regarding nature in the world religions, with their liberating and limiting dimensions. We are clearly indebted to the immense contributions of environmentalists and scientists, many of whom are also motivated by the complexity and beauty of nature to study and protect it. Indeed, some have described environmentalism itself as a religious or spiritual movement.[3] Similarly, our understandings of nature have been broadened through the arts, music, literature, and anthropology. Often these voices, overtly atheistic or humanistic, manifest striking ethical and aesthetic connections to both nature and the larger cosmos. Now, religions are responding to the call of science and the inspiration of the arts to engage environmental issues. Also, scientists are involving the perspectives of religion in environmental studies programs and in discussions at professional meetings.[4] Our stories have led us to explore the interactions of ecology and religion.

The Influence of Asian Religions

In the early 1970s Mary Evelyn went to live in Japan and teach at a university in Okayama. This afforded her the opportunity to travel extensively throughout the Japanese archipelago, from Hokkaido to Okinawa, and to spend time in the ancient capital city, Kyoto. This was the beginning of her encounter with the East Asian religions: Shinto, Buddhism, Confucianism, and Daoism. This expanded her understanding of the very nature of religion as manifest in place-based rituals in both countryside and cities. She was intrigued by the worldviews, symbol systems, ethical codes, and ritual practices of these traditions—so different from anything she had known in the United States or in Europe. But it was not just the worldviews and their shaping of human behavior that fascinated her. It was also the carefully terraced landscapes of Japan and the role of rice-based agriculture in religious rituals. The cities, too, drew her in with their rich display of art and culture, temples and pilgrimage sites. The festival life was robust in both city and country, and she witnessed re-markable seasonal celebrations throughout Japan. This was the beginning of her understanding of religion as having ecological and cosmological dimensions. Her study of religion focused first on Zen Buddhism, and then in graduate school on Japanese Neo-Confucianism.[5] Both of these traditions have rich legacies of cultivating the human within the processes of nature.

Over the next four decades, Mary Evelyn traveled extensively through East and Southeast Asia. It was worlds apart from where it is today. The cities of Taipei and Bangkok, Seoul and Delhi were not yet polluted by an overabundance of cars and industrial processes. This was before rapid modernization overwhelmed these regions, engulfing everything in its path. In many cities, such as Beijing and Bangalore, this tsunami of modernization has wiped away whole sections. Building construction and the influx of cars have caused severe air pollution. The drive toward modern economic progress and the need for energy have resulted in the damming of rivers such as the Yangtze River in southern China and the Narmada River in western India. These are some of the largest engineer-ing projects the world has ever seen, submerging ancient archaeological sites and uprooting millions of people. The environmental impact was so great that in both cases the World Bank withdrew funding. The thrust to-ward economic growth and energy creation is ongoing in Asia and much needed to overcome poverty and improve standards of living. However, the external cost of environmental damage and human health problems are rarely factored into such growth. Such "progress" has had a price for people and the planet. Clearly, there are no easy solutions.

Along with staggering economic growth, the rapid deterioration of the environment in Asia in the last four decades is almost inconceiv-able. The force of industrialization in India and China is changing the face of our planet and putting enormous pressure on ecosystems all over the world as more than two billion people struggle to gain the fruits of modernity and the promise of economic progress. Indeed, Western industrialization was driven by a dream of improving human wellbeing and yet has resulted in unintended environmental consequences. Legiti-mate questions arise: Should people in Asia not have electricity and cars, clean water and computers? How can one balance economic develop-ment and environmental protection under these circumstances? How are modernization processes affecting Indigenous peoples? These are some of the most pressing issues of our global environmental crisis, involving the contested terrain of genuine sustainable development, environmental protection, equity, and eco-justice.[6] These questions give rise to the intersecting field of religion and ecology.

The Impact of Indigenous Traditions

John locates his orientation to religion and ecology initially in his youth in North Dakota, where the high plains afforded him many connections to the natural world. He grew up in a hunting family where wild game was killed and eaten with respect. In his undergraduate years at St. John's, a Benedictine university in Minnesota, he studied the religious traditions of the West. In 1968 John entered the History of Religions program at Fordham University to study with Thomas Berry (1914–2009). It was there that he met Mary Evelyn after she returned from Japan in 1975. While studying the world religions with Berry and working at a local hospital, he became intrigued with healing practices and chose to research shamanism among Central Asian and North American peoples.[7] It was during these studies that he connected religion and ecology.

From 1981 to 1982 John and Mary Evelyn lived in Japan while she was doing her thesis research. During that period in Asia, John traveled to study with shamanic practitioners in urban settings in Korea (*mudang*) and Taiwan (*dang-ki*). He also learned from Indigenous healers ("Black" and "White faced" shamans) in the forest uplands of northern Thailand and with T'boli healers (*tau mulung*) in South Cotobato, Mindanao, in the Philippines. These healers' interactions with land, plants, and animals drew on spiritual practices that were both ancient and innovative. It became clear that these shamanic rituals were not just the actions of individuals but were embedded in their families, communities, and local bioregions. His studies of place-based knowledge increasingly focused on traditional environmental knowledge for healing sickness, loss, and alienation.[8] In 1983 he began to visit and learn from Crow/Apsaalooka peoples in Montana, especially in relation to the Sundance ritual.[9] He also began visiting the Colville Reservation in Washington State to participate in and to research the Winter Dance among Columbia River Salish peoples.

John realized that the colonialist drives that had decimated many native societies were again imposing demands on Indigenous peoples and their homelands in various parts of the world. Industrial mining, logging, and biopiracy were encroaching on tribal peoples, ecosystems, and biodiversity. Increasingly, in both the developed and the developing worlds, extractive claims by multinational corporations were being justified by nation-states as supporting security needs, agricultural production, energy independence, and job creation. Loss of cultural practices often led to environmental degradation as outside economic forces exploited Indigenous lands, whereas preservation of language and cultural identity often led to resistance and survival. Seeing those close relationships being imperiled, he began to reflect on the significance and complexity of lifeways, the integrated character of religion and the environment in these small-scale societies.[10] John was able to experience these lifeways as living cosmologies in daily life and in ceremonials such as the Crow Sundance and the Salish Winter Dance.

The Legacy of Our Teachers

These various experiences in Asia and with Indigenous peoples led to years of research. We were fortunate to study with learned and engaged scholars who were deeply concerned with understanding the world religions: Thomas Berry at Fordham University, William Theodore de Bary at Columbia University, and Tu Weiming at Harvard University. Their interests were not simply in examining the world religions as relics of a historical past, but rather as living traditions that could contribute to the reconfiguration of modernity for the flourishing of the Earth community.

Figure 0.1 Adam Birdinground (Crow/Apsaalooka: Piegan clan) and Violet Medicine Horse (Crow/Apsaalooka: Big Lodge clan); Photo credit: John Grim

Thomas Berry (figure 0.2), a cultural historian, created a comprehensive History of Religions program at Fordham that attracted a lively group of students. He also directed the Riverdale Center for Religious Research, where for several decades we gathered for seminars and discussions along the Hudson River. Thomas passed on to us an abiding interest in the cosmologies embedded in the world religions, that is, the ways in which these orienting narratives bind peoples, biodiversity, and place together. In addition, he had a prescient understanding of the significant challenges of the growing environmental crisis.

Thomas began his studies of Asian religions when he traveled to China in 1949. On the boat to China he met Ted de Bary. Both were intent on studying the history, culture, and religions of East Asia. The two became lifelong friends. De Bary, a specialist in Neo-Confucianism, developed a robust Asian studies program at Columbia and explored the contribution of Confucianism to humanistic education and to human rights.[11] Mary Evelyn did her PhD in Japanese Neo-Confucianism at Columbia with Ted de Bary after finishing her master's degree with Thomas Berry.

Tu Weiming, also a scholar of Neo-Confucianism, collaborated with de Bary on human rights issues and with Berry on ecological concerns.[12] Weiming's essay "Beyond the Enlightenment Mentality" was a seminal inspiration for the religion and ecology conference series.[13] Here he suggests that the eighteenth-century European Enlightenment mentality needs to be reconfigured, drawing on its important contributions to modern democratic understandings of liberty and equality, but also integrating the spiritual perspectives and ethical insights of the world religions. His balanced approach affirmed the liberating aspects of the Enlightenment while also challenging the limitations of its rational and secular legacy, especially with regard to unlimited economic progress. Each of these teachers inspired us to begin a research project at Harvard that continues into the present at Yale.

The Harvard Conference Series on World Religions and Ecology: Collaborative Beginnings

From our concern for the growing environmental crisis, we organized a ten-part conference series on World Religions and Ecology. This was held at the Harvard Center for the Study of World Religions from 1996 to 1998. Because we realized that religions were necessary but not sufficient to solve environmental problems, the conferences included dialogue partners in the fields of science, economics, and policy. They were collaborative efforts over three years of some eight hundred scholars and

Figure 0.2 Thomas Berry (1914–2009); Photo credit: Lou Niznik

environmentalists who were seeking to integrate religious and ethical perspectives into environmental discussions.[14] To this end, they explored views of nature in the scriptures, rituals, and ethics of the world religions.

The conferences and the subsequent books included the Abrahamic religions (Judaism, Christianity, and Islam), the Asian religions (Hinduism, Jainism, Buddhism, Confucianism, Daoism, and Shinto), and Indigenous religions.[15] In October 1998 two culminating conferences were held in

New York at the United Nations and the American Museum of Natural History. It was at the United Nations that the Forum on Religion and Ecology was announced to continue the work of research, education, and outreach. The forum has grown to a network of some twelve thousand people and organizations around the world.[16]

All these Harvard conferences on religion and ecology were based on an acknowledgment of both the problems and the promise of religion.[17] In addition, the participants recognized the disjunction of religious traditions and modern environmental issues, noting the historical and cultural divide between texts written in earlier periods for different ends. They worked within a process of *retrieval* of texts and traditions, critical *reevaluation*, and *reconstruction* for present circumstances.[18] For example, how can the idea of "dominion" over nature in Genesis 1:26–28 be reinterpreted as "stewardship" of creation? They underscored the gap between theory and practice, noting that textual passages celebrating nature do not automatically lead to protection of nature. In fact, many societies with texts praising nature often deforested their landscapes.[19] Thus an important dialogue is still needed between environmental historians and historians of religions to explore the interaction of intellectual ideas and practices in relation to actual environmental conditions, both historically and at present.

The Harvard project identified seven common values that the world religions hold in relation to the natural world: reverence, respect, reciprocity, restraint, redistribution, responsibility, and restoration. There are clearly variations of interpretation within and between religions regarding these values, which have become latent in the modern period. As religions move toward a broader understanding of their cosmological orientations and ethical obligations, these values are being retrieved and expanded in response to environmental concerns. As this shift occurs— and there are signs it is already happening—religions are calling for *reverence* for the Earth and its profound ecological processes, *respect* for Earth's myriad species and an extension of ethics to include all life forms, *reciprocity* in relation to both humans and nature, *restraint* in the use of natural resources combined with support for effective alternative technologies, a more equitable *redistribution* of economic opportunities, the acknowledgment of human *responsibility* for the continuity of life, and *restoration* of both humans and ecosystems for the flourishing of life.

The Forum on Religion and Ecology: Field and Force

One of the outcomes of the conference series at Harvard and the on-going Forum on Religion and Ecology is the alliance of religion and ecology both in academia and beyond. A new field of study has emerged in colleges and secondary schools. Moreover, a new moral force of engagement has arisen within the religions from leaders and laity alike. Both the academic field and the moral force are contributing to a broadened perspective for a future that will be not only sustainable but also flourishing. Thus, ideas and actions cross-fertilize in the Forum on Religion and Ecology, sparking new forms of engaged scholarship and reflective action for long-term change. To assist this synergy, the Forum has developed a comprehensive website and an electronic newsletter promoting research, education, and outreach.[20]

Since 1997 the Forum has supported the first journal in the field, *Worldviews: Global Religions, Culture, and Ecology.*[21] The field has grown rapidly, with numerous monographs, articles, an *Encyclopedia of Religion and Nature*, and another journal.[22] In 1993 scholars of religions established a robust Religion and Ecology Group within the American Academy of Religion (AAR).[23] A master's degree program in religion and ecology was developed at Yale University between the School of Forestry and Environmental Studies and Yale Divinity School.[24] In addition to teaching in this program at Yale, we have organized numerous conferences[25] and helped create the *Journey of the Universe* project.[26]

For a decade we collaborated with evolutionary philosopher Brian Swimme to create a book, an Emmy award–winning film on PBS, and an educational series titled *Journey of the Universe* that narrates the epic story of the unfolding universe and Earth over 13.7 billion years. Within this evolutionary story humans emerged some two hundred thousand years ago and in the last two centuries have radically altered the ecosystems of the planet. This project draws on the perspectives of scientists, religious thinkers, and environmentalists to deepen our understanding of the evolutionary process and to outline new directions for the flourishing of life. *Journey of the Universe* was inspired by Thomas Berry's understanding of the need for a new comprehensive story integrating the sciences and the humanities in relation to the ecological and social challenges we are facing.[27]

Why This Book

Within academia, environmental studies programs are expanding beyond science and policy to include the humanities such as literature, history, philosophy, and religion. In the last 15 years, literary scholars have created the field of eco-criticism.[28] For some 40 years historians have developed a robust field of inquiry regarding the environment.[29] Similarly, since 1970 philosophers have shaped environmental ethics by formulating arguments regarding the intrinsic versus the utilitarian value of nature.[30] In the last two decades, scholars in religious studies, history of religions, philosophy, and theology are creating a field of religion and ecology with implications for policy and practice. Religion and ecology, as an academic field and as an engaged force, is growing rapidly, and there is a continuing need for new introductory texts.[31]

The potential of the field and force of world religions and ecology is varied and significant. These studies broaden our understanding of religion, ground cosmological awareness in relation to ecology, offer fresh insight into holism and particularity in nature, and engage environmental issues with an ethical ecological awareness. This book focuses on the question, "What is religious ecology?" This may be important as we begin to intersect religion with environmental problems such as climate change and biodiversity loss. Although we do not address these environmental issues directly, we are attempting to open up a multireligious context in which the contributions of the religions can be appreciated and made more efficacious. As we observe in chapter 1, we recognize that religions have both problems and promise. Religious adherents have contributed to both the cause of wars and their resolution through peacemaking. Religions can be conservative and unchanging as well as inspirations for change. This was true of the Quakers in the abolitionists' efforts to end slavery in the nineteenth century and of Jewish and Christian leaders in the civil rights movements to halt discrimination in the twentieth century. The potential of religions to infuse an ethical and spiritual dimension into the environmental movement is now emerging around the world.

In chapter 2 we observe that the theory and practice of religion embraces more than Western perspectives regarding monotheism, redemption, and salvation. This chapter explores religious ecology through the processes of orienting, grounding, nurturing, and transforming humans and their communities. Chapter 3 broadly outlines the historically complex views of nature that have unfolded in Western philosophy and religion, giving rise to new forms of ecological consciousness in the modern period.

The field of ecology, as discussed in chapter 4, is defined by various approaches to the study of nature, ranging from holism to biometrics, from aesthetic appreciation of nature to economic valuing of ecosystem services. By engaging in dialogue with the ecological sciences we can also gain understanding of how ecologists have both studied and valued nature. The relationship of these values in scientific ecology to religious ecology needs further examination.

Chapter 5 describes the emerging field of religion and ecology. It recognizes the complexity involved in retrieving, reevaluating, and reconstructing human–nature relations in our modern period without some understanding of what has traditionally shaped cultural attitudes and values. It suggests that religious ecologies may contribute to efforts to form ecological cultures for a sustainable planetary future.

In the four chapters that follow we explore examples of contributions being made to ecological thought and action from particular religious ecologies and their various environmental ethics. Chapter 6 focuses on the orienting quality of Greek Orthodoxy, chapter 7 concentrates on the grounding aspects of Confucianism, chapter 8 is concerned with the nurturing elements of the Winter Dance of the Salish people, and chapter 9 highlights the transforming dimensions of Hinduism. Chapter 10 illustrates how interreligious dialogue has emerged and is contributing toward a global ethics, as in the Earth Charter. The Epilogue points to the need for creating ecological cultures based on an integration of ecological awareness and ethical sensitivity toward the environment.

This book, then, is based on an exploration of religions as vehicles encouraging change of attitudes and values regarding the environment. We are not claiming that religions hold the answers to complex environmental problems, but that they can be active participants in finding solutions along with scientists, economists, and policymakers. Religions are thus necessary but not sufficient in themselves for achieving a sustainable future. For several decades scientists have been calling for dialogue with ethicists and theologians, religious leaders and lay people.[32] Scientists are asking them to join in the ecological work of conservation, mitigation, adaptation, and restoration—work that is more urgently needed than ever before.

This book suggests that by engaging in dialogue with the ecological sciences, religious practitioners can gain insight into how ecologists value nature for conservation, for aesthetics, and for ecosystem management. At the same time, scientists may appreciate how religions have woven humans into nature with rituals, symbols, and ethical practices. The relationship of science and religion may thus be enhanced in a shared concern for our planetary future.

Environmental Ethics across the World Religions

1. The natural world has value in itself and does not exist solely to serve human needs.

2. There is significant ontological continuity between human and non-human living beings, even though humans do have a distinctive role. This continuity can be felt and experienced.

3. Non-human living beings are morally significant, in the eyes of God and/ or in the cosmic order. They have their own unique relations to God and their own places in the cosmic order.

4. The dependence of human life on the natural world can and should be acknowledged in ritual and other expressions of appreciation and gratitude.

5. Moral norms such as justice, compassion, and reciprocity apply (in appropriate ways) both to human beings and to non-human beings. The well-being of humans and the well-being of non-human beings are inseparably connected.

6. There are legitimate and illegitimate uses of nature.

7. Greed and destructiveness are condemned. Restraint and protection are commended.

8. Human beings are obliged to be aware and responsible in living in harmony with the natural world, and should follow the specific practices for this prescribed by their traditions.

Source: Kusumita Pedersen, "Environmental Ethics in Interreligious Perspective," in *Explorations in Global Ethics: Comparative Religious Ethics and Interreligious Dialogue,* ed. Sumner Twiss and Bruce Grelle (Boulder, CO: Westview, 1998), 281.

1

Problems and Promise of Religions: Limiting and Liberating

Contrasting Characteristics of Religions

What might be the contribution of religions to the long-term flourishing of the Earth community? If Earth's life support systems are critically endangered, as the *Millennium Ecosystems Assessment Report* suggests; if climate change is diminishing the prospect of a sustainable future, as the *Stern Review on the Economics of Climate Change* observes; and if species are going extinct, as the *Convention on Biodiversity* notes, should not religions be engaged?[1] How might religions contribute to our present search for creating mutually enhancing human–Earth relations? What of their problems and their promise matter in an era when humans have so radically changed the face of the planet that geologists call our period the anthropocene?[2]

It is important to ask at the outset where the religions have been on environmental issues and why they have been so late to participate in solutions to ecological challenges. Have issues of personal salvation superseded all others? Have divine–human relations been primary? Have anthropocentric ethics been all-consuming? Has the material world of nature been devalued by religion? Does the search for otherworldly rewards override commitment to this world? Did the religions simply surrender their natural theologies and concerns with exploring purpose in nature to positivistic scientific cosmologies? In beginning to address these questions, we still have not exhausted all the reasons for religions' lack of attention to the environmental crisis. Although the reasons may not be readily apparent, they clearly require further exploration and explanation. It may well be the case that the combined power of science, technology, economic growth, and modernization has overshadowed traditional connections to nature in the world religions.

Examples from the past and present make clear that religions have both conservative and progressive dimensions; that is, they can be both limiting and liberating. They can be dogmatic, intolerant, hierarchical, and patriarchal. Or they can demonstrate liberating and progressive elements through compassion, justice, and inclusivity. They can be oriented to both otherworldly and this-worldly concerns—escaping into pursuit of the afterlife or affirming life on Earth.[3] They can be politically engaged or intentionally disengaged, illustrating the complex and contested nature of religion itself. They may invoke a higher spiritual power while still wielding immense political influence. Religious leaders may preach simple living while their institutions have significant material wealth. The nature of religion is complex and often ambiguous, especially in its institutional forms. Moreover, human failings have often led to disillusionment with religions. It is abundantly evident that religious leaders and followers have not always lived up to their highest aspirations.

However, in examining the varied characteristics of religions as liberating and limiting, both historically and at present, one observes that these characteristics are often more dynamically interwoven than rigidly separate. For example, being bound by tradition, religions have been the source of dogmatism and rigidity. They may favor orthodox interpretations of beliefs and practices. On the other hand, they can show flexibility and transformation over time, as with the Reformation in the sixteenth century that gave rise to Protestantism or with Vatican Council II that occasioned deep institutional changes in the Roman Catholic Church. The ambivalence of religions toward modernity has led to both the resistance and the embrace of change. Such resistance has contributed to the rise of contemporary fundamentalism in many parts of the world. Thus, some religious practitioners reject changing social and sexual values. However, openness to change has caused some traditions to advocate justice for the poor and oppressed, as in the work of Catholic Relief Services, World Vision, Buddhist Tzu Chi, and Green Crescent.[4]

Many adherents of religions have become embroiled in intolerant and exclusive claims to truth. Sometimes this has given rise to violence or religious wars, as in the Crusades from the eleventh to the thirteenth centuries and the Thirty Years' War in Europe (1618–1648). At the same time, religious traditions have taught peace, love, and forgiveness, even though imperfectly realized. The New York–based organizations Religions for Peace and the Temple of Understanding have been committed for more than 40 years to promoting peace through religious cooperation and dialogue.[5] The particularist claims to truth in the Abrahamic traditions have contributed to conflicts between Jews, Christians, and Muslims historically and at present. Although intolerance is not absent in East Asia, exclusive truth claims are rare because interaction and syncretism between religions are so common. For example, in Ming China (1368–1644) the phrase "the three traditions are one" was used to describe the mutually enhancing syncretism of Confucianism, Daoism, and Buddhism. This idea extends into the contemporary period across East Asia. In modern Japan one comes of age with a Shinto ritual, practices Confucian ethics in the family and society throughout one's life, and is buried with a Buddhist funeral.[6]

Although most religions have been hierarchical and patriarchal, in the last century they have been increasingly responsive to demands for equity, fairness, and justice. Much more still needs to be done for full inclusivity with regard to issues of race, gender, and sexual orientation. This is especially the case with religious teachings in certain traditions regarding women's roles and reproductive health. However, the expansion of human and civil rights has been an achievement of the last one hundred years, spurred by both secular and religious concepts of justice. Religions have been able to effect change as they participated in this expansion. Now the challenge is to extend this sense of responsibility and inclusivity not only to other humans but also to nature itself.

Religions are often seen as having otherworldly preoccupations, namely concern with salvation in heaven or in an afterlife. Using this logic, some would argue that exploitative treatment of the world is insignificant. These religious practitioners even suggest that degrading the environment hastens the end of Earth and the return of a transcendent paradise.[7] Other religious groups have actively denied the critical nature of environmental problems or rejected the science of climate change.

However, most religions value this world and have rituals that weave humans into the rhythm of natural cycles. This is a dimension of what we would describe as religious ecology. The incarnational and sacramental dimensions of various religions illustrate this-worldly emphases and concerns. That is, Christianity centers on a belief of divine entry into material reality both in the historical person of Jesus and in the Cosmic Christ embedded in the universe. Hinduism has a similar understanding with the idea of *avatar* in figures such as Krishna, an incarnation of the supreme deity, Vishnu. Confucianism and Daoism in East Asia have a strong affirmation of this world, for example in the metaphysics and practices of *ch'i* (*qi*), or life force.[8] *Ch'i* is cultivated in the body movements of *t'ai chi* (*taiji*) and *chigong* (*qigong*) and in the healing practices of traditional Chinese medicine. Most religious traditions have developed sacramental sensibilities in which material reality mediates the sacred. This is evident in the use of water for baptism and oil for anointing the sick. Moreover, offering food and flowers and lighting incense and candles are widespread sacramental practices in the world religions. Such affirmation of material reality is a critical component of our valuing nature.

The role of religion in relation to political power is complicated and highly contested. Religions have often been invoked for destructive or grandiose political ends. During World War II, the Japanese government used Shinto to legitimize their nationalist ideology and the sacrifice of kamikaze pilots. Similarly, after years of severe persecution of the Russian Orthodox Church, Stalin called on ecclesiastical authorities to support the "Great Patriotic War" against Germany. Religions themselves have wielded political power for less than noble ends and often with violent results. This is evident historically in religious wars and with various fundamentalisms present in the world today. The role of politically conservative Christians has been especially pronounced.[9] The Hindu nationalist Bharatiya Janata Party (BJP) is influential in India, as is the Likud Party in Israel.[10]

Yet we can also invoke the powerful examples of nonviolent change, as with Russian writer Leo Tolstoy (1828–1910), who was influenced by the Sermon on the Mount. Tolstoy understood the Christian imperative to live more simply as a call to a personal asceticism, particularly for the affluent. In addition, Tolstoy's pacifism and nonviolence were inspired by a desire for peace as he understood the Gospels. In this quest, his influence extended to Mahatma Gandhi (1869–1948) (figure 1.1) and Martin Luther King (1929–1968). Gandhi also drew on the *Bhagavad Gita* in Hinduism, on *ahimsa* in Jainism, and on the Christian Gospels for his understanding of nonviolence. Similarly, Martin Luther King studied Gandhi, as well as the Christian tradition, in developing his own form of nonviolence. Both Gandhi and King were able to effect political and social change with the spiritual power of their convictions and with the example of their own lives when confronted with violence, hate, and derision. Demonstrations of nonviolent protests were evident in 2011 with the "Arab Spring" and the "Occupy" movement, which highlighted alienation caused by lack of political voice and striking social and economic inequities around the world. Both of these movements manifest the fluid and hybrid character of nonviolent action.

Moreover, there is an emerging movement of religious communities who are participating in transformative social change based on principles of environmental justice. For example, the United Church of Christ

Figure 1.1 Mahatma Gandhi (1869–1948); © Copyright GandhiServe

Commission for Racial Justice published the first statement on environmental justice in 1987, called *Toxic Wastes and Race in the United States*.[11] The Sierra Club has documented many of these efforts in a report called *Environmental Justice and Community Partners*.[12] They are trying to assist in the creation of new attitudes and practices for the flourishing of the Earth community. This is the challenge to which world religions can make a constructive contribution along with environmentalists and secular humanists working toward a sustainable future.

Many people outside the institutional religions share moral values and spiritual attitudes toward the environment. This includes a broad range of environmentalists, nature writers, artists, musicians, secular humanists, and others. Such values and attitudes are more common than has been previously recognized. Indeed, E. O. Wilson and Stephen Kellert claim that *biophilia*, or affiliation with the natural world and its biodiversity, is intrinsic to humans.[13]

In summary, we need to acknowledge the problems and the promise of religions as their perspectives and values are integrated into the academic field of environmental studies and the public force of environmentalism. Within academia it is becoming clear that cultural, ethical, and religious worldviews must be included in the study of environmental issues. This is because historically religions have had ecological dimensions in the ways they ground human communities in the rhythms of nature. This is what we are calling *religious ecology*. An understanding of the roles of religious ecologies is resurfacing with some intensity in an era when religions were thought to be diminishing with the rise of secularization.

The Persistence of Religions

This brief overview of the problems and promise of religion brings us to a consideration of its persistence in the modern period despite the apparent secularization of Western societies. After World War II, secular humanism grew in Western Europe along with the philosophies of existentialism, postmodernism, and deconstruction. Religions were perceived to be ideological, outdated, ineffective, or oppressive. In short, many came to feel that the deleterious aspects of religions had surpassed their achievements. Moreover, there was a widespread assumption among some European and American academics that religions would wither away as modernity brought the benefits of intellectual enlightenment, economic growth, and technological progress.[14] Rationality would replace religion; God was proclaimed to be dead.[15] In this view, sociologists of religion predicted both rejection of religions in secular societies and adaptation by the religions themselves to secularization.[16] This was influenced by Max Weber (1864–1920), who recognized the disenchantment of the modern world through loss of the mythic dimensions of religions.

However, contrary to this thesis regarding the promise of secularization, interest in religion has not declined.[17] For example, the prohibition of religion under Communist regimes did not lead to its demise as many had predicted. Rather, it has flourished in Russia since the breakup of the Soviet Union in 1989 and in China since religious freedom was established in 1981. Moreover, fundamentalisms around the world (Jewish, Christian, Islamic, and Hindu) are stronger than ever in the face of the challenges of modernity.[18] The search for exclusive claims to truth is a response to the relativism of secular values.

The 1979 Iranian revolution signaled for many a turning point regarding the role of Islam in politics and society. With the overthrow of the secular political leader, Shah Mohammed Reza Pahlavi, and the return to Iran of the religious leader, Ayatollah Khomeini, an Islamic Republic was established under *shari'a* law.

In the Christian West some of the groundwork for this resurgence of religion as neo-orthodoxy was laid in part by Protestant theologian Karl Barth (1886–1968). He rejected both Renaissance humanism and the Enlightenment's rational understanding of scriptures and institutional religion. Barth reaffirmed the transcendence of God and the exclusive truth of Christianity. He regarded its biblical scriptures as the primary source of revelation. Thus, other sources of revelation, such as nature, were ignored.[19]

Religion in its various forms, then, has proven to be persistent and forceful despite the increasingly rapid spread of modernization and industrialization around the world. Noted contemporary philosophers such as Jürgen Habermas and Charles Taylor are exploring the implications of this phenomenon. Taylor has acknowledged that the modern secular age is not simply an era of unbelievers. Instead, our contemporary period offers a pluralism of options, which are steadily widening. This results in the emergence of hybrid and fluid identities so that the secular and the religious are not exclusive categories but often mutually interpenetrating.[20]

In recent years, in his lectures and writing Habermas has stated emphatically that philosophy cannot afford to ignore religion. He cites the limitations of the Enlightenment in its singular reliance on reason. The result in the modern period, he observes, is that practical reason is experiencing its own deficiencies in adequately responding to "a modernization threatening to spin out of control." His suggestion is that "enlightened reason unavoidably loses its grip on the images [symbols], preserved by religion, of the moral whole—of the Kingdom of God on earth—as collectively binding ideals." He further notes that such reason "no longer has sufficient strength to awaken, and to keep awake, in the minds of secular subjects, an awareness of the violations of solidarity throughout the world, an awareness of what is missing, of what cries out to heaven."[21]

Habermas is deeply concerned that the moral grounds for transforming the economic globalization that is devouring Earth's ecosystems are unavailable or inadequately stated in secular philosophy alone. He is keenly aware that something important is missing in our efforts to halt the social and ecological ills engulfing the planet. The rational appeal to justice, to enlightened self-interest, or even to the well-being of future generations does not alone seem to have had a significant effect or traction. Religious sensibilities, symbol systems, and ethical concerns are also needed in all their diversity. We will briefly mention some aspects of religious diversity in their historical, dialogical, and ecological forms.

Diversity of Religions

Our understanding of world religions has increased exponentially since the rise of the study of the history of religions in the late nineteenth century.[22] Consequently, even how we define religion has expanded. Although the field of history of religions in its early phases has been criticized as sometimes being orientalist and as imposing patterns of interpretation from a Western perspective, its long-range contributions have been indispensable to the understanding of the diversity and complexity of world religions.[23] Several types of diversity can be identified within religions. By appreciating such diversity we can also recognize that the response of religion to environmental concern will be immensely varied around the planet because these traditions are far from univocal.

First, there is *historical, cultural, and theological diversity* within religious traditions that developed over time in different geographic contexts. For example, there are important variations in Judaism between Orthodox, Conservative, and Reform movements, in Christianity between Catholic, Protestant, and Orthodox denominations, and in Islam between Sunni and Shiite groups. Hinduism has a great variety of schools of thought and practice, ranging from dualism, separating the divine from creation, to nondualism, or monism of unity between creation and the divine. In addition, even in the yogic schools of Hinduism there are practices that are devotional (*bhakti*), intellectual (*jnana*), and physical (*hatha*) that accentuate cultural and theological differences. Moreover, Buddhism arose in India and spread to Southeast Asia and north across the Silk Road through Central Asia to China, Korea, Japan, and Tibet over a thousand-year period. This geographic expansion gave rise to strikingly different cultural and religious expressions of Buddhist thought and practice across Asia. This same variation is true for Islam, which spread from the Arabian Peninsula to Central and South Asia and North Africa. Islam in Saudi Arabia today is quite different from what has developed over time in Indonesia, the largest Muslim country in the world.

Second, there is *dialogic and syncretic diversity* within and between religious traditions. This point does not override the historical and cultural diversity but adds another level of complexity. Interactions between traditions, through trade and dialogue, can lead to new syntheses of religions. This economic and religious exchange often results in new religious expressions that can be described as syncretic, the commingling of religions, or hybrid, the fusion of religions into new forms. Such creative expressions occurred in Celtic Christianity and in the Americas when Indigenous peoples adapted Christianity into local settings, such as the devotion to Our Lady of Guadalupe in Mexico. In East Asia there is an ongoing dialogue between Confucians, Daoists, Buddhists, and Indigenous practitioners that has resulted in various kinds of syncretism. In Japan Buddhist temples manifest this hybridity, for example, with the Shinto gateways (*tori*) placed at the entrance.[24] Moreover, because of such syncretism, new religious movements such as Kurozumikyō and Shinji Shumeikai have flourished in Japan since the nineteenth century.

Third, there is *cosmological and ecological diversity* within and between religions. Religious traditions develop unique narratives, symbols, and rituals to express their relationships with the cosmos as well as with local landscapes.[25] These are what we would call religious cosmologies and religious ecologies. In Daoism and Confucianism religious cosmology celebrated the interpenetration of the microcosm of the self with the macrocosm of the universe that found expression in both intellectual thought and embodied practice. For example, the Celestial Masters School in Daoism perceived the body as an energetic network of breathings-in and breathings-out that expresses basic dialogical patterns of the cosmos.[26] In understanding this process, individuals open themselves to the inner meditative landscape that represents a path of organic unity with the cosmos. Similarly, in Confucianism humans cultivate themselves in relation to the cosmos, linking the virtue of humaneness or love (*jen*) to the fecundity of the natural world (*sheng-sheng*). *T'ai chi* movements align the practitioner with the natural and celestial world. In Vedic Hinduism the identity of an individual with the "great person" of the universe is evident in the *Mahapurusa* hymn. Also, Hindu yogic meditational practices can bring a practitioner into alignment with the sun, moon, stars, and elements.[27] All these are examples of religious cosmologies.

Ecological diversity is evident in the varied environmental contexts and bioregions where religions have developed over time. For example, Jerusalem and Israel are in a larger sacred bioregion where three religious traditions, Judaism, Christianity, and Islam, have both shaped and been shaped by the environment. However, the formulation and expression of symbol, rituals, laws, and communal life within these religions in relation to urban, piedmont, hill country, and desert settings of the bioregion are historically quite different.[28] Among Indigenous peoples, interactions with the environment not only were a significant basis of their religious practices but were themselves highly differentiated. For example, the Kurok, Hoopa, and Yurok peoples of northern California recognized particular spiritual presences in sacred mountains, from the foothills to the summit, that determined where a person was sent for a vision quest.[29] These complex interactions illustrate that religions are not static in their impacts on the environment. Rather, throughout history they have interacted in myriad ways with natural settings. These are what can be called religious ecologies based on varied worldviews, ritual customs, and ethical practices.

Selected Perspectives on Nature in the World Religions

For the most part, the worldviews associated with the Western Abrahamic traditions of Judaism, Christianity, and Islam have created a dominantly human-focused morality. Because these worldviews are largely anthropocentric, nature is often viewed as being of secondary importance. This is reinforced by a strong sense of the transcendence of God above nature. On the other hand, there are rich resources for rethinking views of nature in the covenantal tradition of the Hebrew Bible,[30] in sacramental theology, in incarnational Christology, and in the vice-regency (*khalifa Allah*) concept in Islam. The covenantal tradition draws on the legal agreements of biblical thought that are extended to all of creation.[31] Sacramental theology in Christianity underscores the sacred dimension of material reality, especially for ritual purposes. Incarnational Christology proposes that because God became flesh in the person of Christ, the entire natural order can be viewed as sacred.[32] The concept in Islam of humans as vice-regents of Allah on Earth suggests that humans have particular privileges and responsibilities regarding creation.[33]

In Hinduism, although there is a significant emphasis on performing one's *dharma*, or duty in the world, there is also a strong pull toward *moksha*, or liberation from the world of suffering, or *samsara*. To heal this kind of suffering and alienation through spiritual discipline and meditation, one turns away from the dynamic world of change (*prakriti*) to a timeless world of spirit (*purusa*). Yet at the same time, there are numerous traditions in Hinduism that affirm particular rivers, mountains, or forests as sacred. Moreover, Hindu theology engages the world as a creative manifestation of the divine in the concept of *lila*, the creative play of the gods. This same tension between withdrawal from the world and affirmation of it is present in Buddhism. Certain Theravada schools of Buddhism emphasize withdrawing in meditation from the transient world of suffering (*samsara*) to seek release in *nirvana*. On the other hand, the Zen gardens in East Asia express the fullness of the Buddha-nature (*tathagatagarbha*) in the natural world. In recent years, socially engaged Buddhism has been active in protecting the environment in both Asia and the United States.[34]

The East Asian traditions of Confucianism and Daoism remain, in certain ways, some of the most life affirming in the spectrum of world religions.[35] The seamless interconnection between the divine, human, and natural worlds that characterizes these traditions has been described as an anthropocosmic worldview.[36] There is no emphasis on radical transcendence above the world, as there is in the Western tradition.[37] Rather, there is a religious cosmology of a continuity of being stressing the dynamic movements of nature through the seasons and the agricultural cycles. This organic cosmology is grounded in the philosophy of *ch'i* (material force), which provides a basis for appreciating the profound interconnection of matter and spirit. To be in harmony with nature and with other humans while being attentive to the movements of the *Dao* (Way) is the aim of personal cultivation in both Confucianism and Daoism.[38]

However, it should be noted that these nature-affirming worldviews have not prevented environmental degradation (such as deforestation) in parts of East Asia in both the premodern and the modern periods. In the premodern period centralized governments sanctioned the exploitation of resources, often unaware of ecological limits. In the modern period this degradation is caused by the rapid rate of modernization, driven by population explosion, increased consumption, and the need for new energy sources. In both cases the disjunction between religious ideas about nature and the use of nature is evident. It is also important to note the undermining of Confucianism in the twentieth century, especially its conscious destruction during the Cultural Revolution (1966–1976) under Mao Zedong (1893–1976).

In a similar vein, Indigenous peoples, while embracing religious cosmologies, have in some instances caused damage to local environments through such practices as swidden agriculture.[39] This kind of farming can be sustainable under traditional conditions with fewer people and with subsistence rather than market economies. In more recent times, this ecological degradation is often caused by pressure from neocolonial and multinational intrusions for extractive industry. It is also caused by changing patterns of human migration resulting from climate change. Nonetheless, most Indigenous peoples have religious ecologies in which environmental ethics are embedded in their worldviews. This is evident in the complex reciprocal obligations surrounding life taking and resource gathering that mark a community's relations with the local bioregion. The religious views often seamlessly interwoven into Indigenous lifeways involve respect for the sources of food, clothing, and shelter that nature provides.[40] Gratitude to the Creator and to the spiritual forces in creation is at the heart of most Indigenous traditions. The ritual calendars of many Indigenous peoples are carefully coordinated with seasonal events such as the sounds of returning birds, the blooming of certain plants, the migrations of animals and fish, and cosmological events such as the shift of the constellations and the changes of the moon.[41]

The Force of Religious Environmentalism

The perspectives of the world religions on nature have given rise to new movements of religious environmentalism that are now evident around the world. This illustrates that religions are flexible, able to change from within and to spark change from without. Religions are not simply static institutions with fossilized traditions, despite caricatures by antireligionists and others. They have inspired movements for social change, as the Quakers did in the nineteenth century with the abolitionist movement. In the nineteenth century Catholic social teachings addressed workers' rights, drawing on Pope Leo XIII's encyclical, *Rerum Novarum* (1891). With regard to women's rights, Katherine Bushnell (1856–1946) and others challenged readings of the Bible that denigrated women. From the 1960s the Southern Christian Leadership Conference led the movement for civil rights for African Americans. Indigenous peoples have also marshaled their religious symbol systems to oppose colonial rule, such as the Mau-Mau uprising in Kenya and in the Cargo cults of Papua New Guinea. Moreover, the massive demonstrations against dam building have been led by the Kayapo in Brazil and by the Mapuche in Chile. In each case, as the ethical issues became more evident, shifts in attitudes and behavior occurred.

This is the promise as religions enter their ecological phase, bringing to light the moral dimensions of the environmental crisis. In the last dozen years every major religious tradition has developed statements on the environment, eco-justice offices have been organized, and both clergy and lay people are becoming more active.[42] In the Christian community, the World Council of Churches has been working on issues of "peace, justice, and the integrity of creation" for several decades.

Many of these Christian communities are also addressing climate change.[43] The Evangelical community has been speaking out on the adverse impact of climate change on the poor.[44] The Ecumenical Patriarch Bartholomew organized a symposium in Greenland in 2009 to highlight the effects of melting glaciers. In 2001 the U.S. Catholic Bishops issued a statement on global warming, titled *Global Climate Change: A Plea for Dialogue, Prudence, and the Common Good*.[45] Pope Benedict XVI, Pope Francis I, Katharine Jefferts Schori, and other religious leaders have spoken about climate change as a critical moral issue.[46] The Interfaith Power and Light movement in the United States has sparked thousands of churches and synagogues to change their light bulbs, conduct energy audits, and reduce their carbon footprints.[47]

Religious environmentalism is evident in the numerous statements and resistance movements of indigenous peoples around the world. This is apparent in the "Fraser River Declaration" and the "Calgary Statement of Solidarity" among First Nations peoples protesting the efforts of the provinces of Alberta and British Columbia in Canada to transport tar sands oil in pipelines across their territories. Similarly, the "Idle No More" movement that began in Canada "revolves around Indigenous Ways of Knowing rooted in Indigenous Sovereignty to protect water, air, land and all creation for future generations."[48]

What is striking is that scientists and policymakers are encouraging the involvement of religious communities in environmental issues. This began more than two decades ago with the *Joint Appeal on Religion and Science* in 1991 and the Union of Concerned Scientists' *Warning to Humanity* in 1992.[49] The first declares that "the cause of environmental integrity and justice must occupy a position of utmost priority for people of faith." It continues: "We pledge to take the initiative for interpreting and communicating the theological foundations for the stewardship of Creation in which we find the principles for environmental action." The latter announces, "A great change in our stewardship of the earth and the life on it is required if vast human misery is to be avoided and our global home on this planet is not to be irretrievably mutilated." This statement concludes with a call for moral response: "A new ethic is required—a new attitude toward discharging our responsibility for caring for ourselves and for the earth." More statements have ensued that seek to foster cooperation between science and religion in the service of the larger Earth community.[50]

Conclusion

Religions can no longer be dismissed as irrelevant in environmental discussions, nor can they be seen as ineffective. More than 90 percent of the world's peoples have an affiliation with a religious community, whether nominally or in practice. There are billions of religious adherents around the world; indeed, there are more than a billion Muslims, Hindus, Christians, and Confucians, respectively (see figure 1.2 for further detail). Religions are the largest nongovernment organizations in the world and have significant institutional resources, infrastructure, and financial assets. They claim allegiances that transcend differences of race, class, gender, and nationality. The United Nations Environment Programme has recognized this potential for decades and has been working with religious communities since 1987.[51]

But it is not only for pragmatic or instrumental reasons that religions are important players in environmental issues. There is moral force and spiritual energy at the heart of these traditions, which can contribute to long-term solutions to our complex environmental problems. For millennia religions have fostered worldviews, symbol systems, ethical teachings, and ritual practices in religious ecologies that have the potential to inspire human imagination and evoke human energy for life-enhancing transformation. Such inspiration and evocation are now being harnessed for environmental and social change; moreover, they hold the promise of long-lasting transformation.

As wellsprings of cultures and civilizations, religions have historical experience in articulating sacred–human relations, guiding human affairs, and orienting human–Earth interactions. Religions are repositories of knowledge about these three dimensions of human experience. In this work we focus on the third dimension, human–Earth interactions. In this respect, religions have functioned as religious ecologies that situate humans in the dynamic world of nature. Because of their evocation of symbolic consciousness, they have enduring influence in shaping cultural values and attitudes toward nature and toward other humans. Religious ecologies are thus critical in the transition to a sustainable future at this juncture in the life of the planet.[52] As many would agree, the transformation of attitudes and values is a missing link in creating ecologically concerned cultures at present and into the future. To understand this potential more fully, we will explore the nature of religious ecology. But first let us turn to the broader question: What is religion?

World Religions: Estimated Number of Adherents and Approximate
Percent of World Population.

Religion	Adherents (millions)	Percent of World Population (percent)
Indigenous religions (by region)	405	5.8
Asia-Pacific	365	5.0
Middle-East and North Africa	1	<0.1
Sub-Saharan Africa	27	0.3
Europe	1	<0.1
Latin-America and Caribbean	10	0.1
North America	1	<0.1
East Asian traditions: Confucianism, Daoism, Buddhism, Shinto, and folk traditions	1,566	22.3
Buddhism in South East Asia	231	3.3
Jainism	4	0.1
Hinduism	1,000	14.0
Sikhism	23	0.3
Zoroastrianism	3	< 0.1
Judaism	14	0.2
Christianity	2,200	31.3
Islam	1,600	22.8
Bahá'í	7	0.1
Other	36	0.5
Total	6,858	97.7

Sources:
    The Pew Forum on Religion and Public Life. 2012. *The Global Religious Landscape.*
The Pew–Templeton Global Religious Futures Project. http://www.pewforum.org/
global–religious–landscape.aspx
    Major Religions of the World Ranked by Number of Adherents, Adherents.com,
http://www.adherents.com/Religions_By_Adherents.html
    Gardner, Gary T. *Inspiring Progress: Religions' Contributions to Sustainable Development.*
A Worldwatch Book. New York: Norton, 2006.
    Total 2012 World Population = 7,018 million (according to United States Census
Bureau, International Database). http://www.census.gov/population/international/data
/idb/region.php

Figure 1.2 Demographics of world religions; Credit: Matthew T. Riley

2

The Nature of Religious Ecology: Orienting, Grounding, Nurturing, Transforming

Approaching the Question, What Is Religion?

This is clearly a complex question, especially when we are increasingly aware of the challenges of religious pluralism, ethnic diversity, and multiculturalism. Religion is immensely varied—personally, socially, culturally, institutionally—and continually changing over time. Indeed, there are as many misunderstandings of religion as there are descriptions of religion. Most popular definitions of religion are based on concepts from Western Abrahamic religions of God and salvation. These concepts are presented as universal but generally do not take into account the varied kinds of religious sensibilities in the world religions, especially from Asian or Indigenous traditions. For example, most Asian religions do not require belief in a Creator God or in redemption and salvation outside this world. Some, such as Buddhism, are considered to be atheistic, or not focused on God or supernatural beings. Thus, religious sensibilities are not limited to monotheism or even theism.[1] Nor does religion preclude the inner experiences associated with spirituality. The cultivation of a spiritual path has extensive roots in religious traditions and beyond.

Spirituality involves a search for the sacred in which humans experience their authentic being in relation to a larger whole.[2] This usually entails a spiritual journey of self-cultivation to overcome fragmentation, loss, and suffering.[3] Spirituality is often associated with the mystical traditions that are present in all the world religions as repositories of contemplative insight and practice. There are guides on this path in the form of teachers, scriptures, prayers, rituals, and ascetic disciplines. The spiritual journey situates the human in a larger context so that the small self is seen in relation to the great self. This is what many authentic spiritual journeys aspire to.

For some time in the contemporary period there has been a vibrant interest in spirituality that is seen in contrast to religion, which is identified more with dogmatic institutional forms.[4] This is not always an accurate description of religion that has been sustained and reshaped by the spiritual struggles of adherents throughout history. Currently, the quest to experience spirituality in nature is growing, and various expressions are emerging. The contributions of these nature spiritualities are significant, especially in responding to the environmental challenges we are facing.[5] This book acknowledges the appeal of such spiritualities and suggests that there are important forms of ecological spiritualities within the religious traditions and outside of them.[6]

Among scientists there are also a wide range of religious and spiritual sensibilities involving both nature and a sense of the sacred, evident from Galileo Galilei (1564–1642), Johannes Kepler (1571–1630), and Isaac Newton (1642–1727) into the present.[7] Albert Einstein, who said he did not believe in any god, expressed his convictions in this way: "To know that what is impenetrable to us really exists, manifesting itself as the highest wisdom and the most radiant beauty which our dull facilities can comprehend only in the most primitive forms—this knowledge, this feeling, is at the center of true religiousness. In this sense, and in this sense only, I belong in the ranks of the devoutly religious men."[8] Einstein is not alone in these thoughts, as many scientists manifest a religious attitude without god.[9]

Indeed, Ronald Dworkin (1931–2013) observes, "A religious attitude involves moral and cosmic convictions beyond simply a belief in god: that people have an innate, inescapable responsibility to make something valuable of their lives and that the natural universe is gloriously, mysteriously wonderful."[10] In its comprehensive form, then, religion involves a recognition that there is something beyond the human that cannot be named or defined fully yet calls us to value life, both its material constituents and its living expressions.

If we broaden our definition of religion to include the world religions, we acknowledge religion is not simply a belief in a transcendent deity, nor is it just a means to an afterlife. Indeed, belief or faith is not even a primary category for many Asian traditions as it is in the Abrahamic traditions of the West. This is certainly the case for indigenous traditions as well as Confucianism and Daoism, which are generally more interested in this-worldly practices than belief in a deity or supernatural power.[11] Western religions often emphasize orthodoxy, that is, defined doctrines or teachings. However, orthopraxy, or a concern with normative practices, is as significant as orthodoxy in both Western and Asian religions.[12] Moreover, practice is central to all Indigenous traditions. Religions in the West are also closely identified with ethics regulating human behavior. But even ethics, as critical as they are, do not encompass all aspects of religions in their myriad manifestations across cultures and history. Rather, religions rely on stories and symbols for guidance and rituals and meditations for individual cultivation and community vitality.

Religions thus manifest themselves not simply in texts, statements, and doctrines, but even more directly in practice.[13] The variety of religious practices and rituals around the planet is such that it is difficult to define religion from a single conceptual framework. Moreover, central to these practices and rituals are symbols and symbolic knowing.

Symbol Systems and Symbolic Knowing

For many, religion draws on complex symbol systems that mediate between human imagination and practice. This was the view of anthropologist Clifford Geertz (1926–2006), who understood religion as that which draws together a worldview replete with symbols and an ethos of behavior that creates coherent ways of living. He defined religion as: "(1) a system of symbols which acts to (2) establish powerful, pervasive, and long-lasting moods and motivations in [individuals] by (3) formulating conceptions of a general order of existence and (4) clothing these conceptions with such an aura of factuality that (5) the moods and motivations seem uniquely realistic."[14] Geertz saw that the symbol systems of religion evoked symbolic knowing, thus opening the world to interpretation and meaning. Just as Geertz understood that symbols transmitted in cultural practices have a profound effect on human consciousness in shaping worldviews, so also symbols give expression to empirical knowing.[15] Symbolic knowledge is also used in mathematics and science to communicate and interpret concepts. Greek philosopher and mathematician Pythagoras brought together symbol systems that are now considered separate ways of knowing in science and religion.

Such symbolic ways of knowing emerge out of earlier linguistic and conceptual faculties of the human. Indeed, symbol-making capacities have distinguished humans from our evolutionary origins. Other animals also use symbols, but not in the same way that humans do, to create complex cultures and manage the forces of nature.[16] As early humans awakened to their embeddedness in nature, they created cultural and religious forms that wove them into the natural world—its daily and seasonal cycles and its capacity to nurture with food and water. In this sense, humans developed a rich symbolic consciousness in relation to nature. This was the matrix for meeting the sacred and for articulating this experience in story and ritual.[17] This is evident in the upper Paleolithic cave paintings in France and Spain, such as Lascaux and Altamira, made some 30,000 years ago.[18]

Religions have held in trust and passed on symbolic ways of knowing that are shared with art, music, literature, and poetry. Thus, cultures can be understood as systems of symbolic knowing. Such symbolic knowing is different from, but complementary to, discursive reasoning, or empirical knowing, used in disciplines such as science, law, and economics. Philosopher of history Giambattista Vico (1668–1744) proposed a separation of symbolic knowing in his disagreements with René Descartes (1596–1650). He argued that philosophical critique and analytical geometry provided natural science with tools of understanding and calculation. That is, these ways of knowing could measure what extended into space. However, Vico argued that such philosophical critique could not adequately understand the power of poetry and epic story. Similarly, the quantitative analysis so prized by Descartes and the mathematical community could not interpret imagination or memory that also assist humans to learn, to reason, and to discover truth.[19]

In his *Philosophy of Symbolic Form*, Ernst Cassirer explored this difference. He posited a type of perception of the "facts of culture." This arose from what he called the shared "expressive perceptions" of culture that generate particular forms of symbolic knowing. This differs fundamentally from the empirical knowing of the natural sciences, what he described as "thing perception." For Cassirer, these two forms of perception are primary and cannot be reduced one to the other. However, they can be seen as complementary. Moreover, as neuroscientist Antonio Damasio argues, each form evokes a feeling disposition regarding the nature of objective reality. That is, there is an emotional dimension of knowing in cultural and scientific forms.[20]

To know a tree, for example, from both a biological and a cultural perspective enhances our understanding of the tree. As Yale paleobotanist Peter Crane illustrates in his book on the ginkgo, these ancient trees have become closely associated with the religious traditions of East Asia that value their antiquity, beauty, and endurance.[21] In addition, he points out how scientists have carefully studied the biological complexity, medicinal and nutritional uses, and survival of the ginkgo for more than 200 million years. These varied ways of knowing, scientific and cultural, augment our appreciation of the ginkgo.

Moreover, a feeling dimension for the tree can be seen as a kind of valuing or cherishing. This is expressed by Princeton biologist Steve Pacala, who speaks of his approach to the study of nature as having three phases: "I observe, I cherish, and I conceptualize."[22] He describes this as a pathway for creative scientific discovery that is inspired by an aesthetic sense of beauty and order in nature. Those who express an artistic, ethical, or religious perspective regarding nature's value generally share this sense of cherishing.

For Cassirer, empirical perceptions in science gave rise to scientific laws that extend throughout physical space and time. Cultural knowing constituted for him an analogous type of intersubjective knowing transmitted within various societies. Thus, art, music, architecture, and belief systems could evoke shared expressive perceptions that would be transmitted over centuries. As these "cultural objects" became interpreted and reinterpreted, they could acquire a trans-historical and trans-local cultural meaning and depth of feeling.[23]

For example, food in the world religions becomes a source of symbolic reflection. Rice in Asian cultures is revered as nourishment and is a life-giving symbol for many communities. Similarly, bread in Christian and Jewish religions is central to ritual practices that symbolize historical events, such as the Last Supper and Passover. Corn in Meso-American Indigenous traditions symbolizes the profound interconnection of human communities to the living world, and corn pollen is widely used in ritual. In all these cases, the expressive and detailed knowledge of planting and harvesting of rice, wheat, and corn becomes a focus of symbolic consciousness and celebration.

Such symbolic knowing for the human does not embrace any single interpretation or arrive at a final conclusion. This is because symbols evoke multivalent knowledge and emotions. Humans continue to interpret cultural objects, compounding them with new historical meaning. The potential for adapting and reinterpreting religious symbols as life enhancing or life diminishing is part of the work of theologians, rabbis, imams, and scholars of other traditions. In addition, there is the possibility for an artistic object or place to become universally significant for a community that reinterprets this significance over time. This is evident in the dynamic roles of religious centers such as Jerusalem, Rome, or Mecca in the West and Benares (Varanasi) in India, Chang-an (Xi'an) in China, or Kyoto in Japan.

Religion has been a vehicle for this kind of symbolic cultural knowing and reinterpreting into the present. With secularization, some traditional religious symbols have lessened in import and impact in the modern world as film, media, and the arts have become more pervasive. However, secularization has not diminished the influence of religion in modernity, as is evident in the religious revival in Russia and China and its endurance in the United States. Nonetheless, with the dominance of science and technology, nature has been increasingly divested of symbolic value in favor of instrumental and economic value. This devaluing of nature has been driven in large measure by an economism that reduces symbolic knowing to the marketplace of materialism.[24] Thus, nature is seen as primarily for human use and exploitation.

Some have claimed that the emphasis in the Abrahamic traditions on spiritual transcendence has also led to the desacralization and abuse of nature.[25] In addition, as Max Weber observes, the rise of an elect community contributed to a capitalist mystique that valorized an ethic of monetary accumulation and devalued nature.[26] Admittedly, then, symbols may be invoked and rationalized to increase community cohesion or to ensure community control. The multivalent character of symbols makes them vulnerable to manipulation of political power and the evocation of authentic transformative spiritual power.[27] Discerning between the two is an ongoing challenge for religious leaders, scholars, and practitioners.

In the modern period we appear to have reached something of an impasse with regard to our understanding of the role of nature in human symbolic expression, both religiously and scientifically. Although we have a better understanding of how nature works ecologically, we lack an integral orientation to nature that recognizes our symbolic and biological interdependence. *Homo sapiens* emerged in planetary history with symbol-making capacities that were in direct relationship with the natural world.[28] Human linguistic, narrative, and ritual practices co-evolved within nature's rhythms and restraints. In our later development, our symbol-making capacities functioned, as Cassirer points out, in cultural and scientific modes that came to be seen in the modern period as separated from each other and often from nature.

In summary, the study of religion often emphasizes the cognitive, linguistic, and symbolic capacities of the human, as we have seen in the contributions of Geertz and Cassirer. However, in exploring religious ecology the context is not simply that of human knowing but of nature itself. The question for religious ecology, then, is what is the role of religion within the processes of Earth and its ecosystems? This is different from sociology of religion, anthropology of religion, philosophy of religion, history of religion, or theology where religion is examined through a human lens. It is also different from geography of religion, which puts less emphasis on cosmology.[29] Religious ecology draws on various modes of symbolic awareness and explores human–Earth relations. The shared symbol-making capacity that has endured in world religions can be a source of wisdom in restoring the central value of nature in sustaining humans and shaping cultures. This is the role of religious ecology, which is an important element of religion that needs further exploration, definition, and study.

Defining Religious Ecology

Religious ecologies are ways of orienting and grounding whereby humans, acknowledging the limitations of phenomenal reality and the suffering inherent in life, undertake specific practices of nurturing and transforming self and community in a particular cosmological context that regards nature as inherently valuable.[30] Through cosmological stories humans narrate and experience the larger matrix of mystery in which life arises, unfolds, and flourishes. These are what we call *religious cosmologies*. These two, namely religious ecologies and religious cosmologies, can be distinguished but not separated. Together they can provide a context for navigating the tragic and chaotic dimensions of life. They may evoke energies for encountering these inevitable challenges, thus transforming destructive experiences into creative possibilities for new beginnings.

Human communities until the modern period sensed themselves as grounded in and dependent on the natural world, especially the very elements of life. Thus, even when the forces of nature were overwhelming, the regenerative capacity of the natural world opened a way forward. Humans experienced the processes of the natural world as interrelated, both practically and symbolically. These understandings were expressed in traditional environmental knowledge, namely, in hunting and agricultural practices such as the appropriate use of plants, animals, and land. Such knowledge was integrated in symbolic language and practical norms, such as prohibitions, taboos, and limitations on ecosystems' usage.[31] All

Figure 2.1 Mt. Kilimanjaro as seen from the Amboseli National Park in Kenya;
Photo source: iStock

this was based in an understanding of nature as the source of nurturance
and kinship. Thus the Lakota people still speak of "all my relations" as an
expression of this kinship (*Mitakuye Oyasin*).[32]

Sacred places also manifest these intimate relationships of a people to
the land. These include mountains such as Mt. Kilimanjaro in Kenya (figure 2.1), rivers such as the Yamuna and Ganges in India, waterfalls such
as those used by Yamabushi ascetics in Japan, and rocks that are the site of
piling of stones throughout Central Asia. Pilgrimage sites arise in sacred
places that shape and define religious practices such as the Way of St.
James pilgrim route to Santiago de Compostela in northwestern Spain.
Religious ecologies develop in relation to these sacred places, often finding their own symbolic meanings in ritual. For example, Navajo/Déné
sand paintings involve complex healing rituals in which a patient sits on
colored sands that are ritually laid and symbolize specific sites in their
cosmological stories. As a sacred chant is sung, the sands are rubbed onto
the patient, who partakes of the healing power of this religious ecology
that flows from connection to sacred places.[33]

Through symbols and rituals, art and architecture, religious ecologies
respond to the incompleteness, brokenness, and fragmentation of life and
reorient the human toward the fullness of life. In this spirit, religious
ecological sensibilities have developed sacred architecture to align living

spaces and ceremonial places with the sun and stars and the four directions.[34] Such architecture embodies a religious cosmology and ecology that places a community in relationship to the natural world and the cosmos itself. This symbolic knowing integrates land and structures as well as institutions and practices.

Religious structures of worship around the world do this, from Jewish synagogues to Christian cathedrals, from Islamic mosques to Hindu temples.[35] Across Asia the great Buddhist monuments display this cosmological orientation, such as the massive Buddhist mandala structure of Borobudur in Indonesia (figure 2.2), the Buddhist caves of Ajanta and Ellora in India, and the Buddhist carvings and paintings in Dunhuang, Loyang, and Datong in China.[36] In Indigenous societies, ceremonial houses were built in certain directions according to cosmological symbolisms that also embodied ecological understandings of climate and land formations.[37] In the American hemisphere the ritual lodges of the Northern Plains Indian Sundance and the majestic structures of Mayan and Incan peoples attest to their cosmological symbolism, cosmovision, and geographic knowledge.[38] Similarly, *feng shui* practices—or geomancy—in East Asia reflect this ancient inclination to orient buildings in relation to nature. The elements, the seasons, and directions were all used as correspondences to create an intricate system of microcosm–macrocosm relations.[39]

Weaving into the Fabric of Life: Elemental Dimensions

The elements of earth, air, fire, and water are important in religious ecologies as biocultural realities that literally and symbolically weave humans into the vibrant processes of Earth and cosmos. These elements differ symbolically from the elements listed in the periodic table. However, as biocultural symbols, air, earth, water, and fire can be seen as corresponding to religious ecological processes of *orienting, grounding, nurturing,* and *transforming* humans. *Orienting* refers to the inclination of humans to turn toward air, sky, and celestial bodies, namely, that which moves above us. *Grounding* refers to earth, the soil and land on which we stand and in which we dwell. *Nurturing* evokes water and food, so essential for life. *Transforming* connects to fire and the powerful forces that can be creative, destructive, or healing. A human life that comes out of the elements of Earth and ultimately returns to these elements seeks such deep connections through religious symbols and practices.

Religious ecologies weave humans into the elements of life both practically and symbolically. In a similar way, the scientific discipline of ecology studies the interaction of the elements in ecosystems. Both religious

Figure 2.2 Borobudur Buddhist Temple in Java, Indonesia; Photo source: iStock

ecology and scientific ecology affirm the interrelated components of a system, or parts of a whole. Religious ecologies emphasize correspondences and subjective connections through symbols, whereas scientific ecology draws on empirical observation and objectivity through models. In Han China, for example, an elaborate system of correspondences was transmitted in the thought of Tung Chung-shu (Dong Zhongshu 179–104 BCE).[40] This religious ecology oriented the human to the elements, the directions, the seasons, and the larger world of nature, so that the human is situated in the context of Heaven and Earth, that is, the cosmos and nature.

Correspondences also refer to the complex symbolic systems articulated by cultures for expressing the relationship of the small self of the human (microcosm) to the large self of the universe (macrocosm). This idea is widespread in religious ecologies. In the Vedic hymns of early Hinduism, for example, the *Mahapurusha* is the "great person" whose sacrifice gives birth to all the elements of the universe. By ritual sacrifice in this tradition, a person is integrated into the larger cosmos that holds the ancestors, deities, social structures, and elemental matter.[41] This is the cosmological self that resonates with all living things. In this way religious cosmology and religious ecology are mutually enhancing modes of integrating humans into the social, natural, and cosmic orders of reality.

Orienting, Grounding, Nurturing, Transforming

Religious ecologies can be seen, then, as ways of *orienting* humans to the universe, *grounding* them in the community of nature and humans, *nurturing* them in Earth's fecund processes, and *transforming* them into their deeper cosmological selves. This gives fresh meaning to the Latin root of the word *religion*, *religio*, meaning "to bind back" or "to bind together." This implies a return to, or coming into, a relationship with numinous power.[42] Here we take that "binding" to be an awareness of and commitment to the fundamental wellsprings of life.

Religious ecologies become vehicles for *orienting* humans, experiencing a guiding and sustaining creative force in the natural world and beyond. For some traditions this is a creator deity (Yahweh, God, or Allah in the Western religions and Brahma in Hinduism) or a numinous presence in nature (Great Spirit, *mana*, or *kami* in some Indigenous traditions). For others it is the source of flourishing life (*Dao*, or the Great Ultimate, in Daoism and Confucianism) or Original Mind (the Buddha Nature in Mahayana Buddhism). Theologians and commentators have debated the nature of this creative force, ranging between transcendence above or immanence within nature or some dynamic combination thereof. Some religious thinkers speak of "panentheism," a sense of the divine permeating all of reality and yet maintaining a transcendent presence beyond the world. This is distinguished from "pantheism," which identifies the divine with nature itself. For many in the Abrahamic traditions pantheism is to be avoided because God is understood as a Creator deity above nature.

In the most comprehensive sense, then, religious ecologies provide an orientation to this creative force in the cosmos. This elicits our response by raising such enduring questions as: Where do we come from? Where are we going? How do we fit in? Is there a Creator, or is the universe a process of ongoing creativity? The emergence of galaxies, stars, planets, and life is narrated in the origin stories of many traditions. Through such stories, or religious cosmologies, the human is oriented to comprehensive questions about the larger context of life.[43]

However, it is important to note that not all religions have creation stories that acknowledge a time of origin. For example, both Buddhism and Confucianism suggest that the universe is an ongoing creative entity without a specific beginning. There is no Creator God in these traditions. Buddhism also has a cosmological understanding of the interdependence of life in its teachings about dependent origination or "the together rising up of things" (*pratitya samutpada*). In the Hua Yen school of Chinese

Buddhism this teaching is presented in symbolic form as a cosmic jeweled net of the god Indra. In that cosmic net each jewel reflects all the others, thus mirroring the interpenetrating and interdependent nature of reality. Confucianism has a rich cosmological view of the continuous interaction of the great triad of Heaven (cosmos), Earth, and humans, which is described by Tu Weiming as a "continuity of being." In the Confucian classic *The Doctrine of the Mean*, this relationship of Heaven, Earth, and humans provides a constant teaching of balance and reciprocity. Both Buddhism and Confucianism foster a sense of relational resonance between the myriad communities of life.[44]

Indeed, fostering such relational resonance as a means of *grounding* the human is at the heart of religious ecologies. Humans have a deep desire to belong, to be part of a community or broader fellowship. Such communities include humans in past, present, and future generations—from ancestors and grandparents to parents and children, from the sages and saints of the past to future descendants. For many traditions, the community of life also embraces the larger world of four-legged, winged, and gilled beings along with the meadows, rivers, forests, and oceans in which they dwell. In this light, nature is a revelatory context for orienting and grounding humans amid abiding religious questions about the origins of the universe, the emergence of life—mineral, plant, animal—and the role of humans amid these life processes.

For many practitioners this gives rise to a human desire to enter into Earth's *nurturing* processes that depend on water and food. Most religious communities value water as sacred, using it for ceremonies of purification or initiation. Moreover, individual and communal nurturance is experienced through rituals and ceremonies for gathering and hunting or growing and harvesting food. Planting and harvest rituals, as well as thanksgiving for food and drink, are common in all religious ecologies. When human communities are gifted with nature's bounty in food and drink, the fear of hunger is overcome. This is acknowledged with the Seder in Jewish families, the Eucharist in Christian communities, and Ramadan dinners in the Muslim world. With the offerings of food to the ancestors in Buddhist and Confucian communities, humans are bound to the long lineage of life. Religious ecologies thus link humans to nature's nurturing power through symbols and rituals that help establish patterns of reciprocity with nature, with other humans, with ancestors, and with the numinous forces sustaining life. Nature's fecundity is seen as a source of life, providing rich nourishment for individuals and communities.

Religious ecologies also help in *transforming* individuals from their small self into their greater self. Humans negotiate this transformation in a variety of ways through prayer and meditation, ritual and sacrament, repentance and renewal. In many traditions, prayers and rituals are designed to carry a person through the rhythms of the day—lighting candles and incense in the morning in the Confucian and Buddhist traditions of East Asia, reciting Vedic hymns at dawn tò greet the sun in Hinduism, praying five times a day in the Islamic world. This can be done at home or in the monasteries of Christianity, Buddhism, and Hinduism, where the sun's rising and setting are celebrated at dawn and dusk with prayers and chanting. In addition, visual images can enhance such meditation: icons in Orthodox Christianity, mandalas in Tibetan Buddhism, and statues in Hinduism.

Moreover, religious ecologies mark the great life transitions, or transformations, through birth, maturity, marriage, and death with rites of passage, such as the sacraments in Christianity. In both the daily rituals and in rites of passage, images from nature are used. This places a person within the diurnal alteration of dark and light and the seasonal cycles of death and rebirth. In the yearly calendar these are celebrated as solstice and equinox. Humans are participants in the rhythms of nature—each day, every year, and across the expanse of a lifetime. Thus, loss, suffering, and diminishment are given a larger meaning within the changing and renewing processes of nature itself.

Finally, traditions of atonement and renewal are built into religious ecologies with ascetic practices such as fasting or seeking a vision in nature, namely in mountains or deserts, rivers or waterfalls. Testing oneself in nature, training one's body through discipline and denial, performing austerities—all these practices bring one to a sense of purification and renewal.[45] In this way a person or a community is transformed and restored.

Conclusion

Religious ecologies in their fullest potential orient individuals to their larger role in the cosmos, in Earth's ecosystems, and in human societies. Religious ecologies thus help humans see themselves not as isolated beings in a vast and indifferent universe but as embedded in the cosmic and Earth communities from which they draw nurturance. This realization finds different expressions. For Jews and Christians a human being is made in the image and likeness of God and as such imprinted with possibilities for creativity and love. In Confucianism the human is the mind-and-heart (*hsin*) of Heaven and Earth, the reflective and feeling consciousness of the universe. For Buddhists, although there is no abiding self, humans are dependent on the dynamic processes of an interwoven world. Some Buddhists refer to this perception of relationship as "inter-being."[46] For Hindus, *atman* (self within all things) and *Brahman* (divine self) are mutually indwelling. This is a fundamental insight of the Upanishads, where wisdom is seen as the realization of an inherent identity of all reality with the divine. All these are examples of the pervasiveness of microcosm–macrocosm relationships as a given reality in religious ecologies. However, for humans to realize their place in the larger macrocosm is an achievement through religious practice. For example, the practice of yoga can bring a person into a bodily experience of the rhythms of nature and the cosmos.

Religious cosmologies and religious ecologies—through orienting stories and practices, symbols and rituals, meditation and prayer—are the means by which humans integrate themselves into these interpenetrating communities. They help humans find grounding to negotiate tragedy and loss, contingency and finitude. They nurture individuals and communities to live amid uncertainty and pain with joy, hope, and even laughter. They transform the human to activate healing and reconciliation so that comprehensive compassion may flow into the world.

In the modern period in the West we diminished these multiple relationships so that religion became focused primarily on God–human relations and human–human relations. Human–Earth relations were ignored or attenuated.[47] The aim of the study of religious ecology is to retrieve, reexamine, and reconstruct these human–Earth relations that are present in all the world religions. This relationality with nature, both symbolically and practically, is one of the elements religions have in common as cosmological and ecological systems. Religions thus hold a promise of extending once again care and compassion to the planetary community of life.

3

Religious Ecology and Views of Nature in the West

Religious ecologies in particular cultures provide an integrated milieu for living in community with other humans, with nature, and with the Earth. Similarly, religious cosmologies create a broad narrative context for humans to explore questions of origin and the unfolding of life. Religious ecologies are not static entities but change over time through interactions with complex currents of intellectual, social, and political thought. Such interactions are continually reshaping relations of humans with nature and those of humans with each other and with the divine. With the development of the science of ecology, many of the processes of nature came to be studied using empirical and analytical methods. In this chapter we explore cosmological concepts and views of nature in the West as background for understanding how scientific ecology developed over the twentieth century and how religious ecology is being interpreted at present. Whereas this chapter focuses on the West, religious ecologies in South Asia, East Asia, and Indigenous traditions are discussed in later chapters.[1]

Views of Nature in the West

This overview is intended to illuminate five key movements in Western thought that helped shape human–nature relations: from animism to monotheism, from purpose to ambivalence, from holism to rationalism, from romanticism to transcendentalism, and from anthropocentric to anthropocosmic perspectives. The term *anthropocosmic* refers to a view of the human as having arisen from cosmological and ecological processes, which orient humans in the universe and ground them in nature. It is part of earlier religious ecologies, but a reformulated anthropocosmic perspective is now being rediscovered amid scientific ecology and evolution.

Although painted in broad brushstrokes, the story that this overview tells is one of human struggles to discover our creative roles in the vast processes of nature and the cosmos. This narrative conveys the aspirations and the failures of the human, thus revealing both the intimacy and distance humans have engendered with the natural world. The history of intellectual ideas about nature in the West and their implementation in practice need further study, but the contributions of Clarence Glacken and Peter Coates are noteworthy. Glacken provides a comprehensive survey of views of nature through the eighteenth century, whereas Coates demonstrates the often paradoxical and problematic character of such views.[2] This chapter does not analyze the varied uses of ideas for political power, but we recognize the reality of such inevitable manipulation. We are also aware that the relationships between ideas and practices, and between theory and action, are more complex than such a survey can explicate. Instead, our aim in this chapter is to situate the reader in a Western historical lineage that provides background for understanding how the study of ecology as a scientific discipline arose (chapter 4) and how the study of religious ecology has emerged (chapter 5).

The broad features of this lineage underscore the many diverse strands of thought in Western views of nature. The natural world is clearly viewed as a source of both material benefits and spiritual inspiration for humans. The question in the modern period is, In pursuing material benefits, have we diminished nature's capacity to inspire humans? In other words, have we dimmed down our creative relationship by dismantling nature? Might it be possible to envision a shift from an anthropocentric view of our role above nature to an anthropocosmic view of humans as interdependent with nature? Can we reimagine ourselves as embedded in the ecological and cosmological processes that have birthed us? Because we see ourselves as biocultural beings, it is more likely that we will participate in preserving and conserving ecosystems and species. From this perspective, this journey through Western thought might be seen as a movement from various animistic and anthropocentric worldviews to emerging anthropocosmic and participatory perspectives.

From Animism to Monotheism

Animism, the experience of spiritual forces in nature, is widespread around the world and endures in many Indigenous traditions to the present day. In the early Mediterranean world animism was eventually supplanted by Greek philosophical thought and later by monotheism in the Abrahamic traditions. The shift was from an immanence of the divine within nature to transcendence represented by a Creator God above nature. The order and harmony in nature posited in Greek philosophy were reconceptualized as God's created plan.

The Mediterranean World and Greek Thought: Animism and Cosmological Harmony

Animism is the relationship of humans to forces ("persons") in the landscape rather than simply supernatural powers fixed in natural phenomena.[3] Religious ideas of animism were widespread in the ancient religions of the Middle East. In this region, various Sumerian, Egyptian, Semitic, and Indo-European myths of creation posited a universe of cosmological correspondences between material realities, cosmic bodies, and deities that linked humans, nature, and cosmos. These ideas persisted in Greek religion and mythology. However, Greek philosophers, such as Pythagoras (570–495 BCE), rationalized these personifications as natural forces.

Pythagoras was renowned as a mathematician and cosmologist whose ideas influenced Western conceptions of the cosmos and the natural world.[4] He proposed a mathematical and sympathetic relationship between numbers, or patterns, in the world. Human moral behavior depended on right relations with the rhythms and vibrations of the cosmos. The cosmos itself emanated music from the movement of the stars and heavenly bodies. Humans could orient their lives according to this cosmological music or rhythm. Pythagoras himself became an exemplar of wisdom that brought together mathematics and religion, understanding the patterns of matter and living in harmony with larger cosmological forces.[5]

This notion of living in harmony (*harmonia*) was critical to the Stoics, who also described a cosmological sympathy for the rhythms and vibrations that extended throughout the cosmos, linking all life into a pervasive unity. This linkage between cosmos, Earth, and humans gave rise to a new sense of cosmopolitan citizenship as a way for humans to participate in a cosmological order.[6] The Stoic Chrysippus (279–206 BCE) proposed the idea of citizenship (*cosmopolites*) in which all beings are related in a natural chain of being. From this perspective humans were seen as caretakers of the harmony of nature and the cosmos. They could thus assist transformation in nature by virtue of their unique citizenship in the cosmos.

This hierarchical view of life, imaged as a chain or ladder, was one of the most significant concepts developed in the Hellenistic period. It suggested that the gradations of the natural and human worlds had an inherent order, stability, and harmony. Such a great chain of being brought together Platonic (metaphysical) and Aristotelian (material) worldviews. From a Platonic perspective the chain of being oriented humans to a transcendent reality above nature toward which the human soul journeyed back to the divine. From an Aristotelian standpoint the chain of being situated humans in material reality and affirmed the empirical investigation of nature. This metaphysical and biological model of the great chain of being continued into the medieval period in Europe.[7]

A different cosmological view was presented by Lucretius (ca. 99–50 BCE), who wrote *De rerum natura*, "On the nature of things." This philosophical poem continued the emphasis that Epicurus (341–270 BCE) placed on atoms as the basic dynamic constituents of reality. Lucretius focused first on the microscopic realm of atoms, whose continual movements explained all phenomena; next on human beings, especially the character of the living soul; and finally on the infinite cosmos. Rather than simply a determined causal flux, Lucretius posited an indeterminacy, *clinamen* or "swerve," leading to the possibilities of interrelated changes in the natural world and free will in the animal realm. His emphasis on a purely material world over divine causation or design depended on an infinite plenitude where great variety occurs. Lucretius is distinguished by "his rebuttal of . . . the argument from design, his conception of the organic, and therefore the mortal, nature of the earth, and his ideas of environmental change as a part of culture history."[8]

Abrahamic Traditions: Monotheism and Transcendence

Cosmological concepts also significantly shaped the Abrahamic traditions that attributed creation to a monotheistic God. Greek philosophical thought was used by many Jewish, Christian, and Islamic thinkers to articulate ideas of order and participation in nature as reflecting the power of this transcendent Creator, a Divine Artisan who crafted the world. The Abrahamic traditions developed theologies of both transcendence of the divine above creation and immanence of the divine in the world. The Hellenic influence stimulated views of creation as good and as filled with *harmonia*.[9] This idea of *harmonia* in nature and also as an attribute of the divine integrated the created world more intimately into the sacred in the Abrahamic traditions.[10] This Greek lineage of harmony passed into later philosophical and religious thought, relating the many parts of creation to the whole, especially in Western monotheism.[11]

In these Abrahamic "traditions of the book," the scriptures of the Hebrew Bible, the Christian New Testament, and the Islamic Qur'an were interpreted as living manifestations of the plan from which creation was constructed. Both Rabbinic Judaism and early Christianity drew on the celebration of nature that appears in the Hebrew Bible, especially in the Psalms.[12] In addition, some of the values evident in a traditional Hebraic ethics of place, such as wilderness as a place of encounter with the divine, also passed into Christianity.[13] Similarly, images in the Bible associated with sheepherding and agriculture find distinctive religious expressions in the Abrahamic traditions.[14]

Such images of nature were also linked with the idea of a cosmic center as a sacred city, namely Jerusalem. This was the centering ground from which one could map the entire known world. Mapping the local in relation to the universe, namely cosmography, meant that regional centers could claim cosmological significance and historical relevance. Thus, in the Orthodox tradition of Christianity, Constantinople could become the second Rome and Moscow the third Rome, in which Rome itself—even after its fall in the fifth century—retained its symbolic significance in Christianity as a formative cosmological center.

This notion of a cosmological center was often used to establish political power and was invoked, for example, by Christian missionaries who at times situated churches on older Indigenous sacred sites.[15] Similarly, distinctive cosmological concepts of God's divine plan for creation were woven into Jewish and Christian notions of governance, land distribution, commerce, architecture, and religious authority. In Genesis, the divine plan for the world is laid out in the 6 days of creation that God perceived as good.[16] This goodness of creation is further elaborated as God's ordering of creation and God's care for creation through the human to whom stewardship was given.[17] From this perspective, God is transcendent to nature, although not detached from it.

These biblical themes grounded religious ecologies in Judaism and Christianity. The notion of God's loving care for creation is evident in the imagery of the *Song of Songs* in the Hebrew scriptures and in the parables of Jesus in the Gospels.[18] Love of the divine through the natural world became part of religious practice in the Abrahamic traditions. Some of the singers of such love mysticism, such as Francis of Assisi (1181–1226) and Jalal al-din Rumi (1207–1273), wrote intense poetry highlighting the capacity of nature to praise God. Their devotional exuberance inspired many followers, but the scholastics often sought to circumscribe such enthusiasm with more systematic views of God, humans, and creation.

From Purpose to Ambivalence

Medieval scholasticism celebrated the ordered plan of creation in the image of the Divine Artisan. This sense of divine purpose in nature gave way to new views of human agency in the Renaissance. The Greek classics inspired this renewed humanism that placed the human at the center of all things. The Protestant Reformation that followed encouraged a return to the transcendence of God and reliance on the Bible, more than nature, as revelatory. Nature was seen as imprinted with the divine by such Protestant reformers as John Calvin and Martin Luther, but an earlier sense of purpose in nature was subverted by theologies underscoring the fallenness of humans and nature.

Medieval Scholasticism: Divine Plan and Nature's Fall

Scholastic thought from the twelfth through the fifteenth centuries reflects the influence of classical ideas of a divinely ordained origin, plan, and order to creation. God as manifest in God's works became identified with views of the Divine Artisan who contained within himself the divine forms as articulated by Plato and who imparted form to matter as described by Aristotle. In this spirit, many religious and philosophical thinkers depicted nature as similar to a scripture that reveals the mysteries and mind of the Creator.

However, nature also was understood as participating in human sinfulness and brokenness. Like humans who suffered from original sin, it was widely believed that nature had also fallen and consequently aged like a human and experienced decay. Thus, it might be said that in the Abrahamic traditions there arose an ambivalence regarding nature.[19] In Christianity, for example, nature is seen as good at the Nicene Council (325 CE), in which the incarnation of Christ into material reality was understood as an affirmation of the goodness of nature. The sacramental quality of nature was thus upheld. Nature was also viewed with concern that it could distract humans from acknowledging the Creator. This range of views in Christianity is evident in the writings of Augustine (354–430 CE), who explored both beauty and divine handiwork of creation, as well as a flight from the "groaning and travail" of the Earth described in Paul's epistle to the Romans.[20] Influences from Gnosticism may linger in Augustine's work, namely, the Manichaean denigration of matter and the body. Interestingly, Augustine did not believe that creation fell when humankind transgressed the divine command in the Garden. In fact, he thought only humans had fallen; the Earth, on the other hand, remains in its original state of perfection.[21] Similarly, in Judaism and Islam, nature is at once God's handiwork and a potential place of chaos requiring transcendence. This ambivalence has endured into the present in Western religious traditions.

Nature was worthy of admiration by humans if that wonder and esteem was associated with the love of God. It is in this context that scholastic thinkers such as Jewish philosopher Maimonides (1135–1204), Christian synthesizer Thomas Aquinas (1225–1274), and Islamic thinkers such as Ibn Sina, or Avicenna (980–1037) and Ibn Rushd, or Averroes (1126–1198) reinvigorated the direct investigation of nature based on Aristotle's notion that form is embedded in the world of matter. For example, in the *Summa Contra Gentiles* Thomas Aquinas affirmed the diversity of created forms as coming closest to manifesting the divine. He wrote, "the presence of multiplicity and variety among created things was therefore necessary that a perfect likeness to God be found in them according to their manner of being."[22]

This cosmological order of things also found expression in literature. Dante Aligheri (1265–1321) reformulated the Christian cosmological story as the journey individual humans make to the beatific vision after passing through the moral dilemmas of life. The rise of urban cultures with their dense populations and concentrations of symbolic knowing are prefigured in literary works such as Dante's *Divine Comedy*.

Creating cities and civilization was seen as a devotional act imposing order on nature. This was believed to bring humans farther up the hierarchical ladder to God rather than remaining in wild, undomesticated nature. This exemplifies the dichotomy of nature and culture that pervades much of Western thought into the present. After this split, as Catholicism became dominant in Europe and later in the Americas, it suppressed Indigenous nature-based religions and leveled sacred groves. For example, although Bernard of Clairvaux (1090–1153) experienced a deep mystical union with the Divine Artisan of nature, he also sought to tame the wild growth of the Clairvaux valley in France as an expression of that devotion. Medieval scholastic thought thus reflects ambivalence between the vision of a divine plan in the natural world and human control and transcendence of nature.

Renaissance Thought: From Recovery of Classics to Skepticism

If medieval scholasticism accommodated the Abrahamic traditions to broader cosmological perspectives of a divine plan, the emergence of Renaissance thought from the fifteenth to the seventeenth centuries reformulated cosmology in the context of the human. This shift toward humanism is often identified with the *Oration on the Dignity of Man* of Giovanni Pico della Mirandola (1463–1494).[23] Not only did Mirandola seek accord between the pagan, Greek, and Christian traditions, but he also presents the human as having been created with a distinct *fortuna*, or fate, to formulate his own form and being.[24] Despite the tendency to read Renaissance humanism as completely secular, religious cosmologies and religious ecologies endured in various forms, especially in the arts.

Central to this new humanistic cosmology is the placement of the human as a template or measure for understanding the world. This is strikingly imaged in the *Vitruvian Man* (figure 3.1) by Leonardo da Vinci (1452–1519). Based on a classical Greek text on architecture, da Vinci's perfect human form models the symmetry and patterning of the universe. These ways of thinking about the human as the microcosm of the macrocosm spread across Europe by the seventeenth century.

Four key themes were the basis for the revolutionary thinking of the Renaissance: recovery of classical texts, discovery of empirical method, challenging of received authority, and skepticism of scholasticism. Renaissance humanists such as Erasmus (1466–1536) encouraged direct encounter with classical texts rather than reliance on received scholastic thought. This emphasis on individual literacy, coupled with the proliferation of printed texts from movable type, ushered in new ways of accessing knowledge. Moreover, an epistemological shift encouraged actual observation of the world. The empirical method led to revolutionary understandings of the Earth in the cosmos, such as Copernicus's (1473–1543) discovery of the heliocentric universe and Galileo's (1564–1642) affirmation of this discovery through observational data with the telescope. This Copernican revolution set in motion a new worldview that undermined traditional religious cosmologies.

Authority was being challenged on all sides, from cosmology to natural law and from philosophy to ethics. By freeing themselves from conventional thinking, scientists were able to observe, experiment, and postulate based on case studies. New skeptical attitudes emerged in which knowledge itself was questioned as simply subjective opinion. Rather than

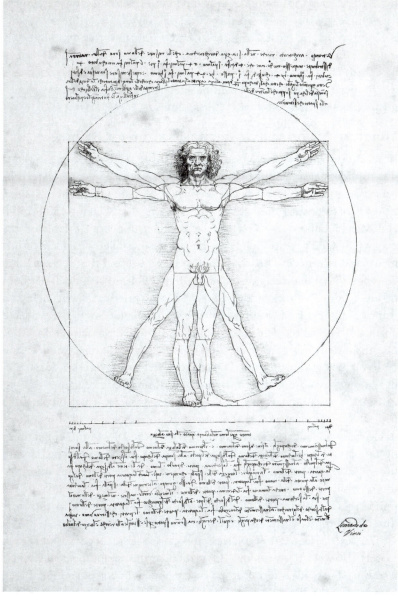

Figure 3.1 Vitruvian Man by Leonardo da Vinci; Photo source: iStock

revealed religious cosmologies, the human was confronted by the empirical complexity discovered in the world. The evidence of the senses and a view that nature existed simply to satisfy human curiosity could only mitigate this skepticism. Thus Michel de Montaigne (1533–1592) took as his motto "*Que sais-je?*" ("What do I know?"), and his *Essays* anticipated the modern critique of rationalism. These perspectives were developed further during the Protestant Reformation.

Protestant Reformation: Ambivalence toward Nature

In reaction to the cosmological thought of the medieval scholastics and the confident rationalism of the Renaissance humanists, the sixteenth-century Protestant Reformation returned to Augustine's fundamental ambivalences toward the natural world. With John Calvin (1509–1564) and Martin Luther (1483–1546) the Reformation both celebrated the majesty of God's creation and meditated on the fallen character of humans and nature.[25] This ambivalent view caused the Reformation churches to emphasize a need to control the wild and chaotic dimensions of the world. As Protestantism spread to the Americas it engendered a fear of both new lands and new peoples as manifestations of the wild and chaotic.[26] This resulted in a justification by both Protestant and Catholic missionaries for converting native peoples as irrational, soulless, and chthonic beings. Furthermore, these views led to the limitless extraction of resources as a productive ordering of irrational nature.

In such a worldview, nature was no longer sacramental but became malleable for human use. At the same time, the divine resided in a more stable transcendent realm, having turned over the keys of the kingdom to his human steward. This early modern religious worldview accorded with the views of the scientist Francis Bacon (1561–1626). Bacon reformed the scientific method by advocating a turn from classical "idols of the mind" to an experimental and empirical method described as the "torture of feminine Nature to make her reveal her secrets."[27]

The discoveries of the Americas also caused major revisions of certain aspects of Western cosmology. In particular, the Columbian encounter introduced new ideas into Europe about land and peoples and reinforced concerns about the aging and senescence of nature. While increasingly observing a balance and harmony in nature evident in the web of life, explorers also noted the limits of the Earth's productivity and the potential loss of harmony through the destruction of nature in early colonization.[28]

From Holism to Rationalism

A return to a sense of order in nature characterized seventeenth-century thinkers at the beginning of the scientific revolution. This organic order was observable by empirical investigation and provided evidence of the design of the Creator. Appreciation of design led to Deism, in which God was a distant clockmaker who set in motion a mechanistic universe. Early scientific rationalism in the Enlightenment period also elevated human ways of knowing above nature.

Natural Philosophy and Theology: Holism and Order in Nature

By the seventeenth century, philosophers such as Baruch Spinoza (1632–1677) arrived at a sense of nature as God, or "nature naturing" (*natura naturata*).[29] For Spinoza a formal religious attitude distanced one from actually investigating nature. Rather, the search for intellectual understanding through empirical observation was the key to "Nature's Substance" as God.

In the English-speaking world natural theologians such as John Ray (1627–1705), Thomas Burnet (1635–1715), and John Woodward (1665–1728) became accomplished amateur observers of European geology and of botanical and zoological species. Indeed, Ray is reported as the first writer to use the term *species*.[30] This group of naturalists emphasized the organic order and wholeness of the universe as evidence of the design of the Creator. Based on nature's inherent design, its interrelationships, productivity, and capacity for positive manipulation, nature responded to human knowledge and control as God had planned.

These religious thinkers focused on observing and understanding the interrelationships in nature as superseding theological speculation on final causes or teleology. This emphasis on observation of nature carried over into new insights regarding the uses of nature for human benefits. Their preindustrial, utilitarian views were oriented to village and local economic exchange and not to larger commodity production. Ironically, however, these utilitarian values lay down strong religious roots for affirming the handiwork of God in creation and consequently for promoting the connection of science and technology to extractive industries as beneficial for society.

Enlightenment Thought: Deism and Rationalism

Enlightenment thought in the eighteenth century helped shift conventional Western cosmology even further from a theological perspective focused on a personal Creator actively involved in creation to a predominantly scientific view of the universe as operating under machine-like principles. As a result of the scientific revolution and an Enlightenment worldview emphasizing rational inquiry, theologians further muted their ideas about final cause and purpose in the universe itself. They broadly accepted the notion of Deism, namely, that God created nature with inherent mechanistic relationships that carried the whole cosmos forward.

Thus, the light of God's revelation in creation was dimmed for many Western religious thinkers. Indeed, the revelatory character of nature was replaced by a linear unfolding of divine creation. This view connected God's care for creation and the ancient design arguments with the Deist notion of a clockwork, mechanistic universe. A conceptual worldview revolving around Deism, observation of nature, and objectified mechanism opened the way for a further distancing of the human from nature as a source of religious awe or guidance. Scientific empiricism moved with confidence into the opening. However, resistance to this distancing from nature arose with the Romantics.

From Romanticism to Transcendentalism

The Romantic thinkers sought to recover an organic holism that accorded with their felt perceptions of a living world. Notions of a unity and harmony in nature seemed to move out of a strictly institutional religious sphere into more secular spiritualities celebrating the sacred in nature, especially in the arts. These intellectual and literary currents influenced the Transcendentalists and the early American nature writers and painters.

The Romantic Movement: Emotion and Beauty in Nature

Romantic thinkers and artists of nineteenth-century Europe, in reaction to the rational, objectifying Enlightenment worldview, came to see nature as vital, dynamic, and, for some, revelatory of the mind of God. Jean-Jacques Rousseau (1712–1778) led this "age of sensibility" by revisioning both religion and nature in such works as *Émile* and *The Reveries of a Solitary Walker*. Rousseau reframed questions about the origins of human morality in relation to the natural world, stating that "there is no original perversity in the human heart." That is, rather than seeing the human as depraved in relation to the Fall, Rousseau linked human goodness with the good in nature. Most importantly, his recurring affirmation of the spiritual beauty of nature found ready acceptance in Romantic writers such as Johann Fichte (1762–1814), whose study of self-consciousness emphasized a deeply sensual experience of the world.

Johann Herder (1744–1803) and Johann Wolfgang von Goethe (1749–1832) gave forceful voice to the *Sturm und Drang* ("Storm and Stress") movement in which extreme expressions of emotions were understood as necessary to counter the excessive emphases on rationality. In their distinctive writings, Herder and Goethe, along with Friedrich Schelling (1775–1854), returned to the direct experience of nature as a way toward unity or harmony with the sacred in nature. Moreover, Goethe saw this as a means toward a more empirical understanding of the complexity of nature. The Romantic poets in England, Wordsworth, Coleridge, Shelley, and Keats, were influenced by their German counterparts and celebrated the splendors of nature.

This type of personal experience of nature as revelatory was troubling to the orthodox teachers of the Abrahamic traditions because it fostered a religious path in nature apart from the revealed scriptures. Consequently, the Romantic return to the embodied experience of nature as sacred was not welcomed into the European or American mainstream religious traditions. Rather, the nature-based spirituality of the Romantics was largely dismissed as emotionalism or transformed into poetry, music, and the arts.

Alexander von Humboldt (1769–1859), a remarkable scientist and synthesizer, was profoundly influenced by the Romantic sensibility of organic holism. Through his extensive travels he collected numerous specimens. Underlying his scientific studies was a sense of the unity of nature embedded in empirical observation and quantification. Affirming holism through the consortium of physical sciences, Humboldt bequeathed to later cosmological thinking a sense of the wholeness of the universe in his usage of the term *kosmos*.[31]

Early American Environmentalism: Transcendentalism

The Romantic contemplation of nature also significantly influenced the American Transcendentalists, such as Ralph Waldo Emerson (1803–1882) and Henry David Thoreau (1817–1862), as well as such early environmentalists as John Muir (1838–1914) and John Burroughs (1837–1921). Both the Transcendentalists and these nature writers established a religious platform of reverence for life underlying the American conservation and environmental movements.

For Ralph Waldo Emerson, the key human exchange with nature came through the imagination, such that examining the whole organic world resulted in a supersensual, or transcendental, experience of the sacred. Henry David Thoreau was anchored in a close empirical observation of nature, even describing forest successions and seed propagation.

Moreover, his romantic and transcendental orientations drew him into a reverence for life as experienced at Walden Pond, the place of his meditations on life and nature. He was often suspicious of the objectivizing and mechanistic tendencies of his day.

In their ecstatic language describing natural beauty, Muir and Burroughs drew on the rhetoric of holism found in both religion and philosophy. In particular, Burroughs was inspired by Henri Bergson's (1859–1941) idea of vitalism, and Muir described nature as an organic whole that was infused with "an essential love, overlying, underlying, pervading all things."[32]

From Anthropocentric to Anthropocosmic Thought

The intellectual revolution associated with Darwin included geological and biological understandings that challenged traditional religious cosmologies. The life sciences especially shifted the story of the human from a special creation to one of a species embedded within evolutionary processes. This tension continues into the present regarding the role of the human and the value of nature. The conflict is manifest in anthropocentric views of humans as dominant versus views of the primacy and integrity of nature's ecosystems, such as in deep ecology. Resolution of this struggle is not immediately forthcoming, but anthropocosmic views of the human as emerging from out of the processes of nature provide new orientations for mutually enhancing human–Earth relations of participation rather than domination.

Darwinian Revolution and Modernism

In the twentieth century, as a result of the revolutionary work of Isaac Newton (1642–1727), Charles Darwin (1809–1882), and Albert Einstein (1879–1955), religious traditions in the West began to relegate cosmology to physicists and the understanding of Earth's geological development and biological diversity to the domain of the Earth and life sciences. This turn from cosmology by the religions also led to a diminished sense of their traditional forms of religious ecology. For example, the idea of a divine plan in nature, though much changed during Christian history, was dimmed down by theologians as science became accepted as the bearer of cosmological and ecological knowledge.

The concentration on the individual that characterized Protestant Reformation views of personal salvation combined with an Enlightenment perspective in which the human was seen as above nature. Salvation history became identified with a Western anthropocentric view of redemption focused almost exclusively on the human condition as alienated from both the divine and nature.[33] Although Darwinism resituated anthropocentrism in an evolutionary worldview, an abiding tension surfaced in some forms of Christianity that emphasized the uniqueness of God's creation and stressed revelation as residing in biblical scriptures, not in nature. This became even more pronounced in the early twentieth century when the Roman Catholic Church condemned "modernism," that is, ideas that challenged the authority of traditional religious beliefs and values. Modernism ranged from critical biblical interpretive methods, to evolution, to social planning such as communism. Catholicism eventually came to accommodate both biblical hermeneutics and evolution, but it retained a largely anthropocentric perspective.

Many critics have cited Western anthropocentrism in its religious and philosophical forms as a major obstacle to the emergence of more comprehensive environmental ethics in the face of an aggressive degradation of nature.[34] Indeed, they suggest that this anthropocentrism in combination with the objectification of nature fostered by the scientific method of empirical observation has resulted in a relentless economic exploitation of nature and consumption of its resources with little sense of restraint or limits.

Such a critique of anthropocentrism was articulated by Lynn White (1907–1987) in his provocative essay titled "The Historical Roots of Our Ecologic Crisis" (1967).[35] There he challenged theologians and biblical scholars to explore the relationship of religion to the environmental crisis. White argued that the technological impact of humans on the planet's ecology has been largely deleterious. This, he suggests, is caused in part by the influence of Christianity as a highly anthropocentric religion emphasizing a transcendent God removed from nature. These notions, he felt, contributed significantly to the desacralization of nature and thus the ability to exploit nature without awareness of the consequences. White recommended alternative forms of Christianity, such as Orthodoxy and the nature spirituality found in the life of Francis of Assisi, whom White proposed as a patron saint for ecologists. In his later work he proposed a spiritual democracy as a new basis for more equitable human relations with nature.[36]

Norwegian philosopher Arne Naess (1912–2009) also articulated an influential corrective to these positions of anthropocentrism and the objectification of nature. Bill Devall and George Sessions introduced Naess's concept of deep ecology, which emphasizes the intrinsic value of the natural world.[37] This perspective draws on Advaita Vedantic thought in

Hinduism, as well as other nature-oriented religious traditions such as Daoism. Deep ecology emphasizes "self-realization" that emerges from awareness of the dependence of humans on the entire community of life. Naess is also indebted to the natural philosophy of Baruch Spinoza, highlighting the unity of nature and the divine. Deep ecology has thus promoted biocentric equality and an understanding of species interdependence as indispensable for protection of both biological and cultural diversity.[38]

Process Thought, Phenomenology, and Embodiment in the World

Alfred North Whitehead (1861–1947), and many subsequent process philosophers and theologians, argued for a dynamic, organic view of nature in which human creativity is a vital part. Whitehead was indebted to Henri Bergson (1859–1941) and his philosophy of change and duration. Whitehead articulated a theory of interrelatedness where internal relations hold all life together in a vibrant web of being. The opposite of this, he suggested, was a mechanistic materialism that emphasizes external, quantifiable relations. He developed a pointed critique of such a worldview as "one-eyed reason, deficient in its vision of depth." He thought this perspective had dominated science for several centuries and stripped away value from nature. In *Science and the Modern World* he called for an age of reconstruction of science and culture.[39] He observed that not only technological applications but also the methods of science have moral consequences. With process philosophy he developed an approach to nature and life that reclaimed complexity and depth of relationality in Western thought.

The twentieth-century development of phenomenology, a philosophy centered on human perception and experience of the world, has had significant influence on ecological thought. Phenomenology is associated with Edmund Husserl (1859–1938), who called for a "return to things" in the world away from more positivist and empirical rationality. Husserl described this return as intersubjectivity, that is, an empathy for the surrounding environment. His student Martin Heidegger (1889–1976) formulated his investigations of being-in-the-world as continuing this intersubjectivity with the world. Heidegger focused on "dwelling," or the ways in which we intimately participate in life. Deeply critical of technology as breaking such intimacy, Heidegger emphasized the fragmentation of the modern world and the need to recover our authentic relationship with nature.[40] Maurice Merleau-Ponty (1908–1961) made a turn toward sensory reflection, emphasizing how our body–mind perceives the world.[41] He rejected modern dualisms that separate the body from the mind and the human from the world. For him the individual body–mind is present to the subjectivity of self and world, participating in all their rich ambiguities. Merleau-Ponty explored the ways speech and gesture open us to the indeterminacy of the world stretching from our embodied being to the horizons. Bodily perceptions of the world are preobjective, that is, they occur before any conscious act. For Merleau-Ponty the body–mind engaged in the world is the source of speech, rationality, value, and existence.

Environmental psychologist James Gibson (1904–1979) helped elucidate phenomenological insights for a holistic understanding of ecology. He saw nature as having both an explicate realm in itself and an implicate dimension connecting various modes of reality. For example, animals, according to Gibson, have evolved capacities for interacting with their environments according to a visual exchange of what the one affords the other.[42] He suggests that both the environment and individual animals are mutually involved in the establishment of affordances. The phenomenologists, then, brought forward a perspective that underscores the intersubjectivity of reality and the participatory role of humans and the more-than-human world. In the contemporary period this has been the work of eco-phenomenologist David Abram.[43]

Universe Story and Self-Organizing Dynamics

The reorientation of human–Earth relations in the context of the evolutionary story of the universe and Earth provides another path beyond the human–nature divide that emphasizes anthropocentrism. This path was articulated by Jesuit scientist Pierre Teilhard de Chardin (1881–1955), who viewed humans as a phenomenon of evolution, not an epiphenomenon or special creation.[44] His concern to activate human energy for building the Earth became a source of inspiration for those interested in an ecologically flourishing future. This included cultural historian Thomas Berry, who also recognized humans as part of an evolving community of life. Berry suggested that evolution should be told as a "new story" that brings together science and the humanities.[45] From this perspective humans could embrace their role or their "great work" to assist in creating a sustainable Earth community. He understood that such mutually enhancing human–Earth relations were critical to reverse the destruction of nature in the contemporary period. With evolutionary philosopher Brian Swimme, he wrote *The Universe Story* as the first comprehensive narrative of universe, Earth, and human emergence.[46]

Figure 3.2 View of the Earth from the Moon; Photo source: iStock

This perspective embraces an anthropocosmic worldview that provides an integrated view of humans as embedded in and dependent on nature. Thus, humans can be understood as a biocultural species. Such a perspective acknowledges the importance of human agency in creating culture but places humans within a vast unfolding universe out of which our solar system and our species have emerged. The work of scientists such as Ilya Prigogine (1917–2003) and philosophers such as Isabelle Stengers has contributed to our understanding of evolution as emerging from self-organizing dynamics.[47] Such dynamics describe the innate characteristics of matter to organize into emergent forms that could not have been predicted by the prior constituents. Terry Deacon, in particular, has done significant work to describe the properties of emergence.[48] Stuart Kauffman and others at the Santa Fe Institute have studied the creative properties of systems.[49] Self-organizing dynamics are seen to occur in physical, chemical, biological, social, and cognitive processes. Many natural and social scientists are studying such processes as evidence of cooperative tendencies in evolution.[50] This has implications for how we are being challenged to evolve culturally toward participation in a larger, cooperative Earth community.

That we live on a watery planet that has birthed an enormous variety of life forms gives humans a new appreciation for life's uniqueness and complexity (figure 3.2). This is the perspective of cell biologist Ursula Goodenough, who wrote *The Sacred Depths of Nature*.[51] This complexity is also the inspiration for the *Journey of the Universe* project,[52] which explores the emergence of the human out of the self-organizing processes of Earth. In this project the scientific understanding of evolution is joined together with a fresh realization of the anthropocosmic character of the human. This new story thus calls humans to the next critical stage of awareness and responsibility in determining the future course of Earth's evolution, namely, toward creating ecological cultures.

Conclusion

This brief overview, while presenting multiple views of nature in the West, can only suggest the immense complexity of the subject. Various problems arise, such as the need to include the voices of minorities in these discussions and the difficulty of realizing ideas in practice. Yet something is gained even by such a broad synopsis as is presented here. Several key themes emerge from specific periods in Western history that endure into the present, often in inconsistent and paradoxical forms. These include views of the roles of humans from such perspectives as anthropocentrism to humanism and rationalism and views of nature ranging from animism to monotheism and romanticism. These dialectics between humans and nature represent a wide spectrum of ways of responding to and valuing the sources of biological life and human creativity.

These themes illustrate the ongoing interaction of nature and culture that remains unresolved into the present. On one hand, there is a recurring appreciation for holism in nature as expressed in order, pattern, harmony, or a divine plan. On the other, there is a more ambiguous view of nature as wild, fallen, random, or to be controlled. These two contested views have resulted in ambivalence as to the nature of the natural world and the role of the human within it. Thus mutually enhancing human–Earth relations for a flourishing Earth community remain elusive. To see humans as a biocultural species is crucial to resolving these dilemmas. The study of the development of ecology as a scientific discipline and as a method of ecosystem preservation or management is a vital component of this resolution.

4

Ecology, Conservation, and Ethics

Forms of Ecology

Just as views of nature have changed radically in the West, so too ecology, conservation, and ethics have their own history and development, which we will survey in this chapter. This will help illustrate ways in which they are now coming into dialogue in the emerging field of religion and ecology. As our understanding of nature deepens and broadens, our role in nature is being reconfigured by questions such as: How do ecosystems work? How do we conserve them? How do humans fit in ecosystems?[1] If we restore ecosystems, what models should guide us and why? Is there a place for precautionary principles?

The idea of ecology as used in this book locates humans within the horizon of emergent, interdependent life and does not view humanity as the vanguard of evolution, nor as the exclusive fabricator of technology, nor as a species apart from nature. The term *ecology* in this sense describes these dynamic interactions of humans with nature more specifically than the term *environment*, which can suggest that nature is something apart from humans. In this chapter, however, *scientific ecology*, or *biophysical ecology*, refers to the empirical and experimental study of the interactions of living and nonliving components of an ecosystem through energy flow and nutrient cycling.

In the last few decades, other forms of ecological studies have arisen in the social sciences such as political ecology, social ecology, cultural ecology, industrial ecology, and ecological economics.[2] Though having a different focus, each of these approaches recognizes the interdependence of human and natural processes as ecologies. These relationships of systems are described, analyzed, and critiqued using methods derived largely from the social sciences in conjunction with the natural sciences. The humanities are also making contributions to the broadening of environmental studies from the fields of history, literature, and art. In philosophy environmental ethics began some 40 years ago, and in religious studies religion and ecology emerged some two decades ago.

In this emerging field, we speak of religious cosmology and religious ecology. Religious cosmologies in world religions describe the origin and unfolding of the universe, Earth, and life. Religious ecologies are functional cosmologies that express an awareness of kinship with and dependence on nature for the continuity of all life. Religious ecologies, then, provide frameworks for exploring diverse religious worldviews, symbol systems, rituals, and ethics as developed in relation to the processes of Earth and the universe. They assume cosmological stories and embedded cultural practices that weave humans into the life systems of the cosmos, of the Earth and of bioregions. These perspectives and practices are very old in the human community. We have described them as processes of orienting, grounding, nurturing, and transforming. Our scientific understanding of holism and of the functioning of ecosystems has changed dramatically over the last century, and this broadens and enhances religious ecologies.

Religious ecology invites us to explore cultural understandings of natural processes and of the depth of symbolic meanings embedded in human–nature relations. The scientific study of ecology brings us to a greater empirical understanding of natural processes in ecosystems. Scientific ecology studies the complex interactions within and between ecosystems; religious ecology examines cultural awareness of these interactions as creative, generative, and normative for the continuity of life. Whereas the former has given rise to various methods of conservation and management of ecosystems and species, the latter represents an important lens whereby humans can understand and reenvision their roles as participants in the dynamic processes of life.

Religion and ecology as an emerging field is closely connected to three key areas: ecology as a research science largely concerned with the study of ecosystems and species, conservation as an applied science concerned with valuing and preserving ecosystems and species, and ethics as ways of shaping human behavior in light of these disciplines. Some ecologists question the idea of holistic ecosystems. This is because in the face of the remarkable diversity of life and ecosystems, it is a challenge to discover holistic connections and to measure or model them. Nonetheless, holism is a persistent theme in the history of ecology, conservation, and ethics.

An organismic perspective shows awareness of the relation of parts to the whole. Indeed, this perspective is shared by both ecology and religion, thus giving a comprehensive basis for understanding and valuing the natural world. In this context, the intrinsic value of ecosystems and biodiversity, not simply their instrumental value, can be better understood.[3] As Aldo Leopold suggested in *A Sand County Almanac*:

> The last word in ignorance is the man who says of an animal or plant: "What good is it?" If the land mechanism as a whole is good, then every part is good, whether we understand it or not. If the biota, in the course of aeons, has built something we like but do not understand, then who but a fool would discard seemingly useless parts? To keep every cog and wheel is the first precaution of intelligent tinkering.[4]

Leopold was interested in understanding how ecosystems worked ("cog and wheel"), but also how each part fit into a larger community of life. Moreover, he brought together ecological sciences, conservation strategies, and ethical principles in the "land ethic." In the land ethic, Leopold saw the biotic community as a whole life pyramid in which humans are responsible members. The implications for how we value the parts and the whole of ecosystems remain to be more fully explicated in the context of a living ecosphere.[5]

Emergence of the Field of Ecology

Ecology as a science has undergone many changes, as has been astutely analyzed by Donald Worster in his pathbreaking book *Nature's Economy*.[6] The etymological definition of *ecology* is knowledge (*logos*) of the house or household (*oikos*). With the appearance of the idea of ecology (*oekologie*) on the European and American scene in the late nineteenth century, a new science of the unity of organisms in the environment emerged. As a study of the "inhabited world" (*oikumene*), this had older antecedents associated with the phrase "nature's economy." These antecedent usages linked understandings of scientific ecology to traditional environmental knowledge, especially connected to the rhythms of agriculture. From its academic inception, ecology was closely tied to biology and that discipline's study of organisms. Consequently, the unity sought in ecology was often limited to the study of organisms rather than the larger, inorganic physical environment.

The historical story of the formation of scientific ecology cannot be fully described here, but even a brief survey reveals significant shifts in the values underlying the study of ecology.[7] One way to characterize these shifts is to suggest that the study of ecology in the last 150 years has moved between *holism* and *bioeconomics*.[8] Holism promotes an integrated understanding of the community of life forms, whereas bioeconomics promotes a managerial style based on efficiency, productivity, and measurement.[9] Thus, as ecology emerged in the twentieth century as a scientific discipline, it faced methodological challenges as it tried to establish credibility as a discipline that has its roots in holism. Although the term *holism* was not used until 1926 by South African statesman and philosopher Jan Smuts (1870–1950), the idea came to characterize an early understanding of ecology.[10]

German naturalist Ernst Haeckel (1834–1919) first used the term *oekologie* in 1866. With this term he implied that all the living organisms of the Earth constituted a unified whole, "a single economic unity resembling a household or family dwelling intimately together, in conflict as well as in mutual aid."[11] In focusing on the inherent order, harmony, and beauty of the many parts of nature, Haeckel stood in a significant lineage of naturalists, including Carl Linnaeus (1707–1778), who described the organic order of nature as an *oeconomy*. Linnaeus's classifications manifested his reverential awe of nature as revealing a divine harmony. Haeckel also drew on the work of Alexander von Humboldt (1769–1859), who came to an empirical and quantitative methodology. Humboldt's emphasis on the holistic harmony of nature eschewed institutional religion but affirmed the spiritual and aesthetic motivations of his work.[12] Haeckel similarly emphasized a unique form of holism, describing the unity of nature in his philosophy of monism.

For Haeckel, species were seen as unified and interdependent in both evolutionary time and ecological space. He wrote, "The orderly course of evolution, according to fixed laws, now leads the human spirit through long eons from a primeval chaos to the present 'order of the cosmos.'"[13] Haeckel observed that not only does evolution situate humans in the larger order of the cosmos, but ecology provides insight into the virtues necessary for humans to live in harmony with nature.

Haeckel understood ecology in concert with Charles Darwin's (1809–1882) notion of evolution involving competition between species. Haeckel promoted Darwin's ideas in Germany, intersecting them with the organismic philosophy of Johann Wolfgang von Goethe (1749–1832) and the evolutionary philosophy of acquired characteristics from

Jean-Baptiste Lamarck (1744–1829). Goethe viewed organic life as formed by internal biological laws that were subject to influence from external environmental forces.[14]

However, this actually differs from Darwin's emphasis on natural selection as the force that altered ancestral forms of life rather than an internal law. Lamarck argued that species acquired characteristics from previous generations that had used those characteristics for survival in their environment. Haeckel's evolutionary views led him to coin the terms *ontogeny*, or a being's development, and *phylogeny*, or a species development, to describe the way in which embryos recapitulate the evolutionary history of their species.

By the last quarter of the nineteenth century, the understanding of ecology as a holistic mutuality of organisms was seen as limited because of its static, harmonic view of nature. In contrast to this, geologist Charles Lyell (1797–1875) presented evidence of the tumultuous and long-term processes of the Earth's surface. This had a strong influence on Darwin. Moreover, in his travels and his empirical studies Darwin came to an understanding of the competitive struggle of species to fit into their environments. This related directly to his articulation of natural selection as an explanation for a species' reproductive success. These discoveries came into the field of ecology just as its practitioners began to establish it as a scientific discipline.

The organic, holistic ecological model was also seen as limited because it lacked a suitable metric, a means to quantify the mutuality it tried to describe in nature. Scientific ecology used empirical analysis to identify patterns of growth (such as the idea of plants, forests, or crops passing through identifiable states to a climax stage) and to observe discrete ecosystems as particular units of the larger interdependence in nature. In addition, understandings of such Darwinian concepts as natural selection and fitness provided means to describe complex biodiversity.[15]

By the late twentieth century, ecology had moved away from its organic, holistic roots and developed scientific methods for measuring ecological complexity. At the same time, there was a renewed recognition that ecology heralded a potential integration of the sciences—natural and social—allowing dialogue across specialized branches that were often segregated. Moreover, ecology was seen as transmitting concerns not simply for the individuated organism and a holistic unity but also for an understanding of processes in the industrial and commercial world that threatened ecosystem survival. The human component of ecology was being more fully examined from both the social sciences and the humanities.

It is in this context that environmental ethics as a field of study arose 40 years ago and religion and ecology emerged some 20 years ago. Over the last several years, scientists with concerns for conservation, such as Thomas Lovejoy, E. O. Wilson, and Peter Raven, have looked to philosophy and religion for ethical assistance on these issues.

Stan Rowe (1918–2004), an ecologist at the University of Saskatchewan, was especially concerned with these ideas, as is evident in his book *Earth Alive*.[16] Rowe affirmed the cosmological character of all reality as activating a "spark of creativity" in humans that flowed from the spirit of place.[17] Rowe consistently made connections between the energy flows in material reality and the human feeling of aliveness:

> Now we know that this Earth planet, in whose skin we live, is an immense, vital, integrated system, the Ecosphere. Nothing that we can see, feel, hear, smell, or taste is separate. Everything has co-developed in complex interaction with the rest. The sense of wonder and affection felt for the splendor and bounty of the Earth is natural to us, an expression of our co-evolution with all that exists on the planet.
>
> We do not understand, and may never fully understand, this miraculous Earth that we briefly occupy. We have made some progress in understanding the intelligence of individual organisms, so that, for example, we know how to plant trees and help them grow. But we have no comprehension of the wisdom expressed in the structure and function of Earth and its geographic ecosystems. For example, we do not understand the complexity of forest ecosystems that humans have blithely destroyed since the time of Gilgamesh and continue to destroy today.[18]

The Development of Ecology in the United States: From Holism to Metrics

The holistic view became a basis for a broad spectrum of interpretations of nature in America. This is evident in the organismic views of transcendentalists, such as Ralph Waldo Emerson (1803–1882) and Henry David Thoreau (1817–1862). Their profound sense of nature as a unified whole has resonated with nature writers, as well as the larger American environmental movement down to the present. A holistic view extended into the "complication" perspective of George Perkins Marsh (1801–1882), the aesthetic preservation focus of John Muir (1838–1914), and the progressive conservation policies of Gifford Pinchot (1865–1946).[19]

George Perkins Marsh was deeply concerned about deforestation, based on his studies in the Adirondacks and the Mediterranean region.

He was influenced by agricultural reforms emphasizing soil nurturance in New England and New York and by his own readings in geology, forestry, and hydrology. He advised caution in management because he saw more "complication," or complexity, in the interactions of nature. Marsh especially emphasized nurturance of soil depleted by human overuse. In 1864 he wrote in *Man and Nature*,

> The object of the present volume is: to indicate the character and, approximately, the extent of the changes produced by human action in the physical conditions of the globe we inhabit; to point out the dangers of imprudence and the necessity of caution in all operations which, on a large scale, interfere with the spontaneous arrangements of the organic or the inorganic world; to suggest the possibility and the importance of the restoration of disturbed harmonies and the material improvement of waste and exhausted regions; and, incidentally, to illustrate the doctrine, that man is, in both kind and degree, a power of a higher order than any of the other forms of animated life, which, like him, are nourished at the table of bounteous nature.[20]

John Muir's love of the Sierras and of Yosemite in California led to a desire for preservation based on an aesthetic and religious appreciation of wilderness.[21] There he felt humans could experience nature's vastness and beauty, without which the human spirit would be much diminished. As Muir wrote,

> No synonym for God is so perfect as Beauty. Whether as seen carving the lines of the mountains with glaciers, or gathering matter into stars, or planning the movements of water, or gardening—still all is Beauty![22]

To help people appreciate and protect nature, he founded the Sierra Club in 1892 and served as its president until his death in 1914. This is still the largest environmental group in the United States. He resisted development, such as damming, that would compromise such pristine settings as the Hetch Hetchy Valley east of San Francisco. It was this aesthetic valuing of nature that led to his differences with Gifford Pinchot, who supported the "appropriate" development of resources. The different perspectives of Muir for preservation and of Pinchot for conservation are reflected in environmental studies and practices down to the present.

Pinchot's progressive conservation policies represented a critical and timely response to the unrestrained utilitarian ethic of random and complete consumption of resources that dominated American forestry in the nineteenth century. Pinchot proposed a more careful management of natural resources that is described as "wise use:"

> Without natural resources, life itself is impossible. From birth to death, natural resources, transformed for human use, feed, clothe, shelter, and transport us. We depend on them for every material necessity, comfort, convenience, and protection in our lives. Without abundant resources prosperity is out of reach.[23]

He drew on the utilitarian justification of both conserving and using forests for the greatest good for the greatest number over the longest time. He argued this was the best approach for sustained use for a common human good that would benefit the nation. Pinchot founded the Yale Forestry School in 1901 based on this philosophy, and in 1905 he became the first chief forester of the U.S. Forest Service. His principles of adaptive forest management implemented a German model of cutting and reforesting trees as crops. As a pragmatic yet holistic view of managing nature, Pinchot's crop model combined utility, morality, and economics.[24]

Because of the work of Marsh, Muir, Pinchot, and others, by the end of the nineteenth century ecology was recognized as a natural science. In addition, the work of Ellen Swallow Richards (1842–1911) contributed to this development from the field of public health. Richards, a chemist at the Massachusetts Institute of Technology, emphasized the need to protect nature in order to protect human health and wellbeing. Her focus on the problem of sewage and industrial waste led to the development of the first water quality standards in the United States.

From Climax State to Food Chain

Departments for ecology existed in some European and American universities by the early twentieth century, although typically they remained within biology departments. Gradually, in these academic settings major theoretical problems were recognized in the early holism model of ecology. For example, holism implied that nature as a whole was more than the sum of its parts. This theoretical model could not be substantiated quantitatively, nor could it be falsified. In other words, there was no metric, or method, for measuring either the parts of an ecosystem leading to the whole or the wholeness of interactions themselves. This search for a metric characterizes ecology as a discipline from the first decades of the twentieth century into the present.

A contribution to an analytical understanding of the holism model was the "climax state" approach of Frederic Clements (1874–1945). His early botanical work was in the prairies of Nebraska at the turn of the century and later in Minnesota. His work in the competition and succession patterns of plant ecology resulted in his description of vegetation communities as "super-organisms." According to this hypothesis, vegetation passed through successive stages until it reached its maturity in a climax stage. After the publication in 1916 of his work on *Plant Succession*, Clements's theory of a climax state became widely accepted among ecologists. His perspective was seen as responding to the perplexing question of an observable whole. However, by the 1940s this super-organism theory was being questioned.

An earlier challenge to Clements's view of ecological communities as super-organisms came from Henry Cowles (1869–1939) in his 1898 dissertation, "An Ecological Study of Sand Dune Flora of Northern Indiana." This investigation of the succession of vegetation initiated a new theoretical focus in which plants were seen in close relationship with the changing nature of their environment over space and time. Cowles's story in relation to the Indiana sand dunes is intriguing, as he traveled by train to walk the dunes and then returned home by a different train route to see them from another perspective. What he found was an ever-changing panorama in which dunes moved, tree lines receded, and wetlands formed and filled over time. Cowles, a professor at the University of Chicago, established a more dynamic succession model for ecology than the climax state theory. In so doing, he helped save the dune coastline and bring forth a new generation of field-oriented ecologists.

Clements's views of succession and climate state were also disputed by Henry Gleason (1882–1975), who built on Cowles's research. Gleason proposed an individualistic concept of ecology, maintaining that plant associations are less structured than Clements suggested, and indeed their distribution was somewhat random. The relationship between species resulted from environmental requirements, tolerance, and chance. Community boundaries were not sharp, and associations of species were not as predictable as in Clements's super-organism framework. However, Gleason's individualistic perspective did not gain traction until the 1950s, when Clements's ideas were superseded. While Clements and Gleason's views were considered to be in opposition, later ecologists built on their ideas for new syntheses in understanding the mechanisms of succession.

In these formative years, plant and animal ecologists significantly differed in their scientific approaches.[25] Whereas plant ecologists focused on understanding the assemblage of species into communities (higher levels of organization), animal ecologists concentrated on individuals and their responses to environmental and biotic interactions (individual-level organization). Plant ecologists early on had little understanding of the demography of individuals forming populations, whereas animal ecologists had many insights into how individual animals interacted.[26]

A major contribution to ecological models was the work of Charles Elton (1900–1991), whose classic book *Animal Ecology* was published in 1927. Elton relied on traditional ecological classification but proposed a radical new idea emphasizing structure and function of what he called the "food chain." This underscored the etymological link between ecology and economics in the root term *oikos*, meaning "household." This new community model of ecology did not focus simply on the dynamics of a natural community but rather on the form and organization of the food chain moving like capital through an economic order. From photosynthesis in plants to herbivorous animals and predators there existed a food chain of beings. Unlike the old philosophical model of the great chain of being that emphasized a taxonomy of ever-higher beings, Elton's food chain described rungs of a food ladder or pyramid that identified "producers" and "consumers," or prey and predators. Thus, the first comprehensive economic model appeared in ecology emphasizing the "corporateness" of survival and nutritional interdependence as an exchange of food as capital.

Through this food chain model Elton provided a comprehensive metric for ecology. First, he located forms of life in a bioregion on a food chain. Later ecologists expanded the linear phrase "food chain" to "food web" so as to emphasize a network of connections. Second, Elton identified a structural relationship between the size of food for a predator, namely, larger eats smaller. Third, he noted the significance of fertility and reproduction in which biomass, especially among plants, defined the base of a pyramid. As one goes up the food chain pyramid, higher predators were fewer in number and had a smaller species population. Fourth, he drew on earlier work, such as Darwin's concepts of "place" and "office" and Joseph Grinnell's idea of "niche" as status or occupation. He connected the concept of niche to what a life form is doing, not merely what it looks like. Niche provided a means of measuring "competitive exclusion" in which, supposedly, no two species were seen as occupying the same food niche.

Elton was aware of serious questions raised by his work, such as "invasion" of species and multiple niche occupants. However, he set ecology on the path of bioeconomics, with the metaphor of nature as a factory-like place in which food was exchanged like currency. The concept of niche was further developed by G. Evelyn Hutchinson (1903–1991) to include the environmental and biotic factors with which organisms interact. Hutchinson's student, Robert MacArthur (1930–1972) played an important role in examining niche separations. MacArthur influenced E. O. Wilson, with whom he published *The Theory of Island Biogeography*, which continues to influence conservation studies, planning, and management.[27] Another student of Hutchinson is Thomas Lovejoy, who has been an important figure in the conservation of the Amazon. In particular, he developed the strategy of "debt-for-nature swaps" to protect forests in exchange for canceling part of a country's national debt. Both Lovejoy and Wilson have been significant figures in promoting an understanding of the critical role of biodiversity in ecosystems.

Ecosystems and the New Ecology

English botanist Arthur Tansley (1871–1955) was a key figure in developing the science of ecology and conservation. He founded the British Ecological Society in 1913, the first such organization in the world. He established and edited two journals, *New Phytologist* (1902) and *The Journal of Ecology* (1917), which helped shape the field of ecology. He sought to move ecology from descriptive biology (static morphology) to a revitalized curriculum that recognized the human role in changing nature.

For Tansley both matter and mind could be explained as biological processes based on physical and chemical laws of energy.[28] In this sense holism was not a helpful concept for the study of ecology. For him nature was a mechanical system in which rigorous science isolated the basic units, splitting up the fictional whole into its very real individual parts. He saw holism as a construction, as "synthesized actions of components in associations."[29] For Tansley, *community* was also an inadequate term arising from a misguided anthropocentrism. For him, there was no psychic bond observable between plants or animals that warranted such a descriptive term. What ecology needed was quantification and analysis devoid of all moralizing and literary projections.

For this new model of organization, Tansley coined the term *ecosystem* in 1935, describing a natural system that followed the laws of physics.[30] In this system there were mathematically measurable quantities of material exchanges of energy, chemical substances, and nutrients as "food." For Tansley, energy replaced the food metaphor of Elton. Nature was reduced to quantifiable energy exchanges that could be graphed and measured.

This became the "New Ecology," focused on energetics and magnitudes of ecological efficiency in energy capture and capitalization.[31]

This approach to nature as a resource to be measured essentially removed ethics from ecological concerns. As Donald Worster observes,

> In reducing the living world to ingredients that could be easily measured and grasped, the ecologist was also in danger of removing all the residual emotional impediments to unrestrained manipulation. To describe nature as an organism or community suggested one kind of environmental behavior by [humans]; to speak of it as but "a momentary stay against entropy" suggested a wholly different behavior and as good as removed it from the ethical realm altogether.[32]

The work of Raymond Lindeman (1915–1942) signaled the success and applicability of this new ecology in his essay "Trophic-Dynamic Concept in Ecology." Unfortunately, Lindeman died before this essay was published, but his teacher and mentor at Yale, G. Evelyn Hutchinson, carried his work forward. This trophic-dynamic model refers to an ecosystem's energy cycles in which energy use at one level is never passed on in its entirety to the next level. The idea is to measure these losses. Thus, an ecosystem, or ecological community, could be measured in a form of productive mathematical analysis that established which organisms were most efficient in energy extraction as one moves up the food chain. Moreover, respiration was noted as a higher percentage of energy use as one moved up the food pyramid described by Elton. This model reached back to Clements, noting that in the early stage of growth in an ecosystem, productivity increases rapidly, leading to large numbers of a species. The energy economic model of the environment was thus firmly established as the basis for the New Ecology. Holism was largely disregarded in the quest for a more quantitative and quantifiable science, particularly after the introduction of economic models and energy budgets, whereas the earlier studies were more qualitative and natural history oriented.

Economic Valuing and an Emerging Environmental Ethics

The New Ecology from the 1930s introduced views of nature not simply as competitive but as energetic circuitry and transfer, geochemical cycling, and an integrated mechanized system that could be quantitatively modeled. Underlying these developments in ecology were methodological adaptations of economic metrics that had proven to be highly successful for undertaking careful analysis of ecosystems and species populations. For example, the analysis of food webs in bioregions allowed ecologists to identify species as producers and consumers in the food web. This capacity for evaluative measurement naturally called for closer assessment of numbers in territories that maintained these food web relationships. Significantly, these species relations were themselves recognized as dependent on the niches that any one species occupied to the exclusion of others like it.

These analytical tools, accompanied by new thinking about energy flows moving through nature, ecosystem services, and biodiversity population dynamics, all gave rise to a New Ecology. The New Ecologists responded to the business ethos of American culture and eagerly promoted ecology as bioeconomics. The exchange within energy systems could be measured by physical and chemical sciences. Thus, there emerged a metric for quantifying and describing the interdependence in nature. These developments drew on the progressive conservation philosophy of wise use and anticipated the economic valuation of ecosystems for the services they provide to humans.

By the mid-twentieth century, the academic field of ecology was established with help from the New Ecologists. This included study of the larger physical environment as an interactive context for organic life. With this move, ecology became somewhat independent from biology's emphasis on individual organisms. Rather than seeing ecology as the analysis of discrete actors on a stage, ecologists realized that the stage itself, namely the interrelated parts of ecosystems, had a critical role to the maintenance of life. Ecologists also refined their analyses of human impact on the environment. These expanding insights into the dynamics of ecosystems, the relationships of organisms, and the transformative character of human intervention on landscapes gave shape to new forms of holistic analysis in ecology linked to ethics, as well as to new forms of environmental management based on efficiency.

This reconsideration of the holism model can be said to return to the etymological roots of ecology from the Greek *oikos*, or "household." An important perspective arose with Aldo Leopold (1887–1948) (figure 4.1), who graduated from the Yale Forestry School in 1909. Aldo Leopold's major technical work of 1933, *Game Management*, goes beyond the progressive conservation policies of environmental management primarily for human use into a concern for wildlife habitat and wilderness preservation for its own sake. Leopold initially embraced Gifford Pinchot's "resource conservation ethic," which he had assimilated while at Yale.

However, he came to believe that maintaining processes of nature would ultimately provide greater long-term value to humans. In light of these changes in Leopold's thought, it is possible to see the gradations of his transformation toward an evolutionary ecological land ethic.[33]

In this way, though aligned with the New Ecology of bioeconomics, Leopold introduced original ethical insights from a holistic perspective. Dissatisfaction had been building among ecologists with the predator reduction and elimination policies of wildlife management for hunting and shooting purposes. The valuable role of biodiversity in ecosystems became apparent, especially when wolves and other predators had been exterminated and deer populations exploded. Conservation efforts were also assisted by the establishment of the National Audubon Society in 1886 and by the Sierra Club, organized by John Muir in 1892. Moreover, ecologists like Olaus Murie (1889–1963) increasingly questioned human interventions in ecosystems without awareness of the differing roles of species. On the other hand, there also developed a strong critique of the "balance of nature" image and the "climax state" of ecosystems as too static. As more dynamic views of ecology became normative, the approach of overly managed ecosystems was critiqued and reexamined.

Aldo Leopold's ethical reflections on these issues were published posthumously in *A Sand County Almanac* in 1949. He questioned the role of ecology as a science serving human progress exclusively. He found insufficient a technological mentality of management that simply implemented utilitarian models. In his essay "Round River," Leopold revisited the holism in which he described land as an interdependent organism that required a higher ethic than simply pragmatic use. He used the model of land as a biotic pyramid rather than "the balance of nature," which he found inadequate to describe nature's dynamic interactions.

In *A Sand County Almanac* Leopold called for a "land ethic" as expanding the boundaries of the human community to include soils, waters, plants, and animals or, collectively, the land.[34] He writes, "In short, a land ethic changes the role of *Homo sapiens* from conqueror of the land-community to plain member and citizen of it."[35] The extension of ethics to the larger environment was for Leopold both an "evolutionary possibility and an ecological necessity." He reflected, "No important change in ethics was ever accomplished without an internal change in our intellectual emphasis, loyalties, affections, and convictions. The proof that conservation has not yet touched these foundations of conduct lies in the fact that philosophy and religion have not yet heard of it."[36] This challenge has

Figure 4.1 Aldo Leopold in 1944; Photo credit: Courtesy of the Aldo Leopold
Foundation, http://www.aldoleopold.org

helped motivate the work of religion and ecology as an academic field
and a larger force engaging environmental issues around the planet.

The tension in approaches to predator management gave rise to a
more inclusive environmental ethics. The major government agencies involved in predator control in the 1920s—the Department of Agriculture
and its Bureau of Biological Management (which became the Fish and
Wildlife Service), the National Park Service, the Interior Department,

and the National Forest Service—responded initially to ideas of preda- tor eradication in ways that favored ranchers. Gradually, as rodents and herbivores increased, there was a realization that the wolf, coyote, bobcat, cougar, and grizzly bear were necessary parts of the balance of ecosystems. Even more dramatic were arguments from forest biologists such as Aldo Leopold, who argued for a new community and land ethic that restored notions of the natural rights of species to exist in habitat that would sup- port them. Thus, ecologists and conservationists were drawn into new dialogue with each other. One result was the Wilderness Society, which drew extensively on the research and inspiration of Aldo Leopold, as well as Olaus and Mardi Murie.[37]

With the founding of the Ecological Society of America in 1915, the disciplines of ecology and conservation in North America acquired a new academic grounding. The society was established "for the purpose of unifying the science of ecology, stimulating research in all aspects of the discipline, encouraging communication among ecologists, and pro- moting the responsible application of ecological data and principles to the solution of environmental problems."[38] The friction in this statement, between studying natural systems and preserving or managing them, re- mained a major issue and continues to the present. The founding of The Nature Conservancy is an example of this tension. Its establishment in 1951 marks a break from the Ecological Society of America as profes- sional ecologists expressed strong ethical concerns to preserve natural landscapes, not simply study them.

Similarly, in 1978, the field of conservation biology emerged and later organized its own society in 1985 in distinction from the Ecological Soci- ety of America. The express goal of the Society for Conservation Biology is to apply ecological principles and environmental ethics to conserva- tion issues. Conservation biology combines practical experience of agri- culture, forestry, fisheries, and wildlife management with the conceptual framework of population biology, biogeography, taxonomy, genetics, an- thropology, and environmental ethics. Conservation biology has spawned a new generation of ecologically trained scientists who use new approaches and methods to preserve species and their ecosystems. Emerging subdisci- plines of conservation biology now include restoration ecology, landscape ecology, and adaptive management. Restoration ecology complements but differs from both preservation and conservation by actively intervening in ecological processes and landscapes in order to try to restore ecological integrity to them.[39] Many conservation biologists recognize the roles of culture and religion in conserving species and ecosystems.[40]

Ecology, Conservation, and Ethics in the American Environmental Movement

The fields of ecology, conservation, and environmental ethics have also developed in relation to emerging environmental problems that became evident to scientists such as Fairfield Osborn, Paul Sears, Walter Lowdermilk, Eugene Odum, and Rachel Carson. Their work anticipated the intersection of ecology and ethics, as did Aldo Leopold's.

Henry Fairfield Osborn Jr.'s (1887–1969) prescient books *Our Plundered Planet* (1948) and *The Limits of the Earth* (1953) continued an earlier call by conservationists for a moral response to the devastation facing many ecosystems. His major concerns as president of the New York Zoological Society focused on species loss and the cascading effects of human population growth. He also proposed the shocking metaphor of an environmentally devastated Earth with a moon-like landscape.[41]

Paul Sears (1891–1990) was an ecologist whose bestselling book *Deserts on the March* provided an ecological understanding of the implications of inappropriate farming practices leading to soil erosion during the Dust Bowl of the 1930s. This caused him to advocate for soil conservation and land management. Sears was brought to Yale in 1950 to chair the new program in conservation. Five years later he was a key participant in the interdisciplinary conference held in Princeton titled "Man's Role in Changing the Face of the Earth." The goal of this historic gathering was to evaluate the current state of human–nature relations. Indeed, Donald Worster suggests that this conference "prepared the intellectual ground for the environmental movement."[42]

Walter Lowdermilk (1888–1974), a forester with the Soil Conservation Service, sought a similar conservation ethic after extensive travel and study of the effects of human civilization on soils.[43] From an understanding of archeological agriculture, especially in China in the 1920s, he observed the massive erosion that often followed the development of intense agriculture. From his research over decades in major agricultural civilizations, he thought that each country needed to appeal to national awareness for stewardship of soil and land for future generations.[44] He called this an Eleventh Commandment.[45]

A conservation ethic for ecology can also be seen in the work of Howard Odum (1924–2002) and his brother, Eugene Odum (1913–2002). Eugene is credited with the first textbook in the newly emerging academic field of ecology, titled *Fundamentals of Ecology* (1953).[46] Ecology appealed to the Odum brothers because "it seemed to be a science that dealt with harmony, a harmony found in nature, offering a model for a more organic, cooperative human community."[47] They reoriented ecological thinking toward ecosystems as a whole rather than simply protecting specific species or addressing only particular environmental problems. For Eugene Odum, ecosystems were self-organizing entities that moved toward maturity and homeostasis. This involved mutualism and cooperation between the organisms.[48] In his later observations about ecology, he spoke of the global interconnection of ecosystems and human responsibility for preserving their integrity. His understanding of ecology as a science led him to policy recommendations such as land use planning, tax laws controlling economic growth, and even birth control. His understanding of the living Earth as comprised of interdependent ecosystems remains a lasting contribution to ecology and to the environmental movement.

Later ecologists who emphasized flux, change, and disturbance in ecosystems challenged Odum's views of homeostasis. This included work by William Drury and Ian Nisbet published in 1973 and work by Stuart Pickett and P. S. White that appeared in 1985.[49] In addition, Daniel Botkin developed an alternative perspective in 1992 with the idea of "discordant harmonies," which stands in distinct contrast with many classical Western ideas of balance in nature.[50] This understanding of disturbance emphasizes the constant flux and change in nature. Disturbances in ecosystems have also been associated with chaos theory.[51] This suggests that sensitive dependence on initial conditions in nonlinear systems can have significant consequences, such as the example of a butterfly's flapping of wings in Brazil linked to a storm in Texas. These new understandings of disturbances in ecosystems came to be understood as having implications for human–industrial interactions.

As scientists began to explore degradation of land by industrial–technological processes, they documented the dangers to biological life caused by new chemical compounds. In particular, the scientific studies of Rachel Carson (1907–1964) (figure 4.2), along with her profound sense of wonder, provided the basis for her wide public appeal. Carson dedicated her bestselling book *Silent Spring* to Albert Schweitzer, citing his ethic of "reverence for life."[52] Many other scientists have been similarly inspired by this sense of reverence. With the publication in 1962 of *Silent Spring*, documenting the devastating effects of DDT on bird life, the contemporary environmental movement was born.[53] In response to Carson's work, the Environmental Defense Fund was founded in 1967 and helped to ban DDT by 1972.[54] Many others contributed to the early stages of environmentalism. These included Barry Commoner, Paul and Anne Ehrlich,

Stewart Udall, Kenneth and Elsie Boulding, Roderick Nash, E. F. Schumacher, and Arne Naess.[55]

Environmental awareness and activism was also sparked by the Santa Barbara oil spill in 1969. A year later the first Earth Day, promoted by Wisconsin senator Gaylord Nelson and organized by Denis Hayes, drew nationwide attention to environmental issues.[56] In 1972 the U.S. Environmental Protection Agency was established, inspired by the United Nations Conference on the Human Environment in Stockholm. Legislation was also passed that updated earlier laws, namely the Clean Air Act (1970), the Clean Water Act (1972), and the Endangered American Wilderness Act (1978). In addition, the Natural Resources Defense Council was established in 1970 to litigate on behalf of the environment. Accidents such as the oil spills in Prince William Sound, Alaska, by the *Exxon Valdez* (1989) and in the Gulf of Mexico by British Petroleum (2010) refocused the environmental movement and renewed attention to environmental ethics.

Two ethicists who have helped shape the field of environmental ethics in relation to ecology are Holmes Rolston and J. Baird Callicott. Drawing on philosophical and religious traditions, they represent a larger exploration of the holistic valuing of nature in environmental ethics. Rolston draws on natural law for articulating an environmental ethics,[57] whereas Callicott draws on Aldo Leopold's land ethic.[58] Rolston appeals to normative guidelines and moral value inherent in nature. Moreover, he understands that ecological studies are not value free but are concerned with identifying the conditions for the flourishing of the biotic community. In his view, scientific facts (what *is*) are not so radically divided from ethical values (what *ought* to be). He writes,

> No amount of research can verify that, environmentally, the right [good] is the optimum biotic community. Yet, ecological description generates this valuing of nature, endorsing the systemic rightness. The transition from *is* to *good* and then to *ought* occurs here; we leave science to enter the domain of evaluation, from which an ethics follows.
>
> What is ethically puzzling and exciting is that an *ought* is not so much derived from an *is* as discovered simultaneously with it.[59] As we progress from descriptions of fauna and flora, of cycles and pyramids, of autotrophs coordinated with heterotrophs, of stability and dynamism on to intricacy, planetary opulence and interdependence, unity and harmony with opposition in counterpoint and synthesis, organisms evolved within and satisfactorily fitting their communities, and we arrive at length at beauty

Figure 4.2 Rachel Carson on the dock at Woods Hole, Massachusetts, 1951; © Copyright 1951 Edwin Bray

and goodness, we find that it is difficult to say where the natural facts leave off and where the natural values appear. For some people at least the sharp *is–ought* dichotomy is gone; the values seem to be there as soon as the facts are fully in, and both values and facts seem to be alike properties of the system.[60]

Rolston has identified an intersection of scientific description and valuing of nature that underlies much of ecology. As researchers describe an optimal biotic community, they are discovering the conditions of its flourishing. From this perspective, ecology is inevitably linked to conservation and ethics. Moreover, the division between *is* (description) and *ought* (prescription) is blurred as ecology works toward understanding how ecosystems thrive. The further exploration of the long-range efficacy of this interaction is still to be undertaken. Both environmental philosophy and religion and ecology are making contributions to this discussion. Here we see ecology as research science, conservation as applied ecology, and environmental ethics as the engagement of theory and practice coming together.

J. Baird Callicott, an environmental philosopher, has developed Leopold's land ethic in ways that are scientifically informed and ethically engaged. Callicott underscores the land ethic as an extension of the idea of community to the soils, waters, plants, and animals. Like Leopold, he calls for a broader environmental ethic:

> An environmental ethic that takes into account the direct impact of human actions on nonhuman natural entities and nature as a whole is called an ecocentric environmental ethic. An ecocentric environmental ethic conforms not only to the evolutionary, ecological, physical, and cosmological foundations of the evolving postmodern scientific worldview . . . but also to most indigenous and traditional environmental ethics.[61]

In addition to the perspectives of Rolston and Callicott, there are pragmatic ethicists such as Andrew Light, Bryan Norton, Ben Minteer, and Willis Jenkins. They have argued for the development of ethical principles from attempts to resolve particular cases, leading to more strategic adaptive management of ecosystems. The idea is for environmental ethics to emerge as directly and reflexively as possible from responsibility for particular biocultural relations with nature. There are also utilitarian ethicists, such as Peter Singer, who have made a strong case for animal protection and animal rights.[62]

Pragmatic and utilitarian approaches have motivated some ecologists and conservation biologists who have joined forces with economists in valuing ecosystems by drawing on market mechanisms. This strategy is based on the view of nature as natural capital and of ecosystems as providing services to humans that can be measured. Such services consist, for example, of the economic value of forests, fisheries, and wetlands. Making their monetary value evident provides a rationale for protecting them from being overexploited. Gretchen Daily, Robert Costanza, and others developed the ecosystem services approach.[63]

This bioeconomic method for sustaining biodiversity in the face of industrial development has had some traction. It is trying to appeal to the business community with a more pragmatic and measurable strategy for conservation. Economists associated with The Economics of Ecosystems and Biodiversity (TEEB) have also analyzed the productive capacities of ecosystems and biodiversity as significant factors in the cost accounting of large-scale development.[64] The effort is to bring the corporate community into an awareness of environmental externalities. TEEB played an important role in the Rio+20 conference, organized by the United Nations Environmental Programme in 2012, which focused on fostering a sustainable green economy along with new forms of global governance.[65] Although this ecosystem service approach is growing, there has also been concern about this perspective from organizations and individuals who are worried about the various consequences of monetizing nature. This includes critiques of enclosing the commons, the market capture of global patrimony, and the concern that the intrinsic value of nature escapes economic valuation. Nonetheless, the TEEB organizers understand that there are multiple ways of valuing nature beyond economic benefits, such as aesthetically and spiritually.

Conclusion

There is clearly a broad spectrum of perspectives for valuing nature, from what it provides for humans to its own inherent value. This spectrum is reflected in approaches ranging from the economics of ecosystem services, the financing of land conservation, and the pragmatic adaptive management approaches, to the aesthetics of landscape ecology, the health of humans in *biophilia*, and the intrinsic value of nature in some forms of restoration ecology. Paradigmatic voices range from the aesthetic and spiritual approaches of John Muir to the utilitarian and wise use techniques of Gifford Pinchot that endure into the present. Continuing the commitment to conservation of biodiversity and ecosystems from both these perspectives has been the work of scientists such as Thomas Lovejoy, E. O. Wilson, Paul Ehrlich, Camille Parmesan, Peter Raven, Michael Soulé, and Susan Clark.

These varied ecological perspectives might be compared with traditional environmental knowledge, which is present in many religious and ethical systems. Such knowledge is based on insights into the functioning of local ecosystems as occurring on a much longer time scale than current economic markets.[66] Despite their more limited understanding of the complexities of ecology from a scientific perspective, religious ecologies demonstrate awareness of the interdependence of natural systems. Religious ecology thus has both practical and symbolic knowledge that help to ground and shape human–Earth relations.

As this chapter has indicated, the field of scientific ecology is dynamic, contested, and still developing. In a similar way, the study of religious ecology is still unfolding. It can be said that both have an appreciation of nature's complexity, beauty, and holism. Therefore, the shared sense of wonder and awe calls scientists and religious communities together for conservation and preservation of ecosystems and species. This is foundational for creating ecological cultures that integrate and balance appropriate use of nature with restoration. This requires a view of nature not simply as a resource but as a source of life.

5

Emergence of the Field of Religion and Ecology

One of the goals of the emerging field of religion and ecology is to understand different ways of valuing and studying nature from cultural and scientific perspectives. This may encourage cooperative efforts between science and religion for conservation and adaptive management of ecosystems. Some ecologists are moving toward an appreciation of the cultural, spiritual, aesthetic, and ethical approaches to nature. At the same time, religious leaders, scholars, and laity are recognizing the need to understand ecology so as to articulate their ethical concerns.

Although the field of religion and ecology arose in Western academic and philosophical contexts, it cannot be dissociated from either changing ideas of nature and ecology or global and local environmental concerns. Social scientific studies in anthropology and sociology describe how a culture mediates between human populations and ecosystems.[1] Historical, textual, and interpretive studies from the humanities are also addressing these issues. This has given rise to creative approaches in the study of religion and ecology, focusing on the ways in which religions conceptualize, classify, and value natural environments. These differentiated studies are illuminating the varied forms of religious ecologies.

Recent historical research has refuted earlier work that tended to fix a culture's environmental practices and ecological ideas as traditional patterns that rarely changed.[2] Now, the mutual impacts of worldviews and environments are more clearly understood as having changed and shaped one another through time. Therefore, studies of local conservation work are being integrated with an understanding of religious ecologies, such as the significance of sacred sites and of place-based knowledge. The mutual relevance of land, life, value, and sustainability are all involved in these interdisciplinary networks of inquiry. This includes the intersection of cultural and biological conservation, as represented in the work of Eleanor Sterling and others.[3]

It should also be noted that postmodern approaches have also affected many contemporary researchers in religion and ecology, attuning them to questions about the ways individuals and groups construct systems of meaning and power. In this sense, religious ecologies have to be analyzed in their use as not simply unequivocally positive for societies but also as potential forms of control used by those in authority to dominate individuals, communities, and ecosystems.[4]

Approaches to the Study of Religion and Ecology

The field of religion and ecology draws on interpretive tools that are helpful for understanding the dynamics of religious ecologies in their historical and contemporary forms. A variety of methods are being used in the study of religion and ecology, but three interpretive approaches are noted here: *retrieval, reevaluation,* and *reconstruction.* Scholars using the *retrieval* approach identify and bring forward concepts and practices that illustrate individual and community interactions with the natural world. For these researchers, *retrieval* thus refers to the investigation of literate, oral, and performative sources for evidence of traditional teachings regarding human–Earth relations. Using the retrieval method, they examine ethics and rituals present in a religion to discover how the tradition actualized these teachings about the natural world in communal beliefs and practices. The retrieval method is primarily descriptive and can be complemented by studies of the environmental history of cultures and bioregions. Reevaluation and reconstruction, on the other hand, tend to be prescriptive of new possibilities for transformation in contemporary circumstances.

Interpretive *reevaluation* occurs when a tradition's religious ecologies are reexamined and assessed once they have been retrieved. In the following section, we see the ways in which the ideas, teachings, or ethics present in traditional religious ecologies are being adopted and adapted by contemporary scholars, theologians, and practitioners. Drawing on these religious ecologies, they have begun the work of shaping more ecologically sensitive attitudes and sustainable practices. Those engaged in reevaluation also sift through and question ideas that have been retrieved and may lead to inappropriate environmental practices. For example, certain religious tendencies promote world-denying orientations and thus may not be helpful in creating awareness of ecological issues and appropriate religious responses. Moreover, exclusively human-centered ethics may not be adequate to address complex environmental problems. Thus, ethics of eco-justice are being developed along with environmental ethics.[5]

Finally, those using the *reconstruction* method suggest ways that religions might adapt ecological teachings and practices to current circumstances in creative ways. This may result in new syntheses or adaptations of traditional ideas that encourage sustainable practices. Certainly, the reconstructive approach challenges the inherently conservative character of religion that preserves tradition. Yet there are numerous historical precedents for creative reconstruction in the ways religions have reshaped themselves over time. Change is evident in theological commentaries, ethical disputations, liturgical practices, and interreligious dialogues. The following section illustrates the changing dynamics of theological discussions of Christianity that have responded to the environmental crisis.

Christian Theologians: Innovations in Religious Ecologies and Religious Cosmologies

Religious and moral reflections on environmental problems emerged in several Christian theological settings in the second half of the twentieth century. One of the first to raise a voice of concern was Joseph Sittler (1904–1987), a Lutheran theologian at the Divinity School at the University of Chicago.[6] He was influenced by the organismic perspectives of the Ecology Group at the University of Chicago, led by Warder Allee.[7] Writing in the 1950s, he decried the forgetfulness and repudiation of the Earth by Christians as a distorted reading of the biblical promise as exclusively oriented toward humans. Urging a larger cosmological vision, Sittler called for Christianity to recover a cosmic redemption of all creatures and of creation as a whole. Sittler's influence in the World Council of Churches led to the founding in 1963 of a Faith–Man–Nature group. For a decade this group brought together other theologians, such as John Cobb, Philip Hefner, and Paul Santmire, to explore Christian understandings of appropriate human interactions with the environment.

Foremost among these theologians who have urged Christianity to reconsider its relationship to the environment is process thinker John Cobb, based at Claremont University. He published *A Christian Natural*

Theology (1965), which reflected a traditional Christian understanding of "natural theology" as theology done within the bounds of reason apart from any extended discussions of the natural world itself. Cobb's work later moved outside this framework of Kantian philosophy to find a basis in the process thought of Alfred North Whitehead (1861–1947) for valuing the natural world and for undertaking appropriate human interaction within it. Encouraged by the early work of Joseph Sittler and biologist Charles Birch, and spurred by his son's concern for environmental degradation, Cobb wrote *Is It Too Late? A Theology of Ecology* (1972).[8] Cobb has critiqued the harmful effects of growth-oriented economies on the community of life, especially in his work with economist Herman Daly, *For the Common Good* (1989). He and Daly challenged conventional economics, seeing it as engineered to promote development despite the environmental and social costs.

In 1972 Harvard theologian Gordon Kaufman (1925–2011) published a seminal article, "A Problem for Theology: The Concept of Nature."[9] Here and in his later work, *In Face of Mystery: A Constructive Theology* (1993), he raised challenging questions about the anthropocentric model of God as developed in Christianity and the relationship of traditional models of God to creation. Kaufman critiqued the nature and names of the monotheistic, transcendent God that can distance humans from a sense of the sacred residing in the natural world. He urged a new bio-historical understanding of humans as embedded in complex processes of "serendipitous creativity" in nature. Thus, humans can become co-creators with the unfolding Earth processes.

Calvin DeWitt, a biologist at the University of Wisconsin and an Evangelical Christian, founded the Au Sable Institute in 1979. There he convened a series of forums on science, religion, and the environment. He also partnered with Sir John Houghton, the Oxford biologist and Evangelical Christian who founded the John Ray Initiative in England in 1997. Together they organized a Climate Forum in 2002 and invited some eighty Evangelical participants, largely from the United States. This sparked significant concern about global warming among U.S. Evangelicals.[10]

Feminist theologian Sallie McFague, a student of Gordon Kaufman, wrote *Models of God* (1987), where she calls for new images of God as not simply a distant and transcendent father but also as friend and lover. Rosemary Radford Ruether in her book *Gaia and God* (1992) draws on the Gaia hypothesis and ecofeminism for the development of a broader ecotheology. Both of these feminist theologians are indebted to the earlier historical work of Carolyn Merchant on *The Death of Nature* (1980), which sees the use and abuse of nature as comparable to patriarchal domination of women and the disintegration of older organic views of nature in which the sacred was experienced as immanent.

Along with ecofeminism there has been an important alignment of social justice and environmental concerns among religious thinkers in both developed and developing countries. The significance of this movement is that it creates new religious syntheses linking awareness of environmental degradation with insights from economic, political, and social analysis. Latin American liberation theologian Leonardo Boff highlights this conjunction in his book *Ecology and Liberation: A New Paradigm* (1995), as does feminist theologian Ivone Gebara in her work *Longing for Running Water: Ecofeminism and Liberation* (1999). Similarly, such writers as Roger Gottlieb and Dieter Hessel have fostered the emerging theologies and practices identified with eco-justice and environmental justice within Judaism and Christianity. In addition, a series of twenty books on "Ecology and Justice" has been published by Orbis Books.[11] Native American concern for environmental justice is featured in the work of George Tinker and Jace Weaver.[12] Asian American theologians Chung Hyun Kyung and Kwok Pui-lan have emphasized the embodied nature of theology, spirituality, and ethics.[13]

Historian of religions Thomas Berry drew on his studies of world religions and cultures to formulate a framework for rethinking the relationships of cosmology and ecology.[14] Berry understood the role of cosmology in world religions as activating self-awareness of human embeddedness in the Earth community. This entails relationship with the natural world that makes possible a communion with the Earth as the basis of an intimate human experience with the larger universe. The challenge of contemporary societies, for Berry, is to realize and implement the transformative energies of a new cosmological story that would affect a radical revisioning of human–Earth relations.[15] Such a story evokes a commitment by individuals and communities to awaken to the epic *Journey of the Universe.*[16]

Berry observed, "This, then, is our challenge—to move from a purely human-oriented or personal-salvation focus in our religious concerns to one that embraces the universe in all its forms. This will require an immense shift in orientation, one that recognizes our emergence out of the long evolution of the universe and the Earth."[17] Berry was suggesting that by moving into a cosmological orientation we would be able to enter into the "great work" of our times: creating the conditions for the flourishing of the Earth community. To do that required the movement of religions into their ecological phase. Indeed, one might say that for Berry a functional cosmology is a religious ecology.

Berry inspired numerous centers of reflection and study on these issues. In Canada Steve Dunn and Anne Lonergan convened summer conferences at Port Burwell with Berry for some 20 years. Dunn established the first graduate program in theology and ecology, based at the University of Toronto. Jesuit priest Jim Profit directed a retreat center in Guelph drawing on Berry and Teilhard. In the Pacific Northwest Fritz and Vivienne Hull founded the Chinook Institute on Whidbey Island. They organized a conference on Earth and Spirit in Seattle in 1990 that drew a thousand people, where Berry was a principal speaker. At Holy Names University in Oakland, California, the Institute for Culture and Creation Spirituality was directed by Matthew Fox, and later the Sophia Center was led by Jim Conlon. All of these centers were indebted to the work of Berry.

Numerous eco-literacy centers were also established by Catholic nuns to explore the universe story and new modes of human–Earth relations. Miriam MacGillis, the founder of Genesis Farm, spoke across the country on these issues and encouraged the nuns in their work.[18] For several decades workshops were held at Genesis Farm in New Jersey and at Crystal Spring in Massachusetts.[19] In Chicago a center called The Well was created by Mary Southard and John Surette. Green Mountain Monastery was established in Vermont to initiate a new monastic community.[20] In the Philippines and later in Ireland, Sean McDonagh worked on spreading Berry's ideas, especially through his books.[21]

Berry's ideas were an inspiration also for James Parks Morton, who for 25 years (1972–1997) was dean of the Cathedral of St. John the Divine in New York City, near Columbia University.[22] Thomas Berry became an honorary canon at the cathedral and helped Dean Morton create one of the most environmentally conscious centers in North America. Morton invited environmentalists such as René Dubos, Amory and Hunter Lovins, and John and Nancy Todd as consultants and speakers at the cathedral. In addition, he welcomed Paul Winter as artist-in-residence along with other artists and poets. Winter helped to create a yearly solstice celebration and an "Earth Mass" (*Missa Gaia*), where animals are blessed annually on the feast of St. Francis. Dean Morton was also a convener, along with Akio Matsumura and others, of the Global Forum of Spiritual and Parliamentary Leaders that held five conferences in Oxford, Moscow, Rio de Janeiro, Jericho, Kyoto, and Konya.[23]

Religious Ecologies in World Religions

As religious ecologies are seen as processes of orienting, grounding, nurturing, and transforming humans, their integral relationships to ecological issues may be recognized. The chapters that follow suggest this is already emerging. The brief overviews presented here are an introduction to their further development in subsequent chapters. Although each overview emphasizes one of the processes, clearly all these dimensions are interacting in religious ecologies.

Christianity as Orienting to the Cosmos

The cosmological orientation of the Greek Orthodox tradition is leading to evocative statements and interdisciplinary symposiums with scientists and religious leaders organized by the Ecumenical Patriarch, Bartholomew. One such example is highlighted in chapter 6 with the 2004 symposium on the Adriatic Sea, which culminated in Venice with a joint statement of the Patriarch and the Pope on the environment.

In Eastern Orthodox Christianity, theology and liturgy provide orientation for humans to the vastness and beauty of the universe. Through sense engagement with the material world this tradition brings the believer into a cosmic spirituality unfolding in the freshness of the seasons and in the taste of daily bread. Orthodox liturgies arouse the senses with choral music, pungent incense, resplendent vestments, and luminous mosaics suffused with symbolic meaning. Fundamental to Eastern Orthodoxy is belief in a personal Creator who orders the world and stands in relation to that creation as present to the practitioner, especially in liturgy. One expression of this spirituality of matter in Orthodoxy is the celebration of creation as seen in a vespers liturgy:

> You set the earth on its foundations . . . you make springs gush forth in the valleys; they flow between the hills, giving drink to every wild animal . . . by the streams the birds of the air have their habitation; they sing among the branches.
>
> O Lord, how manifold are your works! In wisdom you have made them all; the earth is full of your creatures. Yonder is the sea, great and wide, creeping things innumerable are there, living things both small and great.
>
> These all look to you to give them their food in due season; when you give to them, they gather it up; when you open your hand, they are filled with good things . . . when you send forth your spirit, they are created; and you renew the face of the ground.[24]

Confucianism as Grounding in Community

As discussed in chapter 7, Confucianism is a philosophical, ethical, and religious tradition where the human is grounded in an expansive sense of community including both humans and nature. The individual is seen as embedded in concentric, overlapping circles of family, society, politics, nature, and the cosmos itself. The task of cultivation for humans is to continually enlarge the self so as to participate in these dynamic relationships. By such cultivation one becomes grounded not only in the human community but also in the larger harmony of nature and the cosmos. Confucianism is a political philosophy as well as a personal philosophy, whereby order in the state is mirrored by order in the family and in the person.[25]

Through self-cultivation and betterment of society, an individual completes and assists the natural order of the universe, namely, "the transforming and nourishing powers of Heaven and Earth."[26] One of the key texts of Confucianism, the *Doctrine of the Mean*, presents this cosmological role of the human:

> Sincerity is Heaven's Way [*Dao, Tao*]; achieving sincerity is the human Way. One who is sincere attains centrality without striving, apprehends without thinking. One who naturally and easily is centered in the Way is a sage. One who attains sincerity chooses what is good and holds to it firmly. This involves broad learning, extensive inquiry, careful thought, clear discrimination and earnest practice.[27]

Confucianism thus emphasizes the inherent authenticity (*cheng*) of all reality. To realize this authenticity, humans cultivate the virtue of sincerity with learning and sustain the integrity of nature's ecosystems with careful management. Through cultivation of self and of nature humans participate in the cosmological harmony of the Way.[28] For these reasons there is renewed interest in China among government officials, academics, and the public for developing a broader environmental ethic drawing on Confucian values.

Indigenous Traditions and the Nurturing Powers of Nature

The nurturing powers of Earth are displayed in all the world religious traditions that celebrate food with rituals of planting, harvesting, and thanksgiving. The religions thus embed humans in the seasonal cycles that are linked to hunting, fishing, and agriculture. In this holistic under-standing, humans come into relationship with the nurturing powers of food, water, air, and land. This is expressed in rituals such as the Winter Dance among the Salish peoples, located along the Columbia River in the Pacific Northwest. This ceremony, described in chapter 8, especially honors the root crops that nurture the people and animals in this region.

The ceremony includes the singing of vision songs, giveaways, danc-ing, feasting, gaming, and healing. The space in which the Winter Dance is held connects practitioners to the larger cosmos by means of a lodge-pole pine tree that spans from floor to ceiling. The tree is symbolic of a creative cosmic presence that moves with and through the world.[29] Singing reaffirms the old stories that tell how the spiritual beings in the landscape freely gave of themselves to sustain the human. One Salish elder recalled how singing affirms the sacred exchange with food:

> This is our belief at the Winter Dance when the singers come together and pray for our coming year. We have confidence at the pole during the Winter Dance 'cause it's really the animals, what grows on the ground [plants], the water. They're all out there in the four directions, all you have to do is go out and get it.[30]

Visionary songs thus manifest the spiritual presence in food for nur-turing the singers and their communities. This illustrates the cosmologi-cal and place-based spirituality among indigenous peoples nurtured by intimate knowledge of particular plants and animals.

Hinduism and the Transforming Affect of Devotion

The transforming dimension of religion is evident as humans expand their sense of self beyond their individual natures to see themselves as part of a larger universe and unfolding Earth. Practices of meditation and devotion, fasting and prayer, bring individuals into this transformative process, thus letting go of ego to enter a larger self or find union with the divine. The example of the devotion to Krishna connected to the Yamuna River in chapter 9 indicates the potential to transform individuals who could participate in the restoration of the river.

In Hinduism the devotional practice of *bhakti* brings a person into a transformative experience of the divine.[31] *Bhakti* practitioners manifest diverse forms of religiosity, such as meditational and ecstatic commitment to a personal deity.[32]

A classic expression of *bhakti* is in the *Bhagavad Gita*, the "Song of the Lord."[33] This text presents a conversation between the warrior Arjuna and his charioteer and deity, Krishna.[34] Here Krishna reveals himself as the Absolute and advises Arjuna that the simplest act of devotion performed without attachment results in the indwelling of the divine. Krishna says, "If one offers Me with love and devotion a leaf, a flower, fruit, or water, I will accept it."

This devotional act extends into the natural world. For example, the Yamuna River, along which Krishna is said to have walked and played, becomes personified as a goddess, as Krishna's lover. As such, the Yamuna River is a focus of *bhakti* and celebrated in song and verse:

> She came to Earth to purify all beings.
> She is assisted by parrots, peacocks, swans, and other birds with loving sounds.
> Her waves are her arms, her sands pearl-studded bracelets,
> Her banks are her beautiful hips.
> She is honored as the highest lover of Krishna.[35]

The natural world is thus praised in *bhakti* as manifesting the divine.

Conclusion

The field of religion and ecology helps distinguish religious ecologies by means of an examination of past ideas and practices that have formed various traditions. Rather than simply a historical project, however, these studies are concerned with assessing the relevance of these religious ideas and practices with contemporary environmental concerns. This can lead to the types of changes in religions that are evident among theologians in America who have attempted to address the gaps they saw in religious ecological awareness. Even the brief overview of such thinkers presented here emphasizes the range and diversity of religious ecologies within Christianity.

With these examples we can see that religious ecologies are resonant and dynamic systems that have shaped human–nature relations in the past and continue to do so. The processes of religious ecology, namely, orienting, grounding, nurturing, and transforming, are what constitute these shaping forces. These processes have evocative and multivalent expressions, as the following chapters on different world religions illustrate. We have the possibility of drawing on their long histories and traditions and adapting them in relation to modern circumstances through retrieval, re-evaluation, and reconstruction. In this way, we can move toward creating more engaged ecological cultures that would bridge between scientific knowledge and ethical concern for the environment.

6

Christianity as Orienting to the Cosmos

Divine Creativity at the Heart of Matter

Orienting in religious traditions opens one to the universe as an ever-present and all-embracing reality. It provides a sense of direction and purpose to situate humans in a larger cosmological reality. It draws on the skills of theologians and mystics, intellectuals and artists, storytellers and ascetics. No one idea in Christianity can fully express the divine as orienting humans in the present and into an unknown future. This unknown power has been imaged as God the Creator transcending the world. It is also imaged in the book of Genesis as the breath of God moving over the deep chaotic origins of the universe.[1]

These images of a transcendent Creator and an immanent spirit of the divine are found in each of the major branches of Christianity: Catholic, Orthodox, and Protestant. Although much is shared between these branches, their differences flow from historical circumstances and theological doctrines developed over two millennia.[2] The Orthodox Byzantine Church arose from the earliest beginnings of Christianity and split from Roman Catholicism in 1054. Protestantism began with the sixteenth-century Reformation of Christianity in Europe, emphasizing biblical revelation and salvation by faith alone.[3] This chapter focuses on the cosmological dimensions of Orthodox theology, namely, a divine creativity infusing earthly matter and resplendent in the paradise of Eden.

Orthodox Christianity has an abiding concern for this creativity at the heart of material reality.[4] The cosmological wellspring of creation is directly linked in the Orthodox tradition to the incarnation of Jesus Christ in which the divine is said to empty itself and become manifest in material reality. Moreover, the cosmic Christ of the universe is often depicted in the image of *Christus Pantocrator* in the central vault over the altar in Orthodox churches. Religious art in Orthodox Christianity has provided a means for symbolic representation and reflection orienting the faithful toward mystery within the creative process.[5] In these artistic portrayals the many paradoxes of Christianity confront the believer: the cosmological power of the Creator, the "emptying" (*kenosis*) by the divine Christ to become human, and the relationships of secular civic power to religious authorities.

Symposia on Water Led by the Patriarch

It was in Ravenna that we gathered under the luminous mosaics in the Basilica of St. Apollinare in Classe on June 9, 2002 (figure 6.1). The space was redolent with the history of the powerful Christian denominations that enveloped this region of northern Italy for centuries, both Greek Orthodox and Roman Catholic. In the fifth century Ravenna was the

Figure 6.1 Basilica of St. Apollinare in Classe, Italy, UNESCO World Heritage Site. Statue of Julius Caesar (to left) who founded the port of Classe; Photo source: iStock

seat of the Roman Empire and then the center of Byzantine Italy until the eighth century. Dating back to the sixth century CE, the Basilica is now a United Nations Educational, Scientific and Cultural Organization World Heritage site. The noted mosaic of paradise in the apse over the altar had been reflecting the luminosity of the natural world for some fifteen hundred years.

Our gathering this Sunday morning was to witness the first Orthodox celebration of the liturgy of Saint John Chrysostom in this magnificent basilica since 1263, when the Byzantine empire still held sway. It was a high point in an international symposium on the Adriatic Sea titled "A Sea at Risk: A Unity of Purpose," sponsored by the Ecumenical Patriarch, Bartholomew, the leader of the Greek Orthodox Church. It was a historic moment, one of reconciliation and hope, high emotion and drama. More than five hundred people were present, including religious leaders and scientists, environmentalists and journalists. Visitors had traveled from across Italy to witness this event. The sense of occasion was palpable: choral singing lifted the heart, preaching inspired the mind, incense stimulated the senses, and a spirit of communion drew the congregation together, believers and nonbelievers alike.

The great divide between Eastern and Western Christianity that began in 1054 CE was bridged for the moment. The centuries-old differences of dogmas, historical wounds, and rituals were set aside.[6] A unity of purpose emerged, namely, concern for the future of the planet. This was genuine ecumenism—the ongoing dialogue within Christianity to find grounds for tolerance and reconciliation in diversity—experienced in a shared liturgy that moved the participants beyond simply polite conversation and good intentions.

The next day this engaged ecumenism was made even more explicit in a closing service at San Marco Basilica in Venice. There, just after sunset on this warm summer evening, an ecologically oriented liturgy was held in which prayers were recited and hymns were sung for the protection of the environment. These were especially composed for the occasion and performed beautifully by the Greek Byzantine Choir from the island of Patmos, where the *Book of Revelation* is said to have been composed by John the Evangelist.[7]

In between these memorable rituals, a closing ceremony was convened in the evening in the Palazzo Ducale (Ducal Palace) next to San Marco Basilica. In the presence of leading dignitaries, politicians, and religious leaders, the ceremony was presided over by Roger Cardinal Etchegarey, who chaired the Pontifical Council for Justice and Peace for many years, and Mark Malloch Brown, formerly of the United Nations Development Programme. There a Common Declaration was signed by the Ecumenical Patriarch, Bartholomew, and Pope John Paul II, who participated from the Vatican via satellite (see appendix A).

This declaration brought together Catholic and Orthodox concerns about the degradation of creation. It recognized growing ecological awareness and urged further education in this regard. It highlighted the importance of six ethical goals that focused on the world's children, values based on natural law, appropriate use of science and technology, stewardship rather than ownership, and a peaceful approach to disagreements. The declaration concluded with an urgent but hopeful statement: "It is not too late. . . . Within a single generation we could steer the Earth towards our children's future."

The Ducal Palace was an extraordinary setting for this event. Paintings of Venice's history surrounded us, and the golden ceiling displayed portraits of eminent leaders and public figures of the past. It was also a setting filled with the irony of our present moment. Historically, Venice was considered "wedded to the sea." In this spirit, an annual matrimonial rite was held for more than 800 years. The Doge, the leader of the city-state, would throw a golden wedding ring into the Adriatic Sea to commemorate this union. For many centuries Venice was a political and economic leader in the Mediterranean region, linking the Orthodox, Catholic, and Islamic worlds. The result of this dynamic exchange is evident in the rich art and architecture of the city.

Yet these great treasures are themselves endangered by the rising sea to which Venice is bound. Technological solutions, such as floodgates, have been proposed and hotly debated for years. But in the last decade San Marco Square, a historic treasure known around the world, is regularly flooded. To manage the flow of tourists, wooden planks are laid down for people to walk over the immense stone palazzo. The Ducal Palace is situated next to San Marco Basilica at the end of the square and adjacent to the Adriatic Sea, which is rising inexorably. With climate change affecting sea level rise, the long-term fate of this city and its magnificent patrimony is inevitably endangered. Indeed, this is emblematic of our planet as a whole as coastal waters are rising and small island nations are beginning to abandon their homelands. Not only are cultural treasures endangered, but biological and ecological treasures as well. The fate of people, biodiversity, and the planet as we know it is in the balance.

Figure 6.2 Paradise Mosaic over the main altar at the Basilica of St. Apollinare in Classe, Italy; Photo source: iStock

Ravenna: The Paradise Mosaic of St. Apollinare

The religious architecture and art of Ravenna in northern Italy provided a setting for the "Green Patriarch," Bartholomew, in his efforts at bringing Christianity to address the ecological challenges of our time.[8] Ravenna is a city where the mosaics gleam with exquisite beauty. Their intricate patterns have been crafted and preserved in church ceilings and walls for centuries.[9] These images are among the oldest Christian iconography and include a rich display of plant and animal life symbolizing the plenitude of creation.[10] They provide a stunning array of biblical stories and saintly legends that still inspire. In Ravenna the mosaics in the apse over the altar of the Basilica of St. Apollinare in Classe manifest an ethos cultivated in early Christianity (figure 6.2). These mosaics evoke a feeling for creation as a deep orientation toward and prefiguration of paradise. This is one of the great insights of Eastern Orthodox theology, which will be explored further in this chapter.

The imprint of Orthodox Christianity in these mosaics of paradise is evident in their cosmological orientation and grounding in an Edenic nature. This is the first time a historical human figure is depicted in a Christian mosaic. It is St. Apollinare, the first bishop of Ravenna and also a martyr, whose relics used to rest under the altar. His suffering is likened to Christ on the cross, and his luminous transformation corresponds to that of Christ in the Transfiguration. He is portrayed with hands raised to the cross above him, but he is fully ensconced in the natural world of paradise. A relationship is presented in which divine transcendence is wholly immanent in a world of living ecologies.

Deep green grasses hold the trees and the birds. These include plane, olive, myrtle, and cypress trees along with doves, partridges, quails, and phoenix. The twelve lambs below represent the twelve disciples and the coming of the faithful. The three lambs under the cross represent the apostles Peter, James, and John at the Transfiguration. The cross in the center is decorated with jewels and glows against the background of the luminous blue vault of heaven streaming with stars.[11] The unity of heavenly and earthly realms is depicted here. Above it all is the figure of Christ whose hand is raised in benediction, flanked by the four Evangelists in the form of animals: Matthew as the winged man representing incarnation, Mark as the lion representing resurrection, Luke as the ox representing the passion, and John as the eagle representing the ascension.

This mosaic of the mythic Garden of Eden presents the powerful symbolic charge of paradise in all of Christianity. The question of the relationships of this mythic symbolism to the actual reality of animals, plants, waters, and minerals within Christianity has been a vexing one. Historian Lynn White described Christianity as being anthropocentric and ultimately failing in its care for the natural world, but his insights may apply more to religious values transmitted in aspects of Protestant and Roman Catholic traditions.[12] He acknowledged that Orthodox forms of Christianity, as the apse mosaic at St. Apollinare suggests, hold a stronger belief in the connection of the divine and material reality, even calling it a unity.

This unity of heaven and Earth is a fundamental cosmological orientation and grounding in Orthodox Christianity. Images of this unity in Orthodoxy emphasize the Incarnation as an affirmation of materiality. Through the mosaics the luminosity of the cosmos is revealed. The precious materials and brilliant colors draw one into the chromatic spectrum of nature from which the stones originate. In addition, the luster of the materials brings the viewer into an intense experience of divine light illuminating all creation. Earth becomes an icon through which the radiance of the divine shines forth. The mosaics evoke many of the theological teachings of Orthodox Christianity, ones that the Ecumenical Patriarch, Bartholomew, has sought to retrieve and reevaluate in his many symposiums on water. Bartholomew is the titular head of the Eastern Orthodox Church who has shown exceptional leadership regarding environmental issues, especially focused on water.

Role of the Ecumenical Patriarch

In the midst of this critical moment in human history, the Ecumenical Patriarch, Bartholomew, has emerged as a preeminent religious figure responding to the environmental crisis.[13] Some of Bartholomew's breadth of knowledge and understanding is undoubtedly due to his studies at the University of Munich and the Ecumenical Institute in Bossey, Switzerland. He also earned a doctorate at the Oriental Institute of the Gregorian University in Rome.[14]

For some two decades the Ecumenical Patriarch has been visible and effective, both as a spokesperson for ecumenism and as a convener of a substantive dialogue between science and religion around environmental issues. With the able assistance of Maria Becket and Archdeacon John Chryssavgis, he has organized eight major international symposia on "Religion, Science, and the Environment," focused primarily on water. These have taken place on shipboard in the Aegean (1995), the Black Sea (1997), the Danube (1999), the Adriatic (2002), the Baltic (2003), the Amazon (2006), the Arctic (2007), and the Mississippi River (2009).

The symposia have involved leading environmentalists and scientists, religious leaders and scholars, civil servants and statesmen, journalists and educators. Having had the privilege of participating in five of the "Religion, Science and the Environment" symposia that he has convened since 1995, we have witnessed not only the eloquence and commitment of the Patriarch but also his humane manner and compassionate presence with people ranging from dignitaries to children. Moreover, his ecumenical work to bring the Christian churches together around environmental problems is unique. In this respect, the Common Declaration on Environmental Ethics with Pope John Paul II in Venice marks an unprecedented historic exchange between the Eastern and Western Churches since the great schism in 1054.

The Patriarch's enduring legacy will be his long-standing articulation of the environmental crisis as primarily a spiritual and moral crisis. He sees the limits of purely utilitarian responses to the Earth, as well as rational choice policies and arid intellectualism. Rather, he notes the need for an expanded understanding of the relationship of humans to the Earth and to the divine. His insistence on the spiritual and moral nature of the environmental crisis leads to fresh theological insights.

The originality of the Patriarch's contributions as a religious leader includes the following:

- Focusing the science and religion dialogue on the issue of the environment
- Speaking out about the degradation of the environment as ecological sin
- Bringing forward traditional Orthodox theology for new understandings of the relationship of Creator and Creation
- Highlighting the unique spiritual and ethical role of humans in the natural world
- Encouraging the discovery of the extraordinary in the ordinary
- Emphasizing the importance of Eucharist as cosmic liturgy

Science and Religion Dialogue for the Environment

With regard to the dialogue between science and religion, the Patriarch has created the space for vibrant conversations between ecologists, biologists, and chemists on one hand and theologians, clergy, and laity on the other. In his Ecological Institutes, which take place on the island of Halki off Istanbul, he has encouraged scientists to educate clergy on environmental issues. Orthodox priests are beginning to acknowledge their responsibility to speak out on behalf of God's creation. Moreover, in each of the eight symposia he has moved the science and religion dialogue outside the walls of seminary education or academic reflection into the world of environmental policy. Thus, both theology and science benefit from an exchange of ideas regarding the pressing issue of water degradation in various regions of the world. A Halki Summit was held in July 2012 called "Progressing Toward a Sustainable Environment." This was attended by notable environmentalists such as Jane Goodall, James Hansen, Bill McKibben, and Amory Lovins.[15]

Ecological Sin: Crimes against Creation

It was in 1994 in his Encyclical Letter on September 1, a day he proclaimed for prayers for the environment, that the Patriarch began to speak about the destruction of nature as sinful. In November 1997 at St. Barbara's Church in Santa Barbara, California he spoke forcefully about "ecological sin," observing that creation is seen as a gift from God. This was reported in the *Los Angeles Times*:

> It is, therefore, appropriate for us to seek ethical and even legal recourse where possible, in matters of ecological crimes.
>
> It follows that to commit a crime against the natural world is a sin. For human beings to cause species to become extinct and to destroy the biological diversity of God's creation; for human beings to degrade the integrity of the earth by causing changes in its climate, by stripping the earth of its natural forests, or by destroying its wetlands; for human beings to injure other human beings with disease; for human beings to contaminate the earth's waters, its land, its air, and its life, with poisonous substances—all of these are sins.[16]

Orthodox Theology: Ethos and Existential Orientation

The Patriarch's special contribution to contemporary Orthodox theology has been to create the grounds for a comprehensive ecological theology of Creation, along with theologians such as John Zizoulas, known also as Metropolitan John of Pergamon, and Archdeacon John Chryssavgis.[17] Using language that is accessible to academic theologians, engaged clergy, and interested laity, John of Pergamon has long been a major spokesperson for the Ecumenical Patriarch on these environmental issues. At the outset of the 2002 symposium on the Adriatic, John of Pergamon explored the turn that is needed in which ethics themselves become an orienting force toward a more profound ethos, or attitude, for flourishing human–Earth relations. In his overview remarks, he said,

> An ethic which is based on what the human being *does* is very different from an ethic founded on what the human being *is*. It is important, therefore, to establish our environmental ethics on existential rather than moral grounds i.e. by looking primarily not into the human actions but into the *attitude* and existential *orientation* that led to a certain ethical behavior. It is only on such a basis that an environmental ethic can demand universal persuasion and acceptance, something that is so necessary in the case of an ethic of this kind.
>
> There is a fundamental difference between ethics and ethos, which affects directly the subject of the environment. Putting it simply, *ethics* has to do with principles worked out *consciously* or even *rationally*, and perhaps intellectually, whereas *ethos* relates to *symbols*, emerging from shared everyday experience in a particular community.[18]

John of Pergamon presses the issue by calling for a deep change in our fundamental orientation and ethos:

> We may teach people what is ethically right to do, but in order to have this applied in their lives it will be necessary to insert it into their ethos.
>
> I believe that as religious leaders and scientists we must go deeper into the issue. We must be ready to propose not simply an ethic but an ethos, and to root our ethical demands deep in human existence and not simply in human behaviour. We must be prepared to ask not simply how people should behave, but why they must behave in a certain way. What are the compelling reasons for their ethical behaviour apart from fear and utility, which can be easily dismissed as exaggerations? What kind of existential reasons suggest or necessitate an environmental ethic?[19]

In this way John of Pergamon anchors his thought, and that of the Ecumenical Patriarch, in Orthodox theological emphases on material reality as orienting toward the divine. Drawing on this long theological tradition, the Patriarch also speaks of the goodness of Creation that is beautiful and blessed. He underscores the harmonious and interdependent whole of Creation.[20] Most significantly, he speaks of the world as a sacrament of communion with God. The natural world is not a place of exile or imprisonment. Rather, "the entire created cosmos is a burning bush of God's uncreated energies."[21] As it says in Psalm 19, "The heavens are telling the glory of God." Bartholomew also cites a contemporary ascetic who asks why we should venerate the clothing of a saint. "Is it not much more fitting that we should also venerate the flowers and the plants? After all, they enshrine within themselves the energy of God."[22]

Human–Earth Relations: Caring for the Gift of Nature

Creation, then, is a place of beauty that reveals divine sacredness. Humans are invited to partake of, to share in, and to enjoy that beauty. Because nature is seen as God's gift to humankind, humans are called upon to care for this gift—to preserve it and use it responsibly. To abuse nature is to sin against it. Domination of nature is to be avoided. However, humans have a special place in creation. "Any abuse of our power, any wanton or wasteful use of the world's natural resources, is repugnant to God."[23] The orienting role of religions is not simply to teach that humans are immersed in nature but that humans are inexorably woven into profound relationships that constitute life on Earth. Humans are thus called to a priestly role of responsibility and stewardship toward creation.[24] This takes various forms.

Cosmic Liturgy: Sacrament of Thanksgiving

A primary form is to see humans as part of a great cosmic liturgy, drawing on the thought of theologian and monk Maximus the Confessor (580–662).[25] Maximus uses the philosophical concept of *logos*, or inner order, to speak of the divine will and purpose within matter.[26] However, will and purpose for Maximus exist not as spiritual abstractions but as a matrix of relationships inherent in reality. Thus, the *logos*, or intention, of any individual may interact with the will and purpose of the divine. These multiple interactions of intention in a person overlap with the purpose in reality and correspond to the multiple manifestations of this divine will in Creation. Furthermore, not only is the world a revelation according to Maximus, but it is a triple embodiment of the *logos*, that is, in nature, in the historic person of Christ, and in Holy Scripture.[27] This concept of *logos*, then, becomes an orientation that guides one into realization of one's full human potential. In the Greek Orthodox tradition this is understood as "divinization," or *theosis*.

The very movement (*kinesis*) of beings in the world enables them to find their potential. Although this is not an understanding of Darwinian evolution, neither is it a static view of creation. Rather, with Maximus, Orthodox theology posits a dynamic universe orienting humans toward regard for creation as a divinizing process. This "anthropic cosmology" of Maximus results from the union of the invisible *logos* and the visible embodiment of the human.[28] This union is a "cosmic liturgy" of created beings that is also a cosmic sacramentalism. In the liturgical act of a living cosmology, all existence is potentially made sacred in the contemplative activity of the human.

Within that liturgy, as the Ecumenical Patriarch understands it, the Christian ritual of Eucharist is seen as a sacrament of thanksgiving for the fruits of the Earth and for the blessings of God.[29] In these ritual actions, the human is invited to revere the Creator but not necessarily to adore Creation.[30] According to Orthodox thought, this requires a *metanoia*, a radical transformation, in environmental consciousness, spiritual aware-ness, and ascetic practice. Humans are called to be restrained and reduce excessive consumption. Such self-control is not seen as world negating; rather, it is viewed as a joyful participation in the rhythms and limits of Creation. The Patriarch observed,

> Everyone, even the feeblest, can contribute to the restoration of the har-monious operation of the world. We can do so by being in tune with the forces of the divine harmony and not with those which are badly dissonant and oppose the divine all-harmonious rhythm of the universal instrument, of which each one of us constitutes but one of its innumerable chords. . . . It is the recognition of the harmony that should exist between our attitudes and actions on the one hand, and the laws of nature that govern the universe, on the other hand.[31]

Conclusion

One can appreciate the embrace of the Ecumenical Patriarch's concerns with the realization that the term *Ecumenical* is more than an honorific name; it is a way of life. He has clearly expanded the word *ecumenical* to in-clude the need not only for communion between the Christian churches but also for broader interreligious dialogue on the environment. But he does not stop there, for the Patriarch recognizes the profound responsi-bility humans have to one another, to other species, and to the Earth as a whole. Thus, the Patriarch's comprehensive concerns are evident in his continual witness to the magnificence and mystery of the Divine and to his constant call not to destroy or degrade God's Creation. This persistent and powerful testimony to the sacredness of Creation and to the special role of the human as mediator brings new energy and urgency into the ancient Orthodox insight of the human as the microcosm within the macrocosm. Such insight may be one of the most lasting legacies of the Patriarch's ecological theology, namely, retrieval of an orienting cosmology that calls forth an environmental ethos and ethics for our times.

7

Confucianism as Grounding in Community

Ecological Ethics for China

It was a steaming hot day in Beijing in May 2008 as we made our way in and out of meetings with scholars and teachers, deans and directors. All of them professed interest in the environment even as we were surrounded by the intense air pollution of Beijing.[1] By mid-afternoon we found ourselves at the Chinese Academy of Social Sciences talking with scholars who had read the Harvard volumes on religion and ecology. Indeed, not only had they read them, they had assembled a team of scholars and over a period of several years translated the volumes on Confucianism, Daoism, and Buddhism into Chinese. Such remarkable dedication to such detailed work. And why? Because they are living in one of the most polluted countries on the planet and want to find environmental values and ethics based on their own cultural traditions that are applicable to China.

Rapid economic growth and unregulated development have caused an explosion of construction in cities and across the countryside. Migrant workers have streamed into the cities providing cheap labor in the factories. Thousands of coal-fired plants have sprung up, spewing out particulates even though the central government has tried to stop some from being built and is now trying to shut some down. The relentless search for energy resulted in the construction of the Yangtze dam that took years to complete, uprooted more than a million people, destroyed ecosystems along the river, and flooded ancient archaeological sites. The environmental problems surrounding it were such that even the World Bank withdrew funding. Silting is already occurring. It has also been reported that one of the causes of the Sichuan earthquake of 2008, which resulted in nearly seventy thousand human casualties, may have been the massive weight of the water and the concrete dam in the Yangtze River.

In the midst of these pressing realities the Chinese Academy of Social Sciences has indicated an interest in sponsoring conferences on environmental perspectives from the three religious traditions of China: Confucianism, Daoism, and Buddhism. For this reason, they have translated these Harvard volumes. They are aware that environmental attitudes and values may be developed through their own traditions, not through Western religions or philosophy. Moreover, they have an Institute for World Religions that is the largest in the world, with some ninety full-time researchers.[2] A number of them are keenly interested in religion and ecology.

In the late afternoon, as we were preparing to leave the academy and face the searing heat once again, we went to check our e-mail. There was a message that we had hoped for but dared not assume we would receive. It said, "Come to the Environmental Ministry Office tomorrow morning at 10:30. The Deputy Vice Minister for the Environment, Pan Yue, will meet with you then." We were surprised and pleased by the opportunity. The vice minister was visiting Sichuan, where the devastating earthquake had recently occurred. He was arriving back in Beijing that night, and our plane to Japan was leaving at two o'clock the next afternoon. We had just enough time for the meeting, which in his eagerness to discuss the topic, he extended to an hour.

The next morning we were ushered through the security gates at the ministry and were led up to a conference room. We sat in nervous anticipation, sipping green tea and awaiting Pan Yue's arrival. Just a minute after 10:30 he walked in with a translator and two assistants. He immediately came to shake our hands warmly. We, too, were accompanied by a translator, one of the scholars from the Chinese Academy of Social Sciences, Chen Xia, and James Miller, a British scholar of Daoism who teaches at Queens University in Canada.

Sitting opposite one another, like diplomats at a long negotiating table, we exchanged gifts. We gave Pan Yue a copy of the Harvard volume on *Confucianism and Ecology*, and he gave us a book with his speeches that had been translated into English. Many of his speeches explored the importance of Chinese religions for modern China. This arose from the fact that he had earned a PhD in the history of religions. Thanks to the advice of a Chinese professor at Harvard, we had been following Pan Yue's speeches for more than a decade, but his detailed understanding of religions was something we discovered in our discussions. No doubt this prompted his writings about the need for "ecological culture" in China based on Confucian, Daoist, and Buddhist perspectives. This had been one of the major inspirations for the Harvard conference series, that is, the importance of traditional religions responding to modern environmental problems. For Pan Yue the notion of a culture based on ecological values and behavior is evident in his remarks:

> Why is environmental protection considered a cultural issue? One of the core principles of traditional Chinese culture is that of harmony between humans and nature. Different philosophies all emphasized the political wisdom of a balanced environment. Whether it is the Confucian idea of humans and nature becoming one, the Daoist view of the Dao reflecting nature or the Buddhist belief that all living things are equal, Chinese philosophy has helped our culture to survive for thousands of years. It can be a powerful weapon in preventing an environmental crisis and building a harmonious society.[3]

We realized that environmental ethics would be formulated differently in China and India than in the West. A cultural sensitivity was necessary that would be attentive to the emergence of plural forms of environmental ethics. So when we began to read Pan Yue's speeches in 1998 we were struck by his insights. With great care and deliberation he had gone back to read the Chinese texts on Confucianism, Daoism, and Buddhism. He wanted to study the classical traditions and their historical development. There he found a broad understanding of views of nature that were embedded in Chinese cultural understanding and practice. He understood in particular how these traditions were constantly interacting and cannot be studied in isolation from one another. His research was thorough and resulted in his thought-provoking essays, as is evident in appendix B. This is especially noteworthy because Confucianism, Daoism, and Buddhism had been nearly eradicated under the rule of Mao, especially during the Cultural Revolution from 1966 to 1976.

As he described it in our meeting, he was calling for the creation of an ecological culture for China and an ecological civilization for the planet as a whole that respected cultural differences. He explained, "We have environmental laws on the books, but we can't enforce them because we don't have an ecological culture." "This is true in the United States as well," we responded. "At times we have had to sue our own Environmental Protection Agency to enforce standards for clean water and air. This is because we have a weak ecological culture and strong lobbyists for the coal, oil, and gas industries."

As he became increasingly aware of how much we appreciated his cultural perspective, he threw back his head and laughed, saying, "Well, if you came to China to speak with someone about cultural traditions and ecology, you've come to the right guy!" Our meeting was lively, and Pan Yue was animated throughout. He acknowledged that he met with many high-level international environmental leaders, but few were attuned to this point of view. His interest spilled over into his hope to sponsor a conference on this topic. His deep desire to plant the seeds of ecological transformation by means of culture was infectious.

Indeed, what is striking about Pan Yue is that in many ways he is drawing on the model of the Confucian literati. These scholars studied the classics as a means of establishing humane government. To become officials they had to pass civil service examinations based on the classical texts. This was to ensure that they had understood the principles of humane and just governance so as to be effective officials. The model of the scholar–official endured for 600 years, until the end of the Ch'ing dynasty in 1905. Although abuses of power clearly occurred, the ideal of the scholar–official working for the common good was something that still inspired a civil servant such as Pan Yue.

This attention to the welfare of the whole may be one of the reasons why Chinese civilization has endured for so many centuries. The question then arises, What does Pan Yue see in this tradition that may help China shift course from an overreaching industrial revolution to a more balanced sustainability revolution? Surrounding this question is the historical reality that China degraded its landscape through deforestation in the premodern period.[4] Some would say that historically Confucianism did not constrain exploitation of resources. This can be further explored with more studies of environmental history in China.

In the last several decades China has created massive environmental problems with rapid industrialization. During this period it has followed a path of economic growth with little concern for ecological consequences and public health issues until recently. The lure of economic progress and development has been primary. Moreover, in the twentieth century traditional Chinese culture fell under attack as inadequate to modernization. Confucianism was undermined by Chinese intellectuals after the May 4th movement of 1919 and was severely attacked in the Cultural

Revolution under Mao between 1966 and 1976. Thus, there was little moral context to develop an effective environmental ethics in China. Although Confucianism and other traditional values have been under attack in the Maoist period, it cannot be disputed that there is now a revival of Confucianism in modern China. This results in part from a moral vacuum in the midst of excessive consumerism. Although this revival is a large topic with complex political and social implications, it is part of a broad struggle to rehabilitate culture, religion, and values in China today.

In this context some critical questions are emerging. What are the dimensions and values of Confucianism that might still contribute to a flourishing future, especially in creating an ecological culture for China? Why is there a growing interest in that question from government officials and academics as well as a broader public? Indeed, what is Confucianism, its past history, and its present implications?[5] In exploring these questions, we are aware of the gap between the ideals of Confucianism and present-day environmental challenges.

Overview: What Is Confucianism?

Confucianism has conventionally been described as a humanistic tradition focusing on the roles and responsibilities of humans to family, society, and government. Thus, Confucianism is identified primarily as an ethical or political system of thought with an anthropocentric focus. However, on further examination and as more translations become available in Western languages, this narrow perspective is being reexamined and enlarged.

Some of the most important results of this reexamination are the insights that have emerged from seeing Confucianism as not simply an ethical, political, or ideological system. Rather, Confucianism is now being appreciated as a complex religious tradition in ways that are different from Western traditions.[6] This may eventually result in expanding the idea of religion itself to include more than criteria adopted from Western traditions such as notions of God, salvation, and redemption. Moreover, Confucianism is being recognized for its affirmation of relationality not only between humans but also between humans and the natural world, and the cosmos itself.[7] In this sense it has been described as an anthropocosmic tradition.[8]

Confucianism manifests a religious ecology in its cosmological orientation. This cosmological orientation is realized in the connection of the microcosm of the self to the macrocosm of the universe through grounding oneself in natural and human communities, nurturing oneself in ritual relatedness, and transforming oneself through cultivation.

A Confucian religious ecology might be described as a series of concentric circles where the human is the center, not as an isolated individual but as grounded in overlapping rings of family, society, and government. This is especially clear in the text of the *Great Learning*:

> Those in antiquity who wished to illuminate luminous virtue throughout the world would first govern their states; wishing to govern their states, they would first bring order to their families; wishing to bring order to their families, they would first cultivate their own persons; wishing to cultivate their own persons, they would first rectify their minds; wishing to rectify their minds, they would first make their thoughts sincere; wishing to make their thoughts sincere, they would first extend their knowledge. The extension of knowledge lies in the investigation of things.[9]

All these circles are contained within nature and the vast cosmos itself. The ultimate context for human flourishing is the "10,000 things," namely, nature in all its remarkable variety and abundance.

Confucian scholar Tu Weiming has described Confucianism as the cultural DNA of Chinese society. He suggests that this is the reason for its survival down to the present, despite severe persecution under Mao, who wanted to eliminate Confucianism. However, Confucianism lives on within the family and involves the relationship of individuals to others. Family relations are primary, with respect for parents, grandparents, and one's ancestors at the heart of human life. Filial piety is an indispensable part of the obligations of children toward those who have given them life, nurtured them in their early years, and supported them into adulthood. The same sense of filiality is extended in the Confucian tradition to Heaven and Earth as the symbolic great parents of all life. Chang Tsai's *Western Inscription* reflects this:

> Heaven is my father and Earth is my mother, and even such a small creature as I find an intimate place in their midst. Therefore that which extends throughout the universe I regard as my body and that which directs the universe I consider as my nature. All people are my brothers and sisters, and all things are my companions.[10]

For some Confucian thinkers this motivates care for the Earth community. Heaven here is understood as a guiding moral force, like conscience, and Earth is the great web of life—human and more than human.

As such, Heaven and Earth are not ontologically distinctive spheres in Confucian thinking but woven into the human experience of lived reality.

In the Confucian tradition the goal is for the individual to add to social harmony through appropriate relations and ritual practices. The *Book of Rituals* describes in great detail how these rituals should be carried out. In Confucianism, individual conflict is to be avoided, and a communitarian ethics is to be honored. These complex social relations and emphases on harmony are still evident in China, as well as across East Asia. In Confucian cultures, traditionally one was encouraged to pursue education for moral self-cultivation and for contributing to the common good of the society. Today regard for the value of education is still strong in East Asia, although more often for economic gain or engineering prowess than moral edification. Yet there is a remarkable revival of Confucianism taking place in China today.

The Revival of Confucianism

In the twentieth century a modern epoch of Confucianism has emerged, called "New Confucianism." This represents a revival of the tradition under the influence of scholars who came to Taiwan and Hong Kong after Mao's ascendancy in 1949.[11] Mao thought that Confucianism was essentially a feudal tradition mired in ancient history and customs and that for his communist ideas to succeed, a radical break must be made with the past. The anti-Confucian campaigns during Mao's rule were virulent, especially in the Cultural Revolution of the 1960s and 1970s.

However, after Mao's death there was a resurgence of interest in Confucian values, some of this encouraged by the government. Seven conferences on Confucius were convened in China between 1978 and 1989. This culminated in 1989 with major conferences in Beijing and in Confucius's birthplace, Qufu, to explore the future of the Confucian Way. These conferences were held to commemorate the 2,540th anniversary of Confucius's birth and marked a renewed interest in Confucianism to balance the unsettling effects of the rapid industrialization and modernization of China. The China Confucius Foundation, founded in 1984, sponsored them along with the United Nations Educational, Scientific and Cultural Organization. The International Confucian Association was established in 1994.

During this period, overseas Chinese scholars were instrumental in researching, teaching, and lecturing on the Confucian tradition. These included scholars such as Liu Shuxian at the Academia Sinica in Taiwan,

Tu Weiming at Harvard, Yu Yingshi at Princeton, and Cheng Zhong-ying at University of Hawaii. Tu Weiming "contributed more than any other individual to promoting a renewed interest in *ruxue* [Confucianism] through his lectures and networking in China, beginning in 1978."[12] Tu has made significant efforts to articulate the value of Confucianism for contemporary Chinese society and its contributions to philosophy in the modern world.

In the last decade there has been a revival of Confucianism from several directions.[13] On a popular level, books on Confucius have sold millions of copies, such as one written by Yu Dan in 2010. Conferences on Confucian thinkers and ideas are being held in various parts of China, sponsored by philosophy departments in many universities. In the model of the Alliance Française, Confucian Societies are being created abroad to expand knowledge of Confucian culture and values. In the United States, decades of efforts to study and translate Confucian texts have been led by Wing-tsit Chan, William Theodore de Bary, Burton Watson, Yu Ying-shih, Irene Bloom, Roger Ames, Henry Rosemont, and John Berthrong. There is a growing movement in China and across East Asia to reevaluate Confucianism for its role in a sustainable future, that is, creating ecological culture.[14] This has been encouraged by a number of leaders besides Pan Yue, including former president Hu Jintao and current president Xi Jinping.[15] In addition, there have been significant efforts in China toward constructive postmodernism, fostered by process thinkers such as David Ray Griffin and John Cobb.[16] This is inspired by the process thought of Alfred North Whitehead.[17] At Claremont University in California, an Institute for Postmodern Development of China has been created by Zhihe Wang and Meijun Fan along with John Cobb, Jay McDaniel, and others. They have held more than sixty conferences in California and China on topics such as "The Place of Harmony in Ecological Civilization" (April 2012). The retrieval, reevaluation, and reconstruction of the Confucian tradition in response to China's ecological crisis are occurring in the educational world and beyond. These efforts draw on traditional Confucian values to articulate new goals of sustainability for forming an ecological culture.

Models of Confucian Flourishing for Self, Society, and Nature

The effort to retrieve, reevaluate, and reconstruct Confucianism that is now taking place in China is drawing on key thinkers and texts from the early classical tradition, which includes Confucius, Mencius, and Xunzi, and the later Neo-Confucian tradition, such as Zhu Xi. These figures and their writings are gradually becoming known in the West through translations and commentaries. Their fuller significance for ecological ethics in China is now being explored.

Confucius: Moral Rectification Extending Outward

The acknowledged founder of the Confucian tradition was known as the sage-teacher Kongzi (551–479 BCE). His name was Latinized by the Jesuit missionaries as Confucius in the sixteenth century CE (see figure 7.1 for a depiction of Confucius). Born into a time of rapid social change, Confucius was concerned with the goal of reestablishing political and social order through rectification of the individual and the state. The principal teachings of Confucius are contained in his conversations recorded in the *Analects*.[18] Here he emphasized the cultivation of moral virtues, especially humaneness (*jen, ren*) and the practice of civility or ritual decorum (*li*), which includes filiality (*xiao*). Virtue and civility were exemplified by the noble person (*junzi*), particularly within the five relations: between ruler and minister, parent and child, husband and wife, older and younger siblings, and friend and friend. The essence of Confucian thinking was that to establish order in the society one had to begin with harmony, filiality, and decorum in the family. Then, like concentric circles, the effects of virtue would reach outward to the society. Likewise, if the ruler was moral, it would have a ripple effect on the rest of the society and on nature itself, like a pebble dropped into a pond.

At the heart of this classical Confucian worldview is a profound commitment to humaneness and civility. These two virtues defined the means of human relatedness as a spiritual path. Through civility, beginning with filiality, one can repay the gifts of life both to one's parents and ancestors and to the whole natural world. Through humaneness one can extend this sensibility to other humans and to all living things. In doing so one becomes more fully human. The root of practicing humaneness is considered to be filial relations. The extension of these relations from one's family and ancestors to the human family and to the cosmic family of the natural world is the means whereby these primary biological ties provided a person with the roots, trunks, and branches of an interconnected spiritual path. Humans, nature, and the cosmos are joined in the stream of filiality. From the lineages of ancestors to future progeny, intergenerational connections and ethical bonding arose. Reverence and reciprocity are considered a natural response to this gift of life from parents and ancestors. Analogously, through reverence for Heaven and Earth as the

Figure 7.1 Statue of Confucius at the temple in Nanjing; Photo credit: Deborah Sommer

great parents of all life, one realizes one's full cosmological being and one's place in the natural order.[19] This can be considered a model for flourishing from the individual radiating outward. These ideas on cosmic filiality hark back to the early classic of the *Book of History* and are more fully developed in the Neo-Confucian tradition.

Mencius: Botanical Cultivation of Self and Nature

Confucian thought was further developed in the writings of Mencius, or Mengzi (385–312? BCE) and Hsun tzu, or Xunzi (313–238? BCE), who wrestled with the question of whether human nature was intrinsically good or evil. Mencius made a case for the former, whereas Hsun tzu argued for the latter. Mencius's position on the inherent goodness of human nature gained dominance among Confucian thinkers and gave an optimistic flavor to Confucian educational philosophy and political theory. This perspective influenced the spiritual aspects of the tradition as well, because self-cultivation was seen as a means of uncovering this innate good nature. Mencius contributed an understanding of the process needed for self-cultivation.[20] He did this by identifying the innate seeds of virtues in the human ("four beginnings"). Mencius suggests ways in which they could be cultivated toward their full realization as virtues, thus activating compassion for others:

> All human beings have a mind that commiserates with others. . . . The mind's feeling of pity and compassion is the beginning of humaneness; the mind's feeling of shame and aversion is the beginning of rightness; the mind's feeling of modesty and compliance is the beginning of propriety; and the mind's sense of right and wrong is the beginning of wisdom. Human beings have these four beginnings just as they have four limbs.[21]

Analogies taken from the natural world, such as the "seeds of virtue," extended the idea of self-cultivation of the individual for the sake of family and society to a wider frame of reference that also encompassed the natural environment. This can be described as a path of botanical cultivation.[22] In addition to his teachings on personal cultivation, Mencius advocated humane government as a means to promote the flourishing of a larger common good. His political thought embraced appropriate agricultural practices and proper use of natural resources. In particular, he urged that the ruler attend to the basic needs of the people and follow the way of righteousness, not profit.

Xunzi: Ritual Relationship of Humans and Cosmos

Xunzi contributed a strong sense of the importance of ritual practice as a means of self-cultivation.[23] He noted that human desires needed to be satisfied, and emotions such as joy and sorrow should be expressed in the appropriate degree. Rituals provided the form for such expression in daily human exchange as well as in rites of passage such as marriage and death. Moreover, because Xunzi saw human nature as innately flawed, he emphasized the need for education and ritual to shape human nature toward the good. Finally, he had a highly developed sense of the interdependent triad of Heaven, Earth, and Human that was also emphasized by many later Confucian thinkers. He writes, "Heaven has its seasons; Earth has its resources; humans have their government. For this reason it is said that they may form a triad [with Heaven and Earth]."[24] Heaven here is understood as the cosmos as well as a guiding force of the universe; Earth is seen as the natural sphere in which humans lived and flourished.

Zhu Xi: Forming One Body with All Things

Confucianism blossomed in a Neo-Confucian revival in the eleventh and twelfth centuries that resulted in a new synthesis of the earlier teachings. The major Neo-Confucian thinker Chu Hsi, or Zhu Xi (1130–1200) (figure 7.2), designated four texts from the canon of historical writings as containing the central ideas of Confucian thought. In 1315 these texts and Zhu Xi's commentaries on them became the basis of the Chinese civil service examination system, which endured for nearly 600 years until 1905. Every prospective government official had to take the civil service exams based on Zhu Xi's commentaries on the Four Books. The idea was to provide educated, moral officials for the large government bureaucracy that ruled China. Thus, the influence of Neo-Confucian thought on government, education, agriculture, land use, and social values was extensive. Views of nature, agriculture, and resource management were derived from Neo-Confucian understandings of the importance of humans' working to cultivate and care for nature as a means to fulfill their role in the order of things. Similarly, the role of government was to ensure healthy harvests and the storage of grain so as to create a flourishing society.

Zhu Xi's synthesis of Neo-Confucianism was recorded in his classic anthology *Reflections on Things at Hand* (*Jinsilu*).[25] In this work Zhu formulated a this-worldly spirituality based on a balance of cosmological orientation, ethical and ritual practices, scholarly reflection, and political participation.[26] The aim was to balance inner cultivation with outward investigation of things in concert with the dynamic changes of the natural world. Zhu Xi affirmed these changes as the source of transformation in both the cosmos and the person.

Thus Neo-Confucian spiritual discipline involved cultivating one's moral nature so as to bring it into harmony with the larger patterns of change in the cosmos. Each moral virtue had its cosmological component. For example, the central virtue of humaneness was seen as the source of fecundity and growth in both the individual and the cosmos. By practicing humaneness, one could affect the transformation of things in oneself, in society, and in the cosmos. In so doing, one recognizes one's deeper identity with reality as forming one body with all things. As the *Doctrine of the Mean* stated, "Being able to assist in the transforming and nourishing powers of Heaven and Earth, one can form a triad with Heaven and Earth."[27]

Confucian Relationality and Nature: Embodied Transformation

From the classical texts to the later Neo-Confucian writings there is a strong sense of nature as a relational whole in which human life and society flourish. Indeed, Confucian thought recognizes that it is the rhythms of nature that sustain life in both its biological needs and sociocultural expressions. The biological dimensions of life depend on nature as a holistic, organic continuum. Everything in nature is interdependent and interrelated. Most importantly, for Confucians nature is seen as dynamic and transformational.[28] These ideas are evident in the *Book of Changes* and are expressed in the *Four Books*, especially in the *Analects*, *Mencius*, the *Doctrine of the Mean*,[29] and the *Great Learning*.[30] They come to full flowering in the Neo-Confucian tradition of the Sung and Ming periods. Nature in this context has an inherent unity, that is, it has a primary ontological source (*T'ai ji*). It has patterned processes of transformation (*yin* and *yang*), and it is interrelated in the interaction of the five elements and the 10,000 things. Nature is dynamic and fluid with the movements of material force (*qi*).

The Morality of Nature: Affirming Change

For Confucians, humans are anthropocosmic beings in relationship, not anthropocentric individuals in isolation. The human is viewed as a microcosm in relation to the macrocosm of the universe. This is expressed most succinctly in the metaphor of humans as forming a triad with the cosmos and Earth. These relations were developed during the Han period with a complex synthesis of correlative correspondences involving the elements,

Figure 7.2 Statue of Zhu Xi at Wuyi Mountain; Photo credit: Deborah Sommer

directions, colors, seasons, and virtues.[31] This need to consciously connect the patterns of nature with the rhythms of human society is very ancient in Confucian culture.[32] It is at the basis of the anthropocosmic worldview where humans are seen as working together with Heaven and Earth in correlative relationships to create harmonious societies. The mutually related resonances between self, society, and nature are constantly being described in the Confucian texts and are evident in art and architecture as well.

In Confucianism, nature is not only inherently valuable, it is morally good. Nature thus embodies the normative standard for all things; it is not judged simply from an anthropocentric perspective. There is not a fact–value or is–ought division in the Confucian worldview, for nature is seen as an intrinsic source of value. In particular, value lies in the ongoing transformation and productivity of nature. A term repeated frequently in Neo-Confucian sources is *sheng-sheng*, reflecting the ever-renewing fecundity of life itself. In this sense, the dynamic transformation of life is seen as emerging in recurring cycles of growth, fruition, harvesting, and abundance. This reflects the natural processes of flourishing and decay in nature, human life, and human society. Change is thus seen as a dynamic force that humans should harmonize and interact with rather than withdraw from.

In this context, the Confucians do not view hierarchy as leading inevitably to domination. Rather, they see that value rests in each thing but not in each thing equally. Everything in nature and society has its appropriate role and place and thus should be treated accordingly. The use of nature for human ends must recognize the intrinsic value of each element of nature but also its value in relation to the larger context of the environment. Each entity is considered not simply equal to every other; rather, each interrelated part of nature has a particular value according to its nature and function. Thus, there is a differentiated sense of appropriate roles for humans and for all other species. For Confucians hierarchy is seen as a necessary way for each being to fulfill its function. In this context, then, no individual being has exclusive privileged status in relation to nature. Rather, the processes of nature and its ongoing logic of transformation (*yin* and *yang*) is the norm that takes priority for the common good of the whole society.

Humane Society and Government: Grounds for Flourishing

Confucians were mindful that nature was the basis of a stable society. Thus, if humans did not tend nature carefully, imbalance would result.

.

There are numerous passages in *Mencius* advocating humane government based on appropriate management of natural resources and family practices. Moreover, there are various passages in Confucian texts urging humans not to cut down trees wantonly or kill animals needlessly.

The establishment of humane society, government, and culture inevitably results in the use of nature for housing, production, and governance, however. In this sense, Confucians might be seen as pragmatic social ecologists (rather than deep ecologists) who recognize the necessity of forming human institutions—both educational and political—for a stable society. Nonetheless, it is clear that for Confucians human cultural values and practices are grounded in nature and part of its structure, and thus humans are dependent on its beneficence. In addition, the agricultural base of Confucian societies has always been recognized as essential to the political and social well-being of the country. The Confucians were consummate agricultural managers, encouraging irrigation projects and careful planting and harvesting techniques, as well as the storage of grain. Humans prosper by living within nature's boundaries and are refreshed by its beauty, restored by its seasons, and fulfilled by its rhythms. For Confucians, human flourishing is thus dependent on fostering nature in its variety and abundance; going against nature's processes is self-destructive. Human moral growth means cultivating one's desires not to interfere with nature but to be in accord with the great Way (*Dao*) of Nature. Thus the "human mind" expands in relation to the "Mind of the Way."

Conclusion

For Confucians, harmony with nature is essential. Moreover, human self-realization is achieved by being grounded in nature and in the human community. The great triad of Confucianism, Heaven, Earth, and Humans, signifies this understanding that humans can attain their full humanity only in relationship to both Heaven and Earth. This became a foundation for a religious ecology of relationality and grounding applicable to spheres of family, society, politics, and nature itself. This is a broad ethical basis for Confucian flourishing and the foundation of ecological cultures.

Many Chinese ask whether these ethical principles can be retrieved, reevaluated, and reconstructed in the face of such rapid development and relentless modernization. Or will the dream of overarching economic growth inspired by the myth of modern progress continue to be the dominant driver for China? What of the pollution of water, air, and soil undermining the health and livelihood of present and future generations?

There are no clear answers to these questions. But with more than 66,000 environmental protests a year, the Chinese know they will have to make some serious changes as they attempt to balance economics and the environment. Indeed, they are already leading the way in green technologies and alternative energy systems. However, the combination of efficacious environmental values and a robust ecological culture is still on the horizon, as it is for so many countries. This will require the creative interaction of many other disciplines such as science, law, urban planning, and public health.

8

Indigenous Traditions and the Nurturing Powers of Nature

Connecting Food and Ritual

Religious ceremonies often bring participants into the immediacy of vital embodiment, that is, the capacity to feel sacred power in one's body. Indigenous peoples recognize this sacred power residing in the surrounding world of plants and animals that nurture humans. In this sense, embodied beings in the world are food to one another. That which nourishes and that which receives the nurturing stand in intimate relationship and thus shape one another.

In these ways, nurturing, as a process of religious ecology, brings us into consideration of food. Food in its many aspects has been marked by religious reflection and ritual action.[1] As a seminal pathway for transferring sacred power, food comes to be gathered, prepared, and presented at celebrations and in thanksgiving. Here one ritual of Salish/Okanagan peoples, the Winter Dance,[2] is highlighted for connections between the sources of food, the life of the people, and the implications of food in the larger flow of the natural world.[3] A term in the Salish language for this sacred flow is *sumix*, and this powerful concept is at the heart of the Winter Dance, a yearly ritual for the Salish peoples.[4] Reception of this sacred power is understood by Salish elders as coming from guardian spirits, or spirit beings, in the natural world.

This major ceremonial is still practiced among Salish peoples of the Interior Columbia River Plateau region in the Northwest of North

America. It has become especially open and public since the American Indian Religious Freedom Act of 1978.[5] Earlier opposition to Indigenous religious practices in the nineteenth and twentieth centuries had come from the civilizing policy of government agents and from the evangelizing efforts of Christian missionaries. Even though government policies preventing the practice of their traditions have changed, some Salish peoples have internalized skeptical attitudes toward the Winter Dance and criticize such Salish practices as outmoded.[6] Nonetheless, the efforts at revival of the Winter Dance reveal the endurance of traditional lifeways. Preserving such cultural and religious practices of indigenous peoples worldwide is the driving force behind the United Nations Declaration on the Rights of Indigenous Peoples (see appendix C).

Lifeway

Lifeway is a term that helps us understand how the Winter Dance is a religious ecology demonstrating the process of nurturing the people and the land. *Lifeway* refers to a traditional integrated style of life found among many Indigenous peoples that distinguishes them from modern secular societies that tend to make distinctions between economics and ecology, politics and society, science and religion. Among small-scale societies there is a seamlessness between political, economic, religious, and cultural realms in which shared language, kinship names, governance systems, reverence for homeland, and collective narratives of identity bind the people together. Cultural forces coalesce, thus forming a collective symbolic consciousness that transmits values over generations. In this sense, the symbolic values that nurture life are threaded through their worldviews. Thus, a traditional people's worldview—or way of understanding reality—flows from their life in a bioregion where rivers, mountains, animals, and particular sites sacred to the people are profoundly intertwined with their identity and their ways of nurturance.[7] This has resulted in cultural coherence for many Indigenous nations even in the face of the fragmenting forces of colonialism.

Anthropologist Tim Ingold images this concept, which he calls lifeworld, as dwelling in a sphere with a strong sense of the relationships between places and life forms. He contrasts this with dominating or moving over a globe as though lands and species exist to serve humans.[8] These interwoven lifeway connections are practiced in ritual and remembered in stories about the community of living presences in the landscape. Lifeway flows from and renews a people's religious cosmology through mythic stories. Such stories are considered to be vital and alive, so that their

narration during ritual constitutes one expression of their living cosmology that carries them throughout their life. These narratives place the
speaker and audience in the larger community of life.[9] Salish interactions
with the natural world manifest a religious ecology. That is, their lifeway
does not separate out religion and the spiritual life as an autonomous,
individualistic, or separate component of community life.

In presenting this particular example of an Indigenous religious ecology, we are not implying that this represents other First Nations or Native Peoples. Striking differences mark the lifeways and ceremonies of
the many Indigenous peoples around the planet. Nor are we suggesting
that a return to Indigenous lifeways is the answer to contemporary environmental challenges. Instead, we are highlighting this ceremonial as an
example of the resilience of Indigenous cultures as sustained by their religious ecologies. This resilience is evident in the ways traditional thought
has been brought to bear in sovereignty struggles that First Nations peoples in Canada are waging against tar sands pipelines (see appendix D).

Attending the Winter Dance

John attended Winter Dances from 1985 to 1997 and again in 2000. The
dances were sponsored by the Louie family in Inchelium, Washington on
the Colville Reservation. The small village of Inchelium is best reached
by the ferry that crosses Franklin Delano Roosevelt Lake. The Columbia
River forms the lake behind the Grand Coulee Dam. This dam was finished in 1941 and has significantly eroded the lifeways of Salish villages
along the river's shores because no fish ladders were included for salmon
to return to their spawning grounds.[10]

Salmon are at the center of the Salish peoples' traditional symbolic
and subsistence activities. Religious and economic life revolves around
salmon. The loss of this keystone food and religious symbol has had a
cascading effect that devastated the Salish lifeway and subverted their
rituals.[11] For this reason, years earlier elder Martin Louie (also known
as *Snpakchin*, or "First Light at Morning"; figure 8.1) left his home in
Inchelium. Seeking religious freedom, he brought his family to the Canadian side of the border. Having grown old, he came home to Inchelium
after the 1978 American Indian Religious Freedom Act was passed. He
returned to end his years in familiar sacred places in the mountains along
the Columbia River so that he could continue Salish traditional ways.
After his return, he and his sons were instrumental in reviving ceremonial
life, especially the Winter Dance.

Figure 8.1 Martin Louie (*Snpakchin*, or "First Light at Morning," Okanagan/Salish); Photo credit: John Grim

At the first Winter Dance John attended, Martin Louie's son, Tom, brought him over to the site. The dance was to begin before sunset, but there was a problem. The "old man," Martin Louie, was not back from his healing travels to northern reservations that no longer had traditional healers. His two sons, Pierre and Tom, knew the ritual procedures, but they had not led a Winter Dance ceremony on their own before.

The anxiety precipitated by the absent ritual leader was relieved by crackling humor as Pierre observed, "I'll bet the old man is parked right on top of the mountain behind us waiting for us to set up the center-ing tree and begin the dance." So we laughed until he and Tom finally brought in the lodgepole pine for the centering pole and began the dance before sunset. In the end, Pierre was exactly right, and their father arrived soon after the centering tree was set in place.

Over the years as John returned for Winter Dances he became famil-iar with external signs that the dance was in preparation. On those later ferry crossings he would invariably spot the welcoming smoke from the dance house stovepipe. On the opening day there are usually several cars parked nearby. By the third day of the dance, the surrounding area would be crowded with cars, with nearly a hundred people gathered. They were waiting for sunset to go into the dance house. During these years, Pierre arranged for a one-room schoolhouse to be transported to the Louie place as the dance house. This spacious setting for the Winter Dance has a marvelous oak floor that seems to lift the dancers as they circle around the singer at the centering tree.

The dance occurs over four nights into the early morning, during which the windows of the hall are covered with different-colored cloths, some of which are also draped over the antlers of the deer heads on the inner walls. Dimmed kerosene lanterns sitting on small shelves cast a comfortable glow over participants seated in chairs around the room. In the far corner the barrel stove glows with the fire within, while its light plays on the stacks of firewood and throws shadows across the dance floor. In the corner of the room opposite the stove, the door for entry is also covered with a long cloth. A doorman stands nearby to welcome participants and to close the door when a singer stands up, begins to sing, and goes to the pole.

The format and structure of the Winter Dance have changed since the nineteenth century, when dances were held in a large rectangular ritual area formed by tule-reed tipis sewn together. Although archaeological records indicate that Salish peoples may have lived in this region for more than 10,000 years, the evolving form of this ancient Winter Dance ceremony is not known. The ethnology gathered from native peoples in the region during the nineteenth century shows differences between Interior Plateau native peoples, such as the Yakima, Okanagan, Flathead, and Coeur d'Alene. Yet a shared consistency endures among these tribes in the ways they practice the Winter Dance.[12] Earlier ethnographic accounts present the ceremony as John experienced it. For example, a Winter Dance from 1954 is described as follows:

> The dance is held in the largest room, usually the living room of a male or female shaman's house. In the centre of the room is a bare pole affixed to the ceiling and floor. This pole acts as the centre point for all activity during the dance. Only a shaman [or singer] may touch the pole.
>
> Before performing, a shaman [or singer] will begin humming a song softly while he [or she] sits or stands in some part of the room. As he sings louder he approaches the pole. He may walk around the pole singing to it or hold out his arms to the pole as he sings. When he grasps the pole in both hands he has become one with his guardian spirit. As long as he is holding the pole his words are not his own but those of his guardian spirit. Guardian spirits speak unintelligibly and in a low voice, and therefore,

another person must transmit the guardian spirit's words to the audience. For this purpose an interpreter [or announcer] stands by the shaman [or singer] and repeats the guardian spirit's speech in a loud voice. . . . This pipeline from the guardian spirit via the shaman [or singer] and the interpreter continues for as long as the guardian spirit has something to say to the audience. As a rule the guardian spirit makes prognostications of the future, gives free advice, and makes comments on present events.[13]

A Winter Dance may also include other ritual activities such as the symbolic cleaning of the room where the ritual is held in preparation for the arrival of guardian spirits, or spirit beings (*sumix*). Other forms of ritualization include participants singing vision songs and dancing as animals on the move around a center pole. There are also giveaways by the singers and host families, distribution of sacred foods, feasting, sweat lodges, stick-game gambling, and storytelling. Each Winter Dance is somewhat different and comes about through a spirit call to the shaman-sponsor rather than a human-determined calendar or clock time.

Nurturing and Giving

Nurturing is a central moral impulse threaded throughout the Salish worldview. This giving forms a core cultural value within the religious ecology of the Winter Dance. Thus, songs are sung at the Winter Dance to honor the giving of the plants and animals as food for humans. Traditional Salish peoples recognize that most animals, including humans, eat root crops. This is particularly the case for the large mammals such as deer, elk, and bear that hunters bring to the community as food. So songs are primarily about changing the weather to give moisture for the growth of root crops. In the Salish lifeway this is a reverential remembering of what the plants in particular have given to nurture life.

In addition to their songs, individual singers may also give away material goods during the ceremony. After singing and speaking slowly at the pole, they may drape over their backs multiple shawls and cloths. They hold in their hands beaded strings, woven belts, bandanas, and other gifts. Singing softly, they move around the circle of seated participants and wait for each person to take an object. These gifts are given to assist the singer in lifting the burdens of life from his or her shoulders. The giveaways amplify the giving of the Earth especially evident in Salish religious cosmologies. Narratives describe how the spirit beings gave of their bodies to nourish humans. The gifts of food from these plants, animals, minerals, and land are symbolically reenacted in the giving of material goods by the singers.

Individuals sing their special song, given to them by a guardian spirit in the local landscape. By singing they give back what was given to them for the benefit of the whole community of life. Their song reverberates on many levels. For example, the songs are believed to affect the weather so that moisture will reach the root crops. One way for that to happen is for a heavy wet snow to fall during the Winter Dance, followed by increasingly cold weather. This creates ice that seals moisture into the ground for the root crops such as camas bulbs and bitterroot. In the religious ecology of the Winter Dance, gift giving reflects the many levels of reciprocity in life from root crops to animals to humans to spirit beings.

Elders often speak of the significance of these gifts (*en-we-num*) while at the center pole. They chide anyone who attends the dance merely for the opportunity to receive a gift. Such thinking is labeled the "outsider behavior" of acquisitive dominant society and is criticized as damaging to the singers, the community, and the moral order in the world. A gift is a nurturing act that imparts reciprocity between the person who gives and those receiving. Receipt of a gift implies an obligation to help the giver who has undertaken the difficult burden of giving. Thus, giving is a central value symbolizing the reciprocal needs across the community of life most evident in the exchange of food.

At midnight the family members go out of the dance hall to get water and prepare the four sacred foods: bitterroot, camas bulbs, salmon, and deer meat. Water is carried in first and placed before the centering tree. There, the head sponsor approaches the pole, singing softly and speaking of the gift of water to sustain life. Taking a water dipper, he or she pours water on the tree first and then takes a drink. The participants line up and come to the pole, offering a silent or spoken word, a small act of appreciation for water, before taking a drink. After this, the four foods are brought out and distributed with a short comment about their gift to the people. This central ritual moment occurs at midnight, when the guardian spirits are said to draw closest to the dance hall. The sharing of food commemorates the religious cosmology describing the *sumix* beings who both give songs and give of themselves as food. Along with sharing food, ritual singing at the Winter Dance manifests this deep relational exchange at the center of the religious ecology of the Interior Columbia River Salish peoples.

Sumix and Spirit Songs

At the heart of the Winter Dance is the individual guardian spirit relationship made manifest in visionary songs sung at the centering tree, a lodgepole pine. It is believed that these numinous spirit persons in the landscape give songs as a gift of *sumix* power to humans. *Sumix* is a Salish word that has no direct equivalent in English. Thus, it is challenging to interpret *sumix* into a non-Indigenous worldview, especially one with a monotheistic understanding of the divine. Rather than a single defined equivalency in English, *sumix* can be understood as referring simultaneously to the spirit-persons in the landscape, the power that they can transfer to humans, and the manifestation of that power.[14] Such manifestations can be in natural occurrences, such as an earthquake, or in a human demonstrating skills and capacities such as healing, hunting, fishing, or plant gathering.

Sumix is considered present in the powers of growth and nurturance in the natural world.[15] It may also describe a person who has the capacity for generating life, for creativity, and for transforming the ordinary. This capacity can be given to an individual in an exceptional way, such as in a vision song, but even that individual learns about *sumix* in the context of his or her community and culture. *Sumix*, then, is manifestation of spiritual power and may be expressed in a song, a sound, and even in a baby's cry. During a Winter Dance, Martin Louie gently said to those assembled:

> When I was a youngster at Barnaby Creek other villages from Mission Flat, Hall Creek, Roger's Bar, Keller, Nespelem, and Omak, they all gathered for the Winter Dances. . . . I think what we gained in one word was *confidence*. We made a circle and we went around the world [the centering tree] and prayed that we'd be in the circle this time next year . . . and it's not only the Indians that sing the song at the Winter Dance. It's all over the world. All nations, they all have a song. That's what my people say. When you're a baby the first thing you do is to learn to hum, to make a little noise. That's what they call a song. Each nation in their own language in their own way has a song. Clear 'round the world [the centering tree] in all the four directions . . . don't matter what nation it is. The world has a song. The rivers, the creeks, the winds, the trees, everything has a whispering sound.[16]

By naming the villages, this elder draws together local sites into a larger circle of place-based confidence around the collective symbolism of the nurturing tree. The local bioregion in the Salish lifeway is filled with songs that flow from the elements and animals. The sonic quality of a song brings the participants into resonance with the living world that feeds them. For example, in the Winter Dance humans dancing around the centering tree both mimic and make present the animals on the move in that season.

Singing songs and spirit talking take place at this lodgepole pine. As a sacred center with clear cosmological and sacred symbolism, this tree is often called "old man" out of respect. It is symbolically understood as "the world that all of us go around." The singers are the only ones to touch this centering pole. After slowly singing their song and moving gradually to the center of the room, they take hold of the pole and speak to those assembled. Often they tell the story of how they acquired their song. They also sing of the skills they have developed for hunting, fishing, or plant gathering. Singers may also comment on community events and give their reflections.

These are *sumix* skills manifested by the numinous powers who bestow songs and who give of themselves. That is, the hunting and trapping of animals, the catching of fish, and the gathering of plants are all gifts from the *sumix* world that nurtures the human. The singer brings forward this traditional knowledge and accompanying skills in appropriate ways at the Winter Dance by singing the songs, undergoing spirit sickness, speaking to those assembled in spirit voice, and bringing instructions from the spirit beings. As an announcer steps forward to project the words of the singer, he or she is believed to be speaking in a spirit-filled way that mediates sustenance to the community. The announcer gives support, staying with a person through all the stages of singing, dancing, and speaking. Thus, singers bring their personal spirit helpers (guardian spirits) in the communal setting of the Winter Dance, and announcers help mediate those gifts. Both activities reaffirm values in the old stories, the Salish religious cosmologies. In these stories all the mythic spirit beings—Bear, Coyote, Bitterroot, and all the spiritual persons in the landscape—prepare for the arrival of humans who were created after all other creatures. These stories relate the willing sacrifice of these spirit beings who give of their bodies as food to sustain humans. The encounter of humans with the songs of these spirit beings occurs in a special way.

Cosmological Songs: Remembered and Forgotten

In the traditional Salish lifeway, young boys and girls are sent out to fast in specific locations to acquire a song from a guardian spirit. Acquisition of a song not only announces a special relationship between that individual and an animal, plant, or place but also initiates the work of knowing and acquiring skills about the environment. This work of engaging in traditional environmental knowledge is coordinated with religious ecology but not in a straightforward manner. That is, Salish individuals who receive a song are culturally disposed to forget, or set aside, their vision songs until they mature, at 25 to 30 years of age, and begin to attend and sing at Winter Dances. Salish author Mourning Dove described this unusual cultural practice:

> When a man or woman had previously experienced the finding of a supernatural power to guide them, it usually left them alone in childhood. It came back when they were adults, appearing as a dream or vision to remind them of the contact saying, "Sing my song and the world will shine for you."[17]

In the Salish lifeway a vision song imparted at youth is "forgotten." Later that song returns and becomes embodied knowledge that causes the world to "shine." At the Winter Dance, it is sung openly to the people. Yet the youth who receives a song enters into a prolonged search to understand the life purpose imparted in a visionary song even before singing it openly at a dance. A male or female singer-in-formation becomes intent on learning the healing, hunting, fishing, or gathering skills associated with the animal, fish, plant, or place-based spirit that sang to them. This learning forms the basis for his or her entry into traditional environmental knowledge acquired by individuals, ritually shared with the community, and implemented in multivillage activities. Novice singers gradually become proficient in this knowledge as they mature and begin to sing their song. At the Winter Dance they bring to completion one stage of learning.

Singing one's spirit song transmits significant information about beings in the environment that the singer is coming to know intimately, such as salmon, bitterroot, camas, or deer. This religious ecology was crucial for the shared tasks undertaken by the independent Salish villages in the precontact days when foods were communally gathered. For example, singers with deer or salmon songs would lead those respective hunting and fishing activities. Even today knowledge of particular animals and plants announced by a singer at the Winter Dance is important for family and community subsistence activities.

Spirit Sickness

Complementing the gradual learning of traditional environmental knowledge is the spirit sickness. This sickness connects a singer to an empathic experience of sacrifice, namely, the giving of the spirit beings in song and in food. The sickness results in disorientation and prepares participants for the giving of themselves. This disorientation is ritualized in the days before the Winter Dance and harks back to a person's transitional stage of forgetting and remembering whereby a singer recovers his or her song and vision power.

With the acquisition of a song, a mature singer takes on the burden of a spirit sickness that returns with each Winter Dance season. The Winter Dance season runs roughly from late December to March, and spirit sickness may come just as this season begins. Spirit sickness can be described as physical, psychic, or both, and it becomes manifest in a variety of ways. That is, a person may feel physically ill, mentally burdened, or some combination of both. Singing at the Winter Dance relieves this spirit sickness. Moreover, the spirit sickness is understood in the context of the stories of creation, or religious cosmologies, so that the physical and psychic debilitation has a larger meaning than simply individual malaise.[18] It is at this point that the conjunction of religious cosmology and religious ecology becomes clear. That is, the guardian spirits who pervade all reality are integral to the Salish lifeway that affirms the nurturing of humans by spirit beings. Through this spirit sickness, individual singers bring to the Winter Dance a living reflection on health and food, subsistence and nurturance.

The spirit guardians are described in the mythic narratives as giving themselves as food and as a healing force in songs. Spirit sickness places singers in a bodily experience that directly relates them to the original and ongoing gifts of the animal–plant–mineral spirit beings. The underlying tension of the spirit sickness also relates to widespread ideas among Indigenous peoples of the need for a "second gift" by humans to the more-than-human world.[19] The complexity of the gift of food, in this interpretation, requires the additional or second gift of suffering by the singers. Enduring the spirit sickness and celebrating its release by singing at the center tree are modes of acknowledging the maturing interchange of humans with the community of life in the Winter Dance.[20] This is a way for humans to acknowledge and nurture the spirit world. This empathy is at the heart of traditional Salish ethics narrated in the cosmological stories.

Coyote Stories and an Ethics of Empathy Regarding Food

In traditional Salish cosmological stories it is Coyote, the mythic trickster, who raises the question, "How will the human survive?" The first of the guardian spirits to respond is bitterroot, the most handsome of the root crops, who gives his body as food for the human. As the other spirit beings step forward, giving of their bodies, Coyote realizes that more than physical food is needed to sustain humans, the latecomers to creation. "How shall they thrive?" Coyote asks. At that point, the *sumix* beings decide to give songs to humans to orient and nurture them. Coyote, the trickster, thus reveals his sincere concern for humans. Coyote is himself the master of transformation and troublemaking. He is the shape shifter extraordinaire, and alternately buffoon and culture hero. One relevant story connects him to the Winter Dance:

> Coyote and Porcupine were partners. Porcupine told Coyote that the latter's son, Muskrat would lead a dance that night. Coyote replied, "Well, we'll go." When they approached the dance house, Porcupine warned Coyote, "You'd better behave yourself, because your boy is pretty powerful. He's liable to kill us." Coyote answered, "No. My boy's not ahead of me." When they came to the house, Porcupine said to Coyote, "Don't enter first; let me." But Coyote said, "No. My power's better than yours. Let me go ahead." So when they entered, Coyote went first. Muskrat had a lot of little maggots dancing for him. When Coyote saw his son dancing and heard him singing, he himself started to do likewise and told the maggots to come to him. Coyote told the maggots to feed on him, and they all rushed upon him and ate him. Before he had danced once around, the maggots had eaten him all up. His partner Porcupine was behind him, but as soon as the maggots got on Porcupine he shook himself and they dropped off. Porcupine danced 'til he got to Coyote, and looked at him. He was nothing but a skeleton lying there dead. Porcupine took him by the wrist and told him to get up. Coyote yawned and made believe he had been asleep, saying, "I went this far and lay down and went to sleep." And Porcupine replied, "I guess you were asleep alright!"[21]

The *sumix* or power of Coyote's son, Muskrat, causes Coyote to die when he claims to have abilities that he does not actually have. Coyote oversteps his limits by claiming to be first and by arrogantly calling the maggots onto himself to feed. Coyote does not show mature judgment or experience of either the proper respect for another's power or the correct ethical understanding of food, eating, and nurturance. Yet in the myth Coyote comes to the dance and undergoes a death experience that marks all singers who endure the spirit sickness and are liberated by the power of their song.

This story describes the Winter Dance among the spirit animals during the mythic time of beginnings in which the patterns for all of life were established. In the story several Salish ethical teachings are flagrantly violated by Coyote. Among them are recognizing personal limitations regarding *sumix*, awareness of the sacrifice of food, and reciprocal giving. The story presents an inflated individual whose self-importance is clear to the audience as a denial of proper respect for power and a singular lack of awareness of personal limitations. The story also intimates Salish cultural reflections on the numinous aspects of nurturing. The maggot power of Muskrat eats to the bone when limits are surpassed and arrogance leads a person.

The singers' experience of spirit sickness at the arrival of Winter Dance season can be seen as the moral reversal of Coyote's arrogance. In the loneliness and discomfort that comes over a singer before the Winter Dances, there is a personal and psychological connection to ecological knowledge regarding limits. The seasonal features of this recurring sickness during the ritual year are intricately tied to the Salish lifeway that connects the sacred, food, and personal growth together. Spirit sickness gives force to the teaching that all members of the community are, in time, food to one another.

Conclusion

This brief overview of the Winter Dance ceremonial gives some idea of the ways in which Salish peoples have ritually integrated the nurturing power of spirit beings in the acquisition of songs along with hunting, gathering, and fishing skills. Human reciprocity is ritualized in giving back to the world by singing, by spirit sickness, and by giveaways. Being mindful of the natural environment in the Winter Dance ceremonial constitutes a religious ecology that fosters personal maturation, stronger community relations, appropriate subsistence activities, and renewing ties with spirit beings. According to the Salish, the *sumix* beings have a central role in nurturing humans and teaching them limits and gifts of life. For the Columbia River Salish peoples, the Winter Dance is a religious ecology that facilitates traditional environmental knowledge of land, species, and food that nurtures the village community.

In many ceremonials Indigenous peoples present remarkably stable patterns of human–Earth interdependence that have been sustained over generations in one location. So also some Indigenous peoples migrate with the seasons, and other native peoples transmit stories of their movements over time from distant settings to the places they now inhabit. What is striking is the manner in which Indigenous peoples are committed to establishing sacred relations with landscape and local biodiversity. They have made significant efforts to maintain their religious ecologies despite historical challenges of conquest, disease, and colonization. These pressures continue into the contemporary period with sovereignty disputes, invasive extractive industries, resource depletion, and cultural subversion. That many Indigenous peoples have endured is a testament to their religious ecologies that survived the arrivals of peoples with other songs and dreams.

9

Hinduism and the Transforming Affect of Devotion

Yamuna: A Goddess Deified and Defiled

We had come to the city of Vrindaban along the Yamuna River, some 100 miles southeast of Delhi. This is one of the most significant pilgrimage sites in India. Both the city with its many temples and the river that is considered sacred draw millions of pilgrims each year. However, the river has become intensely polluted over the last several decades by the effects of rapid industrialization. To draw attention to this problem, we had helped organize a conference bringing together religious leaders, policy experts, and scientists. The aim was to consider interdisciplinary solutions for the long-term health of the Yamuna River.[1] This involved hydrologists and ecologists studying the state of the river, policy experts analyzing government action plans for the river, historians of religion discussing religious practices along the river, and religious leaders trying to educate the laity and encourage monsoon rain retention and water usage reduction. Chancellor Rajendra Pachauri supported a prior conference at The Energy and Resources Institute (TERI) University in Dehli, through which the Yamuna flows. There, scientists reported on their studies of oxygen depletion in the river and on government plans to decrease industrial pollution and urban sewage.

The hope was that new policies might emerge on how to increase the flow of clean water for both human and aquatic life. This was an effort to open up the dialogue to diverse perspectives regarding the needs of humans, of the river, and of adjacent ecosystems as a whole. Mutually beneficial relations between humans and the river need to be reenvisioned, supported, and implemented, and this is the motivation for the Yamuna River Declaration in appendix E. These are significant challenges, but so is daily life in India for many people. Loss of fresh water is a problem for millions of people along the river.

Even walking through the narrow winding streets of Vrindaban can be hazardous. With wandering animals at our feet, one loses track of the monkeys. They perch on the edges of buildings waiting to jump unexpectedly onto one's shoulder and snatch one's glasses. They may return the glasses in exchange for food, or they may take them as an offering to Krishna. As a study in animal behavior, the purloining of glasses is remarkable. Gradually, all the monkeys in Vrindaban have learned how to jump and snatch glasses. However, John did not speculate on who taught the monkeys their trick. Rather, he held his glasses tightly as we made our way to the Yamuna River. Nonetheless, at a distracted moment one monkey leapt onto his shoulder, knocking his glasses to the ground. John managed to retrieve them before the monkey did, but he sensed that the monkey-god, Hanuman, was making a larger request of us than simply holding onto preconceived ideas or solutions.

We continued to the well-known Radharaman Temple. There we took off our shoes and entered the cool interior of the temple to make an offering and take our view (*darshan*) of the black rock image of the god Krishna. This particular image is legendary for its natural beauty, elegance, and grace. All during this visit to the temple, a chanter sang hymns of praise to Krishna and his lover, Radha. This love mysticism, like the *Song of Songs* in the Hebrew Bible, is reflected in the joyful devotion of practitioners to Krishna. This devotional worship, known as *bhakti*, is extended to the Yamuna River itself as a goddess.

As we came out of the temple, the hymns were still ringing in our ears. We followed the back alleys to *Keshi ghat*, a prominent pilgrimage site whose steps lead down to the river for placement of offerings on the water (figure 9.1). We removed our shoes and walked down to where the water was lapping against the steps. One woman in our group sat near the water's edge with a friend who was introducing us to the Yamuna River. A larger view of the dark river was denied us as mist shrouded it. Behind us the young temple priest tended the flower offerings he was selling to pilgrims coming to the river. We hunched down on the middle steps watching the two friends gently release their gift on the river. A small, lit candle shone from that gathering of flowers set in a leaf, shaped as a boat. Gently the woman pushed it into the river. Ever so slowly this delicate craft moved out into the sluggish current. Then it seemed to stop as if mired and unable to move with the river's flow. She was weeping now, her hands joined in front of her on her lap, and he was softly singing. One could see how polluted the river was here in this sacred city of Vrindaban. Black sludge and garbage floated by the temple. How could we not weep, as some 60 million people depend on this river? This is the river that runs through Delhi, that flows behind the Taj Mahal in Agra and irrigates much of northern India's agriculture.

The devotional literature of Hinduism speaks of the endless love of the pilgrim for Sri Yamuna, the riverine goddess who is herself a lover of the god Krishna. Yet here the river is dark and dank with industrial pollution and urban waste from Delhi. Only about 30 years earlier people bathed and drank easily from the river. With rapid industrialization has come intense degradation of the water. The irony is that for centuries the Yamuna River was a vibrant example of the confluence of religion and ecology that joined together the natural and the sacred. But now it is a dying river.

Suddenly the fog cleared, and the river stretched out in front of us. Dappled waves reflected the morning sun briefly as the mist rolled back, giving us a sense of the expansiveness of the river in this ancient pilgrimage site. Unexpectedly, several tour boats with pilgrims were passing by and making offerings (figure 9.2). Our friend and guide gestured toward the boats: "See how the pilgrims continue to come to Vrindaban even though the river is so polluted. They say that the river can be dirty (*gandi*) but never loses its purity (*pavitra*)."[2] This expresses the force of religious belief but also shows how religion can stand in the way of a scientific understanding of the hazards of pollution.

Some religious practitioners are reluctant to confront the dangers of river pollution. They cannot reconcile that a goddess can be deified with religious devotion and defiled with industrial development and waste. "How can we awaken those who cannot see the pollution in the river as a real ecological threat? We are in a transformative time," our friend quietly observed, "where traditional devotional service (*seva*) to the Yamuna as goddess must change to loving service focused on the restoration of the river." Transformation of the river and religious practices are needed. Such commitment might help restore this river that is so essential to the lifeblood of India. To understand the problems of the Yamuna River it is helpful to have an overview of its path from its remote mountain source across the northern plains of India.

Figure 9.1 Keshi ghat—the pilgrims' stairway down to the Yamuna River; Photo credit: Elizabeth McAnally

Figure 9.2 Pilgrimage boat on the Yamuna River; Photo credit: George James

Pull of Tradition: Religious Views of the Yamuna at Its Origin

The Yamuna River originates in a pristine area of the Himalayas at the Yamunotri glacier and at a hot spring in the region. Both of these sites have long been pilgrimage destinations. This revered river then drops down into the plains, where it meanders for 873 miles until it joins the Ganges at Allahabad and makes its way east to the Bay of Bengal. The religious relationships with the Yamuna at its glacial origins are different from those of the city of Vrindaban. In his insightful discussion of religion and ecology issues related to the Yamuna, David Haberman writes,

> All of the pictures of Yamuna Devi [goddess] . . . portray her seated on a lotus on the back of a turtle floating on a river, with high mountains in the background. . . . She is four-armed, holding a pot in her upper left hand, a lotus flower in her lower left hand, and a string of meditation beads in her lower right hand. . . . The symbols of the bountiful pot and creative lotus make it evident that Yamuna Devi is a powerful goddess who manifests life-giving forces and blessings.[3]

The river is ecologically robust at Yamunotri and is imaged as Mother Yamuna. Even guided fishing trips are promoted on this part of the Yamuna River, with images that present her beauty and her sacredness as connected to the vitality of fish and bird life.[4] As this religious imagery suggests, the river transforms those who come with reverent devotion to her.

The other source of the river is at a hot spring that gushes from a crevice in a massive rock face. This hot spring lies at the juncture of the Indian tectonic plate that has collided with the Eurasian plate for more than 70 million years. The force of the Indian plate slipping beneath the Eurasian plate has raised the Himalayas, the youngest and highest range of mountains in the world, generating the largest accumulation of ice and snow outside the polar ice caps. This tectonic collision also generated heat from contact with Earth's mantle. As water trapped in reservoirs deep in the crust of Earth is heated, it ascends through vertical channels to Earth's surface to generate hot springs, the signature of geothermal activity from shifting tectonic plates.

For the priests at the temple complex at Yamunotri there is another explanation for this thermal activity, a more poetic one that expresses the meaning of this source for the devout. The Yamuna is a living goddess who descended to Earth in answer to the prayers, austerities, and penance of seven great *rishis*, or sages. For many years the *rishis* resided at that pond and underwent austerities entreating her to come down to Earth to instill loving devotion among the people. Moved by their austerities and touched by their prayers, she descended to the summit of Mount Kalinda at 20,000 feet, but finding the place too cold for devotees to visit her, she prayed to her father, Surya, the Sun, to make the place more pleasant. With this request, the Sun gave his daughter a single fiery ray that struck the rock face at the base of the waterfall, giving birth to a hot spring.

Pilgrims bathe in this hot spring to commune with the goddess. The temple complex there is dedicated to devotion of the goddess Yamuna through her image as Mother. Her devotees consider the natural form of the river to be a more important manifestation of the goddess than her image. The goddess is embodied in the river; the divinity is the river herself. Therein lies a paradox. Some argue that it is only in the mountains where the river is free and clear that the goddess is truly alive, for now as the goddess descends to the plains her evident purity and holiness seem to be compromised.

The Yamuna as goddess is consistent all along her route as selfless and giving of her sacred waters of life. But the endless giving of the Yamuna has come up against the demands of a new worldview, that of industrialization, to build a modern India. Just as the religious devotion to the river changes along the route of the Yamuna, so the ecological and economic relationships with the river have changed with rapid development over the last 40 years. The question now is, Can there be reconciliation between the demands of tradition and modernity? Can religious devotion and economic development be mutually enhancing? Is the sacred in nature becoming replaced by the sacred in technology?

The Call of Modernity: Sacred Technology and Engineering

The Yamuna River, like all the sacred rivers of India, is a significant site for orienting and grounding religious practitioners in the flow of time.[5] As providers of nurturance and purification, these rivers are themselves places for transformation of mind and body. However, many of these functions, such as ritual and pilgrimage, have been subsumed by the allure of "sacred technology." Technology has become a means of transcending limitations and thus transforming the human condition.[6] In this sense, technology becomes a religious dream of liberating humans through modern progress.[7] This is evident in the statement of the first prime minister of India, Jawaharlal Nehru: "Dams are the temples of a modern India regarding their capacity to provide hydroelectric power for massive production projects."[8] Here we see that dams, not the rivers, are now considered sacred.

This engineering mindset has dominated India's political leaders as a way for the nation to enter into the modern status of an economically prosperous country. Much has been accomplished, but at great cost, and the Yamuna River bears witness to these costs. Dams have provided irrigation in the Doab region between the Yamuna and Ganges Rivers, but this management of the river has been almost totally oriented for immediate human needs. Rather than enhancing the flow of the river, it has radically altered and diminished it. Sustainable development has not been realized.

Guiding this engineering perspective is a bureaucratic mentality focused on centralized planning that largely ignores the human and natural communities along the river. This style of ecological management easily bypasses potentially creative local solutions regarding water usage in favor of a top-down model in which one size fits all situations. Thus, many residents remember interacting intimately with the Yamuna in religious rituals, recreation, and fishing into the 1970s. But centralized governance manipulated the river system so that these diverse local interactions were erased rather than incorporated into managing the river.

The situation in Delhi is instructive for understanding how centralized and provincial Indian governance has impaired regional water sources, knowingly and inadvertently. Lakes, natural catch basins, and wetlands along the river in the Delhi region have been largely drained for housing. Moreover, developers were allowed to use portions of the riverbed and the floodplain for buildings for the 2010 Commonwealth Games in Delhi. Before the Yamuna River reaches Delhi there is life in the river; after Delhi it becomes nearly impossible to sustain aquatic life. In Delhi eighteen drains channel urban waste directly into the river.[9] Delhi officials recommend that even animals should not be cleaned in the river. Yet more than 20 million people live in Delhi and depend on the Yamuna for their water supply.

With population growth and rapid modernization, human demands for energy, drinking water, and waste management have increased in the last 40 years at rates that the Indian government was unable to anticipate. Moreover, the increased demand for food has led to massive irrigation projects and increased use of chemical fertilizers. The consequence is river diversion, diminished flow, and extensive pollution. Central government decision making has guided the types of agricultural practices chosen.

For example, "green revolution" crops that held such promise have in fact required high chemical and water usage.

In 1993 the government of India launched the Yamuna Action Plan to clean the river, mainly through the construction of wastewater treatment plants located around the urban centers. Ironically, despite huge investments totaling US$308 million between 1993 and 2005, pollution levels have increased dramatically. With the huge expenditure of funds spent on the river and the lack of concrete results, the question arises why the approaches taken have not proved effective.

One response is that research on the Yamuna and implementation of recommended policies are fragmented on many levels. In the first place, studies of conditions of the river in different regions are generally unrelated to research in other regions of the river. For example, studies of river issues in the mountain regions related to deforestation are not connected to research concerning river issues on the agricultural plains. Investigations of urban issues such as wastewater management are not related to rural concerns for drinking water, irrigation, and fishing. Scientists examining the hydrology of the river tend to dismiss the initiatives of grassroots organizations for local watershed management. Second, writing and research are fragmented in terms of the disciplines that examine the river. Hydrologists use a different language from ecologists, and natural scientists speak a different language from that of social scientists in fields such as sociology, anthropology, and policy that also pertain to the river. Third, government policy has not been able to anticipate fully the tremendous population growth along the Yamuna River, especially in the urban centers such as Delhi, Mathura, and Agra. This population expansion has been matched by increased water usage by people and by industry. These developments have overwhelmed the wastewater treatment plants that the government has managed to create. Fourth, research and implementation seem to be divorced from the values concerning the river that are embedded in the religious and cultural traditions of Hinduism. Bringing these studies into relationship with one another is one of the motivations for religion and ecology as a field. Finding ways to bring local voices of civil society and religious communities into centralized planning for water conservation, tree planting, landscape restoration, and rain runoff management is one of the transformative long-term goals for religion and ecology. This type of civil advocacy on the part of religious organizations working on behalf of natural systems is not new in India, but new forms are emerging with policy implications.[10] Thus the conferences were organized in Delhi and Vrindaban.

Tension between Development and Devotion

With the influence in India of modern values of efficiency and growth, the relationship with the Yamuna has become more exclusively an economic resource to be exploited than a sacred source that transforms devotees. Life along the river has had to accommodate massive engineering projects driven by new economic agendas. It is the combination of numerous dams, unregulated factories, and untreated urban waste that diminishes the flow and pollutes the river. Whereas religious pilgrimage and tourism represent ancient and enduring relationships between Hindus and the Yamuna, more contemporary industrial and agricultural uses have undermined these religious and ecological relations with the river.[11]

In 1991 a shift in official Indian development policy from the earlier Soviet-style socialism to Western-style capitalism did not alter the centralized planning or engineering mindset.[12] This shift was from a nationalist development ethos focused on large-scale state planning to more market-motivated expansion driven by competitive profit making and economic gain. The impact on the environment in both state planning and the market-driven development was deleterious and significantly increased with the latter. Flowing water, glaciers, mountains, minerals, soils, and biodiversity ceased to be manifestations of a unified reality evident in the ancient religious devotion to the river. To counter this economic exploitation, political rhetoric is invoked and gestures are made toward a religious appreciation of nature, but they rarely result in effective river cleanup. Some religious leaders, such as Srivatsa Goswami, have challenged the domination of economic profiteering, central planning, and massive engineering as the only acceptable approaches to treatment of the Yamuna River.

In subtle ways the older religious relationships allowed riverine biodiversity to flourish even as human populations increased.[13] This is evident in the Yamuna image at Yamunotri, where the presence of turtle, lotus, and mountains highlights awareness and respect for nature's beauty. It is manifest as well in the loving relationships of devotees to sacred forests along the Yamuna that are now mostly cut for development, except for small remnants left for tourism.[14] The centrality and value of biodiversity along the Yamuna reflect an enduring religious ecology within Hinduism. That is, it is understood that animal, plant, and human life occur in symbiotic relations with mountainous watersheds, mineral flows, and soil movements. This is an ecological vision that is present in the devotional practices found in Vrindaban, a vibrant pilgrimage city southeast of Delhi.

Devotion to Krishna and the River

Vrindaban is the setting for so many of the myths describing the life of the god Krishna. These stories of Krishna, and the religious ecology that has flowed out of them, suggest that in Hinduism the natural world is something beloved.[15] Krishna is considered by many Hindus to be the most significant *avatar*, or incarnation, of the supreme being, Vishnu.[16] In the stories of Krishna in Vrindaban, he plays (*lila*) with the Gopi maidens, the beautiful cow-herders who delight in him. Among the Gopi women, there is an intense devotion to Krishna and to Radha, his lover. Such devotion, known as *bhakti*, is a central religious practice of Hinduism, as seen in the *Bhagavad Gita* ("Song of the Lord").

Devotion to the god Krishna has resulted in an extensive religious ecology in Hinduism in which the natural world is interpreted as the manifestation of God's body.[17] Transformative images of the divine are believed to occur in the natural world. Natural objects such as trees, stones, or monkeys may manifest themselves as an icon of the divine (*murti*). For the devotee these natural manifestations are not the absolute fullness of the sacred but fitting expressions through which reverent devotion can be given to the sacred deity.

In the stories of Krishna, the Yamuna River is presented as a *murti*, or appearance of the sacred. Many of these mythic stories are collected in a twelfth-century religious text called the *Bhagavata Purana*. The religious practices, stories, and commentaries constitute expressions of a religious ecology that can be retrieved and reevaluated for transformative reconstruction of Hinduism in relation to the Yamuna.

The *Bhagavata Purana* gives the life story of Krishna at Vrindaban and describes his miraculous birth in the nearby city of Mathura:

Then there was the supreme hour . . . with all the stars and planets in a favorable position. Everywhere there was peace, the multitude of stars twinkled in the sky and the cities, towns, and pasturing grounds . . . were at their best. With the rivers crystal clear, the lakes beautiful with lotuses and flocks of birds and swarms of bees sweetly singing their praise in the blooming forests, blew the breezes with a gentle touch fragrant and free from dust and burned the fires of the twice-born steadily undisturbed.

The sages and the godly joyous showered the finest flowers and the clouds rumbled mildly like the ocean waves when in the deepest dark of the night Krishna, the World's Well-Wisher, appeared [was born] from the divine form of Lord Vishnu . . . that wonderful child was resplendent with lotus-like eyes . . . with yellow garments and a beautiful hue like that of rainclouds.[18]

The details are dazzling and highlight the cosmological character of the birth of Krishna, the World's Well-Wisher. The stars and deities, rivers and lakes, birds and insects all attend to and pay homage to his birth. The intimate relationships between Krishna and nature, especially the purity of the rivers, are evident. Throughout these stories, the love of Lord Krishna with and for the natural world is central. This is the *bhakti* that resonates between devotee and deity and is believed to be at the heart of all reality. In this religious tradition the heartfelt empathy for humans and nature is capable of transforming everything.

The numerous stories of devotion in the *Bhagavata Purana* tell how Krishna played as a child along the river and performed legendary deeds as an adult. There is a delightful human character to the stories of Krishna as a boy and culture hero. Krishna's divine and human character is layered in episodes that reflect dangers he faced. For example, in one story the demon Kaliya takes the form of a giant cobra who, motivated by revenge, completely poisoned the river.[19] In the mythic stories of the *Bhagavata Purana*, Krishna dives into the river and subdues the demon, dancing on his seven cobra heads until Kaliya cries out for mercy. This mythic incidence of toxicity in the Yamuna is seen by many as a remarkable prefiguring of contemporary pollution.[20]

These tales reflect the ancient mythology of Krishna, as lover and beloved, becoming one. In one of the famous hymns, an aspirant sings of this mystical vision yearning with devotion to partake in the river's embrace, the love bower itself. Hindu poet Chaturbhujadas extends this religious ecology into other symbiotic relationships in the natural world:

> Shri Yamuna favors her devotees and grants entrance into the love bower.
> There Krishna, the Supreme Connoisseur of Love, makes love night and
>   day.
> To what extent can one describe that gathering of love?
> Hearing Krishna's flute, the river stopped flowing
>   and the women of Braj became enraptured.
> No one can resist its sound.
> Chaturbhujadas says: Yamuna is like a lotus,
> My mind buzzes around her like a bumblebee.

As a mystical vision of union with the beloved god Krishna, these chants move the listener beyond divisions of the human from the divine. This religious ecology dispels sharp separations of nature from the human realm.

Indeed, this hymn reflects the devotion, *bhakti*, that strongly affirms the natural world as expressive of a larger unitive vision. This religious vision of the unity of all reality is present in the ancient literature of the *Upanishads* from the sixth century BCE. This oneness is named *Brahman*, and it is understood as residing within individuated reality as its *atman*, spiritual essence or self. In *bhakti* this experience of mystical union joins with emotional longing for the deity.[21] One undertakes song, dance, and gestures such as reverently laying a flower before a manifestation of the sacred or placing a drop of water on one's chosen deity. These devotional acts are considered comparable to the meditative acts of a yogi or the denial of worldly pleasures by a *sadhu*, or ascetic.

In this *bhakti*, devotees are not taught how to turn from the world toward a distant paradise or empty themselves of material attachments. Rather, the *Purana* teaches transformation by filling the practitioner with love of Krishna and thus becoming united with all reality.[22] In this vision, then, the devotee is welcomed into the love bower of the Yamuna River. In this loving interaction with the river, the pilgrim is affirmed by gazing on, bathing in, or sipping the water. This embodied knowledge provides insight into how devotion to natural systems enables transformation. That is, the practitioner forms deep experiential and symbolic bonding with such a natural feature as the Yamuna River. Traditionally, devotional practices have been largely personal, family, class, and caste related.

Throughout India these ancient practices are undertaken with sacred rivers, such as the Yamuna, Ganges, and Narmada. The water, or *jal*, of the river is understood as itself sacred and purifying of those who participate in its nurturance. For centuries, pilgrims have come to the rivers to express *bhakti* for personal transformation. Many Hindus come to die and be cremated along the banks as a final passage and purification for the next round of rebirth. These expressions of personal transformation are now being recognized to have implications for environmental civil advocacy, especially as the paradox of purity and pollution is becoming more evident. The overwhelming feeling of the Upanishadic unity of all reality and the goodness of nature experienced by the practitioner of *bhakti* now confronts the diminishment of the unity and the degradation of nature in the river.

Paradox of Purity and Pollution: The Need for Transformative Action

As many in India have observed, the very rivers that are considered sacred and life giving are themselves becoming loaded with toxicities and thus death bringing.[23] It is evident that the river is dying with its toxic burden. Why the overwhelming pollution of a sacred river such as the Yamuna? How could such a paradox arise that a deified river goddess could become so defiled? What can inspire committed and long-term action to clean up this river?

Within the Krishna tradition it is possible to find many levels of realization of these environmental problems. In Vrindaban among religious leaders, laity, and civil society there is growing awareness that more must be done to restore the river. Still, some practitioners remain so absorbed by the powerful religious orientation to the purity of the river that they fail to acknowledge the reality of the river's pollution. Or, if they concede the pollution, they distinguish cleanliness from purity, saying the Yamuna could never lose its religious power to purify, no matter how intense the pollution. Thus, there is a tendency for some to deny the reality of the widespread pollution and hold only to the symbolic transformation offered by a religious ecology that developed over the centuries of the river's nurturance.[24]

As indicated earlier, the sacredness of the natural world in India is anchored in the ancient wisdom of Upanishadic unity, often connected with religious devotion. Yet the connection of this deeper unity and of service (*seva*) with environmental transformation remains to be fully realized. In this regard, there is need for dialogue between scientific ecology and religious ecology that is informed and fully aware of the realities and complexities of the situation. Scientific research is useful for gathering data to understand the sources of diminished flow and river pollution. Moreover, scientists are seeking efficacious public policy and community support. Also, religious practitioners are becoming educated about river pollution rather than simply retreating into rigid doctrinal beliefs or unsanitary ritual practices. Religious leaders and practitioners are playing a role in helping to formulate local restoration plans that address riverine environmental problems.

Conclusion

Many questions remain unanswered. How will India find the political, economic, and moral will to do what has proven so difficult over the past decades of the government-sponsored "Yamuna Action Plan"? Can religious leaders help to stem the tide of increasing pollution of the river from industrial and human waste?

Efforts to make positive changes in the flow and quality of river water have foundered in the face of political corruption, bureaucratic inefficiency, and economic greed. In many ways an ancient religious ecology of devotion and transformation shows more awareness of the interdependence of humans with biodiversity than much of the contemporary attention to development and engineering that has transformed the river for human needs. Yet just as religious ecology is necessary for mitigating the dire situation of the Yamuna River, it is insufficient without the empirical insights of science and the pragmatic contributions of effective policy. The future flourishing of the life of the Yamuna and the millions depending on it is a challenge of immense proportions whose outcome is still uncertain. Is restoration possible for this sacred river and for so many other rivers and bodies of water around the world? Can renewed devotion and sustained development find ways to collaborate?

10

Building on Interreligious Dialogue: Toward a Global Ethics

The challenge of the contributions of religious ecology in relation to sustainability is clear from the preceding four chapters. In particular, the tensions between traditional values regarding nature and modern industrial processes driven by economic profit show no signs of abating. There are no uniform views of nature, and indeed, there are ambivalences toward nature in the religious traditions. However, these case studies in religious ecologies make us aware of the complex perspectives and differentiated languages regarding human interactions with nature. For example, Christianity acknowledges immanence, Confucianism highlights interdependence, Indigenous religions emphasize relationality, and Hinduism underscores unity. Yet the realization of these ideals is compromised by political manipulation, economic exploitation, technological power, and regulatory weakness. Each of these obstacles calls forth the need to create ecological cultures with deeper awareness of human embeddedness in nature.

This can be the contribution of religious ecologies and religious cosmologies. Even though there are ambivalences in some of the world religions regarding nature, for millennia the traditions have provided a context in which humans could see themselves as part of the larger community of life. Religious ecologies bring innovative cultural viewpoints to these questions of the value of life, both human and natural. Religious cosmologies locate the human in the larger contexts of universe and Earth processes that provide a deep time framework for valuing nature.

This comprehensive and long-term perspective that religions can provide is needed in our own time to create ecological cultures. Recent efforts to formulate a global ethics suggest that humans are broadening the basis for caring for life.

Expanding Care for the Earth Community

Despite the world wars and regional conflicts of the twentieth century, it can be said that over the last century there have been movements in the human community, motivated by necessity and moral reflection, to expand the arc of care and compassion beyond one's own family, race, nationality, or religion.[1] After the tragedy of genocide in World War II, the United Nations drafted the Universal Declaration of Human Rights, which builds on Enlightenment principles of individual freedom and religious principles of the dignity of humans with their striking diversity.[2] In theory, this has guided the extension of rights to all peoples, thus broadening the promise of Enlightenment thought that influenced the American and French revolutions. There have also been significant academic and political efforts to identify theories and practices related to human rights in non-Western cultures.[3] In practice, the realization of these rights is still being affirmed and actualized around the world. Now these rights are being expanded even further to embrace the Earth community so as to promote the flourishing of life, human and other than human. This is leading to movements toward a global ethics coming from both secular and religious perspectives. An important contribution to such a global ethics is a result of several decades of interreligious dialogue searching for a shared and sustainable future for the planet.

We are keenly aware of the contemporary impact of religious, ethnic, and cultural pluralism in the anthropocene era.[4] The study of the history of religions has given us deeper insight into the varied nature of religion and of the multiple interpretations of texts, traditions, and practices. An understanding of such diversity has led to interreligious dialogue over the last several decades. This is an important step for the world religions as they are meeting on a global scale as never before in human history. Earlier claims to absolute truth by various religions often gave rise to intolerance and even hostility. For example, with Vatican Council II (1962–1965), the Catholic Church made a significant shift beyond claims to exclusive salvation within Catholicism. It recognized truth in other religions and helped to launch a new period of exchange of ideas between traditions.

This exchange has resulted in greater appreciation of pluralism as well as open-mindedness and common understanding among the religions.

A parallel movement of ecumenism or reconciliation within the Christian churches reaffirmed the basis for unity of belief in the revelation of Christ. The World Council of Churches has taken leadership in this regard for better understanding between the Protestant denominations themselves and with the Orthodox and Catholic churches as well.

On an international level, the Council for the Parliament of World Religions has assisted this interreligious dialogue by organizing major conferences involving practitioners and scholars of the world religions. First initiated in 1893, the Parliament has held four conferences since 1993. This has significantly deepened and broadened the exchange between religious practitioners in face-to-face dialogue. With its headquarters in Chicago, it continues to provide leadership for convening the world religions and for fostering respect for both diversity and commonality.

All these efforts toward appreciation of diversity and engaged interreligious dialogue have created the possibility for articulation of a shared global ethics. Indeed, theologian Hans Küng drafted such a global ethics for the 1993 Parliament, and Leonard Swidler called for exploring a global ethics at the American Academy of Religion that same year.[5] The world religions are beginning to realize that cooperation for the flourishing of the planet is a compelling moral imperative. This is because environmental issues transcend national and religious boundaries and need to be linked to issues of social and economic justice. It was with this awareness that the world religions could contribute to the formation of the Earth Charter.

Earth Charter

The Earth Charter arose from the United Nations Conference on Environment and Development in Rio in 1992.[6] This Earth Summit was called to adjudicate between the increasing global demands of economic development and environmental protection. An international committee, chaired by philosopher and historian of religions Steven Rockefeller from 1996 to 2000, drafted the Charter.[7] A distinguished group of international civil servants served as Earth Charter commissioners for the drafting process, and the Earth Charter International Council has guided the activities of the Charter. There is a Secretariat and a website based in Costa Rica at the University for Peace, run by Mirian Vilela.

The Earth Charter is both a document and a movement (see appendix F). It draws on scientific knowledge, legal principles, sustainability practices, ecological economics, the precautionary principle, and equity issues. In its decade-long drafting process, it involved thousands of individuals and groups from around the planet and is the most inclusive civil society document ever negotiated. The world religions weighed in on the drafting of the Earth Charter during the Harvard conference series on religion and ecology. As a people's treaty it is a soft law document that is complemented by the hard law of international covenants and laws.[8] It has been endorsed by such international agencies as the United Nations Educational, Scientific and Cultural Organization and the International Union for the Conservation of Nature, the largest body of conservationists in the world. It is also endorsed by thousands of individuals and groups and by a number of countries and cities. The implications for the application of the Charter are seen in *Earth Charter in Action*, a book of inspiring stories from around the world, ranging from youth to civil servants and government officials.[9]

The Charter points toward an integrated framework of ecology, justice, and peace as a context for sustainable development. With the Earth Charter it can be said that the ethical compass of the human is expanding. For this is not only a document proclaiming the independence of humans but also a movement that celebrates our interdependence with one another and with the entire community of life. Throughout this process the world religions, with all their diversity, are playing a role in providing theoretical contexts and practical applications of this expanding awareness.

We are in search of shared cultural, artistic, and religious symbols as well as ethical norms, such as the Earth Charter, that point toward a viable future for the planet. Discursive reasoning in science and policy alone cannot make the shift. Neither information (scientific facts) nor regulations (laws) are sufficient to motivate humans for long-term change. However, a fresh synthesis of religious ecology and ecological knowledge may make a significant contribution. This is the promise of the emerging alliance of religion and ecology and of a global ethics such as the Earth Charter. As the religions deepen their dialogue, they are beginning to realize that their common concern for the planet may override their differences.

Interreligious Dialogue

In the last 50 years, just as diversity of religion has been better understood, significant progress has been made in interreligious dialogue.[10] The effort to find unity and community between religions has made progress through study and meetings. This dialogue provides an important base for religions to cooperate on environmental issues and a shared global ethics as they realize that their differences may not be as significant as their concern for the common good of a flourishing Earth community. Since Pope John XXIII called for an updating of Catholicism in the early 1960s and convened a worldwide gathering of cardinals called Vatican Council II, interreligious dialogues have been initiated between Christians and Jews and between Christians and Muslims.

Organizations have been created to foster this dialogue in conferences, statements, books, and articles. Buddhist–Christian dialogue has also been vigorous in both academic exchanges and monastic interchange in the United States, Europe, and Asia.[11] Some of this monastic dialogue began with Thomas Merton (1915–1968), a Trappist monk at Gethsemani Monastery in Kentucky, whose writings revitalized spiritual life in Catholicism. Issues of tolerance and openness have been encouraged through these dialogues on both academic and experiential levels.

Increasingly we realize that such dialogue is not a luxury but a necessity on a planet where religious encounter, cultural exchange, interreligious marriage, and sectarian conflict are ever more common. We are experiencing difference in societies all over the world through expanded travel, immigration, Internet use, and social media. Pluralism has become widespread in modern societies, challenging the ways they negotiate difference. Although much more work needs to be done, the interreligious ground for religious cooperation over ecological issues has been tilled over the last several decades. Because better understanding of different beliefs and practices has arisen through various publications and dialogues, religions are recognizing that they can work together on issues of common concern. For example, Friends of the Earth Middle East has drawn together the Abrahamic religions for protection and restoration of the Jordan River, on which the local region depends.[12]

On an international level, the Parliament of World Religions, with its five major conferences, has tried to support and encourage interreligious dialogue. The initial conference in Chicago in 1893 was an occasion for Asian and Western religions to come together in a new spirit of exchange. This first formal gathering of the major world religions was a watershed moment.[13] Swami Vivekananda from India captured the imagination of the conference and subsequently the American public with his electrifying speech on the need for religious tolerance. His spiritual charisma touched a deep chord in American society, caught up in the materialism of the late nineteenth century.[14] After the lapse of a century the Parliament was revived, and international conferences have been convened in Chicago in 1993, Cape Town in 1999, Barcelona in 2004, and Melbourne in 2009.[15] Although there is no formal representative structure for the Parliament, the conferences have been occasions for the gathering of some five thousand to seven thousand people. The Parliament in Melbourne in 2009 had a dozen panels on world religions and ecology, organized by the Forum on Religion and Ecology.

Parliament of World Religions and the Earth Charter

An example of the cooperation of religion toward building a sustainable future occurred in December 1999 with the embrace of the Earth Charter at the Parliament of World Religions. The Parliament was meeting in South Africa, a country still recovering from decades of apartheid rule that officially ended in 1994. During that time hundreds of African National Congress Party members were imprisoned, including Nelson Mandela. After 27 years in prison on Robbins Island, just off the coast of Cape Town, he brought back a spirit of civility and tolerance, compassion and forgiveness. A country on the brink of bloodshed began the transition to a multiracial democratic society under Mandela's skilled leadership. His inspiration was his Christian affirmation of the dignity of each person and of the principles of justice and nonviolence. Mandela was able to initiate and sustain a great transition, indeed, a revolutionary nonviolent change, with an appeal to rise above differences for a common good for the South African nation.

During a plenary session at the Parliament Mandela greeted the audience members who represented religions from around the world, both large and small. The participants were gathered in a huge auditorium in Cape Town, some seven thousand strong. In a moment of high celebration he was presented with a copy of the Earth Charter, a declaration of global ethics. Steven Rockefeller and Kamla Chowdhry, two Earth Charter leaders from the United States and India, respectively, made the presentation. The symbolism of these representatives from the world's largest democracies offering this newly drafted Earth Charter to the first president of this fledgling democracy was striking. Mandela was delighted and expressed his appreciation with great warmth.

At the Parliament the representatives of the world religions witnessed an important shift in our planetary history toward a global ethics. Clearly, dialogue and cooperation were needed for the articulation and implementation of such a planetary ethics. Just as the Universal Declaration of Human Rights depended on ethical principles from the world religions on the dignity and independence of humans, so the Earth Charter relies on ecological and religious principles of interdependence and connection. The Charter highlights the fact that we are different yet related through the long evolution and emergence of life; we are one human family participating in an encompassing planetary community. This recognition of our interdependence marks a new moment for the world religions. Interreligious dialogue was focusing not simply on tolerance and respect but on cooperation for the future of the planet. How to bring these aspirations into further realization remains a challenge amid immense religious diversity and ongoing dialogue. This was what was launched in the Assisi Dialogues in 1986[16] and was brought to another level with the Earth Charter being honored at the Parliament in 1999. Religious communities were recognizing their role and responsibility as planetary citizens in support of an integrated global ethics for ecology, justice, and peace.

Contributions of Religious Values and the Earth Charter

It is thus at a moment of immense significance for the future of life on the planet that the world religions may be of assistance as they further develop their own environmental ethics. The common set of values for human–Earth flourishing identified from the Harvard conference series on World Religions and Ecology can be seen as compatible with the ethical principles of the Earth Charter. Recognizing the complementary nature of these two may be a helpful framework for linking religion, ethics, and sustainability.

The Charter offers a comprehensive framework for revisioning sustainability as balancing the needs for economic development with environmental protection. It presents an integrated set of principles to guide our emerging planetary civilization that is multinational, multicultural, and multireligious. It provides a platform for universal commitment to the flourishing of biocultural planetary life systems along with differentiated responsibilities.

The key components of the Earth Charter are the following: cosmological context, respect and care for the community of life, ecological integrity, social equity, economic justice, democracy, nonviolence, and peace. These seven components for a planetary future have their counterparts in the seven values for human–Earth flourishing that are shared by the world religions, as identified in the Harvard conference series: reverence for the cosmos, respect for life, reciprocity with ecosystems and humans, restraint in the use of resources, redistribution for justice, responsibility for democratic processes, and renewal through a culture of peace. A planetary future that is flourishing, not simply sustainable, will be enhanced by the seven components identified by the Earth Charter along with these seven shared values in the world religions. The Earth community requires something more robust than simply "sustainability" that can be technologically or economically driven. Rather, Earth's fecundity requires the flourishing of mutually enhancing human–Earth relations. Such a framework that integrates values for flourishing from the world religions with the central component of global ethics in the Earth Charter may be an important context for expanding sustainability principles and practices.

Cosmological Context: Earth Our Home

All cultures have been grounded in the stories they tell about the nature of the universe, the evolution of the Earth and life, and the destiny of humans in this context. These cosmological stories provide accounts of the creation and evolution of life and the purpose of humans. As humans are trying to navigate their way between scientific accounts of evolution and the multiple religious stories of creation, the Charter articulates a broad, simple, and inclusive sensibility that Earth is our home, our dwelling place.

This enlarged perspective of home may be a critical foundation for articulating a future that is both sustaining and flourishing. The Charter recognizes that we are part of a large family of life, including not only other humans but also other species. The interdependent quality of the Earth community is celebrated along with the fact that the conditions for life have been evolving for billions of years. The preamble states, "Humanity is part of a vast evolving universe. Earth, our home, is alive with a unique community of life. The forces of nature make existence a demanding and uncertain adventure, but Earth has provided the conditions essential to life's evolution."[17]

Thus, to speak of the broadest context for the health of biosocial systems, we need to be reminded of the cosmological, evolutionary story of life's emergence. The religious response to this is one of *reverence*, a quality shared by many scientists who are deeply inspired by their study of nature from cells to galaxies, enhanced now by powerful microscopes and telescopes. The intricacy and complexity of life are valued from both a spiritual and a scientific perspective. Awe and wonder become expressed through the shared experience of reverence.

Respect and Care for the Community of Life: Ecological Integrity

The broad context for a sustaining and flourishing future from the Earth Charter is preserving ecological health and integrity. Without such a basis for healthy ecosystems, there can be no long-term basis for the continuity of human life. It is expressed succinctly in the preamble: "The resilience of the community of life and the well-being of humanity depend upon preserving a healthy biosphere with all its ecological systems, a rich variety of plants and animals, fertile soils, pure waters, and clear air."

The response of the religious communities to this call for biological protection is the principle of *respect* for the rich diversity of life and the ecosystems that support life. This requires reciprocity for the community of life, human and more than human. Without such *reciprocity*, environmental exploitation will continue, and we may irreversibly damage the ability of ecosystems to renew themselves and humans to prosper. This is further spelled out in the Charter as protecting and restoring Earth's ecosystems, preventing harm through the precautionary principle, adopting effective patterns of production, consumption, and reproduction, and advancing the study of ecological sustainability.

Social and Economic Justice

The next section of the Charter highlights social and economic justice, which are also key concerns of the world religions. The religious virtues of *restraint* in use of resources and *redistribution* of aid and technology through charitable means complement the Charter's principles. All the world religions encourage moderation in personal behavior and in the accumulation or use of material goods. In addition, the world religions express a strong concern for the suffering of the poor and for inequality between the wealthy and those in need. Charitable giving is valued as a fundamental religious act.

The Charter calls for eradication of poverty, equitable development, gender fairness, and nondiscrimination regarding minorities and Indigenous people. Thus, justice is seen as working toward a balance of ecological, economic, and social factors. The term that many religions are using to describe this is *eco-justice*, where biological and human health are seen as indispensable to one another. Indeed, preserving ecological integrity and protecting social and economic justice will require an integrated understanding of human–Earth relations. This will involve protecting traditional environmental knowledge, especially as preserved among Indigenous peoples in many parts of the world.

Democracy, Nonviolence, and Peace

Finally, the Earth Charter recognizes that democracy, nonviolence, and peace are necessary ingredients for a sustaining and flourishing future. From the perspective of the religious communities, democracy requires a fundamental sense of *responsibility* to future generations of the community of life, human and more than human. Nonviolence and peace encourage the *renewal* of inner and outer peace, something that the religious communities have tried to foster for millennia. Spiritual practices such as prayer and contemplation, yoga and *t'ai chi*, rituals and rites of passage have been developed to foster peace and nonviolence for individuals and communities. Of course, it should be noted that nonviolence has not always been practiced, but it is one of the reasons why Leo Tolstoy, Mahatma Gandhi, Martin Luther King, and Nelson Mandela are so widely admired. The Earth Charter promotes the following principles: strengthening democratic institutions, encouraging sustainability education, respecting non-human animals, and promoting a culture of nonviolence and peace.

Conclusion

This integration of the principles of the Earth Charter with the virtues for human–Earth flourishing from the world religions provides a unique synergy for rethinking sustainability. Such a synergy can contribute to the broadened understanding of sustainable development as including ecological, economic, social, and spiritual wellbeing. Such an inclusive perspective may be a basis for long-term policies, programs, and practices for a planetary future that is not only ethically sustainable but also sustaining for human energies. For at present we face a crisis of hope in the possibility that we can make a transition to a viable future for the Earth community. The capacity of the world religions to provide moral direction and inspiration for a flourishing community of life is significant. The potential of the Earth Charter to create an ethical framework for sustainable development plans and practices is considerable. Together they may offer a comprehensive orienting and grounding for creating ecological cultures.

Epilogue

Challenges Ahead: Creating Ecological Cultures

In the Presence of a Glacier

It was a cool, crisp September morning in 2007 off the coast of southwest Greenland near the city of Ilulissat. The sun shone brightly over the water, and the glacier sparkled with reflected light. This, one of the largest glaciers in the world, was magnificent and overwhelming. We were in awe of its powerful presence, dwarfed by its sheer size and scale. The colors across its surface were unexpectedly varied in shades of white, blue, gray, and turquoise. This pure glistening ice—frozen water in huge sheets—was moving slowly out of granite ravines and rugged mountain slopes into the waiting arms of the Arctic Ocean.

Here we were facing the glacier as it entered the turbulent waters, cold and teeming with marine life. Whales, seals, otters, fish, and plankton were abundant in this region. Inuit people have made their livelihood from these rich seas for millennia. But now their very way of life is at risk. The marine life on which they largely subsist is tainted with toxins, and their climate is changing rapidly, making winter hunting on the ice treacherous.

Because of climate change, this monumental glacier is melting more quickly than expected and calving off huge chunks of ice (figure 11.1). The mile-high ice sheet that covers Greenland is also receding. Global warming has created large ice holes—moulins—into which massive amounts of water are flowing, thus lubricating the movement of the ice cap. To fly over the expansive ice sheet is a numinous experience, both awesome and humbling.[1] To realize that human activities are melting the Greenland ice sheet is arresting and troubling.

What was the response as we witnessed this powerful glacier from our passenger ship? We gathered on the deck, 150 people from many backgrounds and nationalities: Europeans, Asians, Africans, and North and South Americans. We were scientists and religious leaders, politicians and diplomats, scholars of religions and theologians, economists and educators. We were part of a symposium led by the Greek Orthodox Ecumenical Patriarch, Bartholomew, titled "The Arctic: Mirror of Life." We were exploring—indeed witnessing—the effects of global warming in the Arctic region of Greenland. Ironically, we were also aware that we participate in the industrial world causing this loss. With all that had been written about climate change, here it was before our eyes. To see this was deeply disturbing; our human impact on global warming was evident.

As we began our symposium, we wondered what gesture is possible in the face of such stupendous beauty and incredible loss. The Ecumenical Patriarch, Bartholomew, gathered religious leaders of various denominations at the bow of the boat. A few words were said, and then silent prayer was offered. A penetrating quiet settled in, passing across all the participants. The only sound was the lapping of the waves against the boat. The aquamarine water was brilliant against the blue-gray sky.

Then, with gracious humility in the presence of such natural splendor, the Patriarch turned toward the glacier in silence. No words could capture this moment fully as we drew in the shimmering glacier with its occasionally calving icebergs. Nature was speaking; humans were listening.

Suddenly the stillness was broken as a small boat drew near, and the sound of music drifted across the water. Inuit in traditional dress were singing songs of welcome. In the distance we could see other Inuit coming to meet us in kayaks. As they drew closer, some hundred strong, and as the music swelled, there were few dry eyes. We were visitors from around the globe being met by Indigenous peoples in this remote region. We were bound by a common concern for the fate of the planet.

The Ecumenical Patriarch sees our period as a *kairos* moment—a moment in time that has eternal significance. He observes, "We will either act in time to protect life on Earth from the worst consequences of human folly, or we will fail to act. May God grant us the wisdom to act in time." He describes our current destruction of the environment as "ecological sin" and "crimes against creation." Many share his outrage and urgency and his call for people to move toward a more sustainable future.[2]

Figure 11.1 Glacier in Ilulisat, Greenland; Photo source: iStock

One of his leading theologians, John of Pergamon, is calling for a shift not just in short-term behavior but also in longer-term transformation of ethos that recognizes our dependence on being part of nature's processes.[3]

This is a significant part of religious ecologies, namely, what Buddhists see as engaged Buddhism, what Hindus recognize in acts of service (*seva*), and what has also caused resurgence among Indigenous peoples around the world.[4] This deeper shift is similar to what some Chinese government officials, academics, and environmentalists are identifying as the need to create ecological cultures. Such cultures can be characterized by environmental awareness and action that is seen in society, education, religion, politics, and economics. Diverse cultures have been shaped by religious ecologies that transmitted ecological values and behavior through generations. Now we need to retrieve, reevaluate, and reconstruct those values in conjunction with ecological understandings from science.

The Challenge Ahead: Creating Ecological Cultures

It is becoming apparent that this ultimate challenge for humans will require all the skills and wisdom we can muster to create ecological cultures. The skills will come from science and technology, policy and law, economics and business. Already significant efforts are being made in these fields to create the framework and tools for a sustainable future. Wisdom will also come from the world religions and philosophies, spiritualities and psychologies, ethics and moral reasoning, as well as from music and the arts. This transformation of mind and heart will be critical in creating lasting change, both among those who embrace religious traditions and among those motivated by the spiritual dimensions of environmentalism.[5]

This broadened sensibility regarding nature may not be evident in environmental policymaking in secular societies. For many decades we have relied on scientific facts to awaken people to the scope of the environmental crisis. These have been published in various scientific journals, such as *Science* and *Nature*, as well as in policy papers by think tanks such as the Worldwatch Institute and World Resources Institute in Washington, DC. These carefully researched papers have been critical instruments for increasing awareness. But if such detailed reports on the *State of the World* have been distributed to thousands of people over many years and have not significantly changed behavior, what will?

For more than four decades many nation-states have drafted laws and issued environmental regulations to legislate change.[6] This, too, has often proven inadequate, as existing laws tend to remain on the books but are not enforced on the ground. In the United States we have had to sue our Environmental Protection Agency to implement laws regarding clean air and water. Moreover, we have seen economic growth take precedence over basic precautionary principles, for example, in the face of unrestrained extractive activities and toxic emissions. In many countries around the world this is also the case. Thus, neither scientific facts about the multiple environmental crises we are facing nor punitive measures and regulatory acts have shifted attitudes and behaviors for making changes on a sufficient scale to shape ecological cultures.

In large measure this is because we have created societies dominated by principles of market-driven economics rather than principles of ecological interdependence. The health of our economy is not perceived as tethered to the health of the life systems of the planet. Nature has been viewed through a utilitarian lens, as something to be exploited, not valued intrinsically or aesthetically. More than 35 years ago Donald Worster noted, "The split in ecology between [the] organic communal ideal and a more pragmatic utilitarianism remains unresolved. . . . The ethical–economic debate continues."[7]

We are addicted to unlimited extraction rather than intelligent reciprocity with nature's bounty. Such reciprocity requires integrated views of nature where holism and biometrics are woven together. We need to create ecological cultures where economics is seen as a subsystem of ecology, where nature's economy is not ignored but honored. This is what the ecological economists have been trying to do for several decades, as they remind us that the paradigm of unlimited economic growth is undermining the web of life.[8]

Ecological cultures require fresh sensibilities regarding nature. These sensibilities involve renewed spiritual, aesthetic, and moral responses to the plenitude of the natural world.[9] Where do we turn to renew those sensibilities? To nature itself, of course, but we also turn to the arts, music, poetry, and religious ecologies. In the presence of nature and also in artistic and spiritual reflections on nature we can draw guidance, inspiration, and fresh language. This is where awe and wonder can be reignited. For sustainability is not only about devising new social, political, and economic metrics for a viable future, as important as these are. Ecosystem service analysis is an example of monetizing nature that is, no doubt, a necessary contribution to the preservation of nature.

However, we also need a fuller means of valuing nature beyond economics alone. We are searching for new approaches to highlighting the intrinsic, aesthetic, and relational value of nature. Examples of these are the New Economics Institute, the New Economics Foundation, and the

Gross National Happiness indicators promoted by Bhutan.[10] The Bhutanese are inspired by a Buddhist understanding of the interdependence of all life and have been influential in beginning to reshape values regarding profit, consumption, and quality of life.[11] We are also looking for deeper motivations for transforming and sustaining the human spirit in the face of impending ecological collapse.

Conclusion

This book has focused on a critical but sometimes missing element in environmental discourse: the worldviews, ritual customs, and ethical practices of religious ecologies that embody mutually enhancing human–Earth relations. Religious ecologies draw on modes of symbolic awareness and explore mutually enhancing human–Earth relations. The shared symbol-making capacity that has endured in world religions can be a source of wisdom in restoring the central value of nature in sustaining humans and shaping cultures.

Many questions remain. How have such relations been shaped by processes of orienting, grounding, nurturing, and transforming? How can those beneficial perspectives and practices be retrieved and reformed for our modern challenges? What are the obstacles and possibilities for creating a flourishing presence of humans on the planet? Can we expand our social ethics to include environmental ethics? As Thomas Berry suggested many years ago, we have developed a social ethics for homicide and suicide and even genocide, but we have not yet developed an environmental ethics for biocide or geocide.[12] This is our collective challenge: how to respond with a more inclusive ethical understanding and more comprehensive ecological knowledge to the diminishment of planetary ecosystems. In this way we can create the grounds for the flourishing of life.

Revaluing nature is at the heart of this discussion. We are coming to see nature not simply as a resource but as the source of life—for humans and the entire Earth community. If we recognize humanity as part of complex evolving ecosystems, we may become more beneficial participants in the planetary ecosphere. Our reciprocal exchange with the living Earth may be a means whereby we, too, nurture life. Through such reciprocity we may enhance life rather than diminish it. In so doing we may fulfill our deepest role as humans within the Earth community.

Questions for Discussion

Questions for Chapter 1

1. What do Grim and Tucker mean when they observe that religions can be both limiting and liberating? Give at least two examples in which this is the case.

2. Why might appeals to justice, to enlightened self-interest, or to the wellbeing of future generations be insufficient in addressing the social and ecological problems facing humanity today? What can religious sensibilities and ethical concerns provide that secular philosophies cannot?

3. Research how religions have led to instances of social change in the past. In what ways have religions shaped both ideas and practices in the larger culture?

4. What might be the contributions of religions to the long-term flourishing of the Earth community? In what ways might their problems hinder these contributions or their promise foster these contributions?

Questions for Chapter 2

1. What is the importance of symbolic knowing for religion and for science? Give examples in which symbols are used in these disciplines.

2. What is a "religious ecology," and how does religious ecology help humans better understand and envision their roles as participants in or caretakers of the dynamic processes of life?

3. How do religious cosmologies empower individuals to understand and enact relationships between the individual and the larger self of the cosmos? How is this empowerment and understanding ecologically significant?

4. Grim and Tucker state that all religions have pathways for orienting, grounding, nurturing, and transforming. Choose one of these terms and explore its meaning within a particular tradition and across different religions.

Questions for Chapter 3

1. Describe some of the contrasting views of nature in Western thought associated with animism and monotheism, purpose and ambivalence, holism and rationalism, romanticism and transcendentalism, or anthropocentrism and anthropocosmic thought.
2. Grim and Tucker ask, "In pursuing material benefits, have we diminished nature's capacity to inspire humans? In other words, have we dimmed down our creative relationship by dismantling nature?" After reading this chapter, how would you answer these questions?
3. Although some have criticized Western philosophy and religion for their anthropocentrism and for their utilitarian views of nature, what are some ways in which Western philosophy and religion have promoted biocentric thinking and nonexploitative ways of viewing nature?
4. What is an anthropocosmic worldview as it relates to religious cosmology or scientific cosmology?

Questions for Chapter 4

1. Give three examples of how the term *ecology* has transformed over time. Even though ecology today is a diverse topic with a constantly evolving vocabulary, what are some of the commonalities of ecological thought?
2. Research one of the ecologists listed and relate him or her to the question of holism and biometrics.
3. In what ways are holism and biometrics part of contemporary ecological studies?
4. Aldo Leopold has famously stated that "a land ethic changes the role of *Homo sapiens* from conqueror of the land-community to plain member and citizen of it." Based on the chapters you've read before this one, how are religions also challenging humans to be "plain members and citizens" of the larger Earth community?
5. Reflect on some of the differences between scientists and ethicists on questions of value and describe how they are similar in their response to the wonder of the natural world and the larger universe.

Questions for Chapter 5

1. Drawing on the interpretive approaches of retrieval, reevaluation, and reconstruction, show how a particular religious tradition can contribute to the discussion of religion and ecology.
2. In what ways do images or models of God affect the ways in which religions relate to environments?
3. Research how ecofeminism has raised new questions about human interactions with the environment.
4. Discuss the contribution of Thomas Berry's idea of a "new story" in relation to both religious cosmology and scientific understanding of the emergence of the universe.

Questions for Chapter 6

1. What are the theological contributions of the Patriarch, and why are they ecologically significant? How do his theological contributions compare with the strands of Christianity that you are familiar with?
2. How do both theology and science benefit from an exchange of ideas about the pressing issue of water degradation in various regions of the world? Give at least two examples.
3. What is ecological sin? What kinds of behaviors (or nonbehaviors) do you think the Orthodox thinkers in this chapter might view as ecological sin?
4. How does Orthodox theology work to orient individuals in relation to the Earth and to the environment? What do Grim and Tucker mean when they speak of Orthodox Christianity as providing an "orienting cosmology" at the end of this chapter?

Questions for Chapter 7

1. Pan Yue describes the attempt to make China into an ecological culture. What might an ecological culture look like to you? What criteria do you think would need to be met in order to call a culture ecological?
2. What aspects of Confucianism make it a cosmologically orienting religious ecology? In what ways can it help to ground individuals in the world?
3. How does Confucianism understand the role and location of the human in relation to the rest of the natural world? How does this differ from your own understanding of the human, and how might this alternative perspective lead to environmentally friendly ethics and action? What does it mean to describe Confucianism as an anthropocosmic tradition?

4. What is the "great triad of Confucianism," and how does it provide a different way of understanding humans and sustainability?

Questions for Chapter 8

1. What is a lifeway? How does a lifeway differ from other ways of living and from other ways of being religious? How is it similar?
2. How is reciprocity ritualized by the Salish peoples? Describe how this is accomplished through singing, spirit sickness, or giveaways.
3. Describe the Salish Winter Dance in your own words. Then, explain how the Winter Dance relates to the idea of nurturing as discussed by Grim and Tucker in this chapter.
4. How do rituals enable Salish peoples to generate and sustain a deep connection to their place and to the foods, animals, and other people in their community?

Questions for Chapter 9

1. How might religion be a transforming force in the case of the Yamuna River? In other words, how can religion help to restore, reenvision, and implement mutually beneficial relations between humans and the river?
2. The state of the Yamuna River remains a paradox. Do a case study exploring how the Yamuna River is both revered as a goddess worthy of devotion yet also overwhelmingly polluted. What tensions exist in this relationship, and how can those tensions be creatively transformed and overcome in order to inspire action to clean up the river?
3. How is the religious ecology described in this chapter both an ancient force for ecological preservation and a vital, contemporary force for restoration? In what ways does religion promote and sustain ecological restoration that modern economic and engineering models cannot?
4. What do Grim and Tucker mean when they say that it is evident that the river is dying with its toxic burden? What would a living, flourishing river look like in both an ecological and a religious sense?

Questions for Chapter 10

1. Grim and Tucker emphasize the flourishing of the Earth community rather than sustainability. What is the difference between these terms, and why do you think that emphasizing flourishing is significant?

2. What has the Parliament of World Religions contributed to the dialogue of world religions? Research the sessions on religion and ecology at the Parliament in Melbourne in 2009.
3. Documents such as the Earth Charter expand the ethical sphere beyond the human to include the entire community of life. Why is it important to broaden the boundaries of the moral community, and how might religions contribute to this expansion?
4. These are the key components of the Earth Charter: cosmological context, respect and care for the community of life, ecological integrity, social equity, economic justice, democracy, nonviolence, and peace. Explore one of these concepts in relation to one of the world religions.

Glossary

Abrahamic traditions: refers to the traditions of Judaism, Christianity, and Islam that trace their lineage back to the progenitor, Abraham of Ur.

Ahimsa: a term for nonviolence associated originally with Jainism and later assimilated into Hinduism and Buddhism.

Anthropocene: a term first proposed by geologists Eugene Stoermer and Paul Crutzen in 2000. It is now widely used to name our current era due to human-induced changes on the planet.

Anthropocentric: a perspective that prioritizes and focuses on the human apart from other species and life forms.

Anthropocosmic: an understanding that locates the human within the cosmos and within the community of life on Earth.

Avatar: an incarnation of a deity born into material reality with special powers, often for the purpose of performing a particular cosmogonic or world-creating act. In Hinduism, among the *avatars*, or incarnations, of Vishnu, the deity Krishna holds a unique place for many devotees as the source of all other *avatar* incarnations.

Bhakti: devotion to a god in the Hindu tradition. This devotion takes various forms: emotional outpouring in song or ecstatic dance, literary production, or exchange with images of a deity (*murti*).

Biodiversity: this term for biological diversity was originally formulated by biologists Thomas Lovejoy and E. O. Wilson. It refers to the variety among living organisms in ecosystems and to genetic complexity. The United Nations Convention on Biological Diversity has been working since 1993 to promote conservation, sustainable use, and equitable sharing of biodiversity on the planet.

Biometrics: a term for the measurement and quantification of life processes and systems.

Cheng: in Chinese thought this refers to authenticity in the cosmos and sincerity in the human.

***Christus Pantocrator*:** a Christian icon or image of Christ's face surrounded by a halo and often placed in the central dome over the altar.

Conservation: originally this term referred to an ethic of maintaining the health of nature and natural resources for the benefit of the human, in contrast to preservation of nature for its inherent value. This perspective was associated with Gifford Pinchot. *Conservation* has now become a complex term that is used to refer to the protection and care for an increasingly broad range of life forms, human habitat, energy, soil, and activities that promote sustainability.

Cosmology: the studies of and stories about the universe. In the humanities, *cosmology* refers to the myths of the origin and ongoing character of the universe, whereas in the physical sciences cosmology focuses primarily on the emergence of the early universe.

Dao **or *Tao*:** a central term in Chinese religion and philosophy that can also mean a path. It refers to the great unfolding processes of nature and the pathway of humans amid these processes. As in the Daoist text, *Daodejing*, it cannot be fully named or described.

***Darshan*:** a concept in Hinduism of seeing and being seen by a deity, especially in the form of an image (*murti*).

***Dharma*:** a concept in Hinduism for duty and responsibility, especially regarding one's life path; often the term is used in this tradition for "religion."

Earth: the scientific term for our planet. In East Asian Confucianism, *Earth* refers to the entire community of life, human and natural.

Earth community: a phrase developed by Thomas Berry and used in the Earth Charter. It refers to the interrelatedness, interdependence, and co-operative character of organic and inorganic existence. Using the term *community* highlights the scale, intimacy, and affective nature of those relationships.

Ecological culture: a term developed in contemporary China to refer to cultural awareness and effective environmental action of individuals and communities.

Ecological phase: a term used by Thomas Berry to describe an emerging stage in human history in which humans reorient themselves toward mutually beneficial human–Earth relations. He also referred to it as the ecozoic era.

Ecological sin: a teaching by the Greek Orthodox Ecumenical Patriarch, Bartholomew, that intentional pollution of the environment or degradation of ecosystems is an act that defiles creation.

Ecology: a term that refers to a branch of biology that studies the interrelationships of organisms and their surroundings.

Ecotheology: a term that refers to a branch of theology concerned with the relationships of the divine with the Earth and humans with the Earth.

Environment: the natural setting and conditions in which a biological entity lives. Can refer to smaller ecological niches or larger bioregions or used broadly to refer to the entire natural world on which life depends.

Environmental ethics: the study of the religious and philosophical understanding of the human moral relationship to the environment.

Ethos: a way of being in the world that leads to certain behavior. For example, excessive consumption of goods exemplifies a consumerist ethos, whereas an ecological ethos implies sufficiency and living lightly on the Earth.

Evangelical: a term in Christianity referring to the spread of the "good news" of the Gospels, often used today to refer to particular groups within the Christian tradition.

Flourishing: a term used to describe the mutual thriving of human life and all other life. Preference is given in this book to this term (rather than *sustainable*) to describe an ecological future in which the health of ecosystems is emphasized rather than the maintenance of an extractive economy and a consumerist lifestyle.

Giving: this refers to a lifeway among Indigenous peoples based on sharing across families and clan that was in accordance with an observed giving in the natural world that surrounded them; in phenomenology this refers to an understanding that the world offers itself to human perception.

Grounding: in religious ecologies grounding is a means of fostering relational resonance between the myriad communities of life. Such communities may include both past and living humans, the larger world of four-legged, winged, and gilled beings, along with the soils, meadows, rivers, forests, and oceans in which they dwell.

Harmonia: this notion of living in harmony was conceived by the Stoics, who described it as a cosmological sympathy for the rhythms and vibrations that extended throughout the cosmos, linking all life into a pervasive unity and giving rise to a sense of cosmopolitan citizenship.

Heaven: in Christianity this refers to an afterlife state for the blessed. In East Asian Confucianism it refers to a guiding force for the universe that imparts to humans their heavenly nature.

Holism: a term used in ecology that emphasizes the wholeness or completeness of ecosystems rather than simply a collection of parts. This term stands in contrast to reductionistic or mechanistic views that see natural systems in terms of independent, separable components rather than as a whole greater than the sum of its parts.

Human–Earth relations: the moral, physical, cognitive, and spiritual relationships between the human community and the Earth community. Here this set of relationships is described as being either ecologically destructive or as mutually beneficial.

Icon: a religious work of art in Greek Orthodoxy depicting Christ, Mary, or a saint. These images are said to have symbolic power that serves as an opening to the sacred.

Immanence: a sense of the sacred within matter, or divine presence and activity within the world. A theological example in Christianity is the belief that Christ as Logos became incarnate in the human person Jesus of Nazareth. An example from Chinese thought is *ch'i* or *qi*, in which matter–energy is understood to activate and course through all reality.

Indigenous: people who are native to a place. Used in political and social understandings for people located in a place before the colonial settlements in which military and economic power set them aside or marginalized them, hence "First Nations."

Jal: a term for water in Hinduism. This is especially significant if the water comes from a sacred source such as the Yamuna or Ganges River. This water is believed to carry the purifying possibilities of the riverine goddess herself.

Jen or ren: the Confucian notion of humaneness or love, which is present in the human order, the natural order, and the cosmic order. Humaneness is bestowed by Heaven but must be cultivated by humans to be fully realized.

Junzi or chuntzu: the Confucian ideal of the noble person who cultivates himself or herself so as to achieve full humaneness (*ren*) and relatedness to family, society, and cosmos. Such a person gives back to society through family, education, or public service.

Kenosis: the concept of Christ's becoming human, namely, his sacrificial act of emptying himself for the sake of all humans. See Paul's Epistle to the Philippians 2:6.

Khalifah Allah: the Qur'anic concept in Islam of the human as the "trustee" or "vicegerent" of creation for Allah.

Li: in Chinese thought, one character refers to ritual practices used for self-cultivation and the creation of harmonious societies. Another character for *li* refers to the inner ordering principle of reality that is related to material force (*ch'i, qi*).

Lifeway: a traditional integrated style of life found among many Indigenous peoples in which shared language, kinship names, governance systems, reverence for homeland, and collective narratives of identity bind the people together.

Lila: a term in Hinduism for play, namely, the play of the gods Krishna and Siva. Such play may result in worlds being created or destroyed. Creative play is associated with the love of the deity.

Liturgy: the performance of the central ritual act within a tradition, typically used in Christianity for the Mass, namely, the ritual remembrance of the Last Supper at which Jesus of Nazareth blessed the bread and wine as his body and blood.

Logos: a Greek philosophical concept that had various meanings but often referred to an inner ordering principle within every existent reality, namely, the spiritual or metaphysical pattern that gives something its structure.

Mandala: a term for a cosmological image that centers the human among spiritual presences such as Buddhist figures, Hindu deities, or Navajo *yei*. Often place based, a mandala elicits a meditative journey for a religious practitioner.

Metanoia: a Greek term for a radical transformation of consciousness and of practice, usually of a spiritual awareness that profoundly changes one's life and behavior.

Moksha: a Hindu term for liberation from the world of suffering through spiritual practice and meditation.

Murti: an image or icon of the divine in Hinduism that is experienced as a place where the sacred manifests.

Nirvana: a term used in Buddhism for entering into a state of enlightenment and extinguishing craving desires.

Nurturing: in religious ecologies, the term for Earth's processes of fecundity that sustain the community of life with water and food. Individual and communal nurturance is experienced through rituals and ceremonies regarding gathering and hunting or growing and harvesting food. Planting and harvest rituals and thanksgiving for food and drink are central to religious ecologies.

Orienting: in religious ecologies, the term for experiencing a guiding and sustaining creative force in the natural world and beyond. For some traditions this is a creator deity (Yahweh, God, or Allah in the Western religions and Brahma in Hinduism) or a numinous presence in nature (Great Spirit, *mana*, or *kami* in some Indigenous traditions). For others it is the source of flourishing life (*Dao* or the Great Ultimate in Daoism and Confucianism) or Original Mind (the Buddha Nature in Mahayana Buddhism).

Panentheism: stresses the presence of God, or the sacred, in the world. If pantheism collapses everything into God, panentheism preserves a sense of differentiated reality in relation to an immanent or transcendent divine. *Panentheism* has had very different meanings throughout history; for example, Spinoza's sense of *natura naturata*, or nature naturing as God, is quite different from Whitehead's sense of material emergence in evolution as manifesting God. Yet both have been described using the term *panentheism*.

Pantheism: identifies God, or the divine, as within the cosmos, giving rise to feelings of reverence for nature or awe in the omnipresence of the sacred. The usage may be positive, such as in Hinduism, where millions of gods are acknowledged as in the world, or contested and negative, as with some theistic objections that if everything is God, then the problem of evil is ambiguous.

Prakriti: a term in Hindu thought for the world of ceaseless change, in contrast with **Purusha,** the abiding, changeless world.

Preservation: refers to care and concern for the inherent dignity and value of the natural world in itself. This perspective was associated with John Muir, founder of the Sierra Club, who sought to preserve large tracts of land as wilderness in California that led to the formation of Yosemite Park.

Qi or *ch'i*: material force. This is the understanding in Chinese thought in which nature is dynamic and fluid with the movements of matter–energy.

Religion: an attitude, orientation, or conviction that there is something beyond the human that calls us to value life. Religion is a multivalent and complex concept that can be characterized by a set of practices, rituals, beliefs, stories, symbols, or ethics that orient humans within the larger Earth community.

Religion and ecology, field of: an interdisciplinary and multireligious academic field of study that is concerned with questions about the complex and evolving set of relationships between religion, the natural world, and ecology.

Religious cosmologies: stories or understandings that orient humans to the unfolding of the cosmos in relationship to a larger context of life.

Religious ecologies: ways of orienting and grounding human communities in the context and rhythms of nature. This term also implies an orientation toward mutually enhancing modes of integrating humans into the social, natural, and cosmic orders of reality.

Scientific ecologies: a framework for understanding ecosystems that relies on models, scientific theories, and empirical observation to interpret and explain ecosystems and other aspects of the natural world.

Secularization: a description of modern societies proposing that as scientific, humanistic, and materialistic understandings of reality grow in explanatory power, religious ideas and institutions lose their ability to provide meaningful frameworks for orienting and grounding humanity in relation to the world around them.

Seeds of virtue: the botanical metaphor developed by Mencius, the fourth-century BCE Confucian teacher, suggesting that self-cultivation was like an agricultural act that required tending, nurturing, and gradual growth of behaviors and characteristics that would eventually result in a "seed" or "crop" of virtue.

Self-cultivation: a discipline in religious traditions, especially in East Asia, in which a person undertakes practices considered spiritually efficacious. Self-cultivation may lead to mental insight and awareness, physical tranquility, and moral strength of character.

Seva: service to the divine in Hinduism, typically associated with a devotional act but increasingly being understood as environmental service for restoration of rivers, forests, and ecosystems. In an ecological sense, it has sometimes been translated as "loving service" to an ecosystem.

Shari'a: a term in Islam for the righteous path, especially as expressed in law and the legal schools of thought.

Sheng sheng: the fecundity of life, that is, a Chinese understanding of the dynamic transformations of life manifest in recurring cycles of growth, fruition, harvesting, and abundance.

Spirituality: involves a search for the sacred in which humans experience their authentic being in relation to a larger whole. This usually entails a spiritual journey of self-cultivation and discipline to overcome fragmentation, loss, and suffering.

Stewardship: used in the Jewish and Christian traditions to focus on human responsibility for the environment.

Sumix: a manifestation of the sacred power in the Salish world in meteorological events, human skills and songs, and the spirit persons present in the landscape who gift humans with their power.

Symbolic knowing: a mode of consciousness in which images, sounds, or words evoke relational response. Rather than objectifying or quantifying (empirical knowing), symbolic knowing relies on shared cultural understandings and tends toward more affective and emotional tones for identifying with and remembering persons, objects, or events.

Teleology: religious or philosophical affirmation of purpose in the world.

Theosis: related to *theos*, or God, in Christian theology in which a human person can become divinized or godlike through divine grace rather than any specific human act.

Transcendent: beyond the material world, a sense that the sacred is located outside matter, namely, that the divine is external to the world. Examples are the Islamic understanding of Allah as God who creates the whole of reality but exists beyond that reality.

Transfiguration: the event in the life of Jesus in which he became luminous while on a mountain with the apostles Peter, James, and John is found in three gospels (Matthew 17:1–9, Mark 9:2–8, and Luke 9:28–36). Many of the early Christian church fathers described it as the moment when temporal matter met eternal spirit.

Transforming: in religious ecologies, the turn in which individuals or communities go from their small self into their greater self. Humans negotiate this transformation in a variety of ways through prayer and meditation, ritual and sacrament, repentance and renewal. Loss, suffering, and diminishment are given larger meaning within the changing and renewing processes of nature.

Trickster: widespread among many peoples is the concept of a creative person, either animal in form or in the shape of a human, who alternates in behavior as a trick maker, a buffoon, or the creator of differentiated life on Earth. Implied in this ambiguous mythic personality is a cosmogonic insight that all reality changes and holds unexpected possibilities.

World religions: refers to the location of religions in the surrounding world. Rather than a reference to the universalizing character of a religion, *world religions* situates the religious phenomenon as engaged with the natural world. Formerly the idea of world religions arose from criteria in which a colonial prerogative, a monotheistic belief, or a unifying dogma was believed to be appropriate for, and spreading to, all peoples.

Xiao **or** *Hsiao***:** the Confucian virtue of filiality, the sense of responsibility to one's parents and, by extension, to that which gives birth to a person, for example, Heaven and Earth.

Yin **and** *yang***:** the fluctuations in *qi* that manifest throughout the differences in reality. *Yin* is associated with the dark and moist, *yang* with the light and dry, but rather than dualities, yin and yang are co-relational entities.

Appendix A

Common Declaration of John Paul II and the Ecumenical Patriarch His Holiness Bartholomew I

Monday, 10 June 2002

We are gathered here today in the spirit of peace for the good of all human beings and for the care of creation. At this moment in history, at the beginning of the third millennium, we are saddened to see the daily suffering of a great number of people from violence, starvation, poverty and disease. We are also concerned about the negative consequences for humanity and for all creation resulting from the degradation of some basic natural resources such as water, air and land, brought about by an economic and technological progress which does not recognize and take into account its limits.

Almighty God envisioned a world of beauty and harmony, and He created it, making every part an expression of His freedom, wisdom and love (cf. *Gen* 1:1-25).

At the centre of the whole of creation, He placed us, human beings, with our inalienable human dignity. Although we share many features with the rest of the living beings, Almighty God went further with us and gave us an immortal soul, the source of self-awareness and freedom, endowments that make us in His image and likeness (cf. *Gen* 1:26-31;2:7). Marked with that resemblance, we have been placed by God in the world in order to cooperate with Him in realizing more and more fully the divine purpose for creation.

At the beginning of history, man and woman sinned by disobeying God and rejecting His design for creation. Among the results of this first sin was the destruction of the original harmony of creation. If we examine carefully the social and environmental crisis which the world community is facing, we must conclude that we are still betraying the mandate God has given us: to be stewards called to collaborate with God in watching over creation in holiness and wisdom.

God has not abandoned the world. It is His will that His design and our hope for it will be realized through our co-operation in restoring its original harmony. In our own time we are witnessing a growth of an *ecological awareness* which needs to be encouraged, so that it will lead to practical programmes and initiatives. An awareness of the relationship between God and humankind brings a fuller sense of the importance of the relationship between human beings and the natural environment, which is God's creation and which God entrusted to us to guard with wisdom and love (cf. *Gen* 1:28).

Respect for creation stems from respect for human life and dignity. It is on the basis of our recognition that the world is created by God that we can discern an objective moral order within which to articulate a code of environmental ethics. In this perspective, Christians and all other believers have a specific role to play in proclaiming moral values and in educating people in *ecological awareness*, which is none other than responsibility towards self, towards others, towards creation.

What is required is an act of repentance on our part and a renewed attempt to view ourselves, one another, and the world around us within the perspective of the divine design for creation. The problem is not simply economic and technological; it is moral and spiritual. A solution at the economic and technological level can be found only if we undergo, in the most radical way, an inner change of heart, which can lead to a change in lifestyle and of unsustainable patterns of consumption and production. A genuine *conversion* in Christ will enable us to change the way we think and act.

First, we must regain humility and recognize the limits of our powers, and most importantly, the limits of our knowledge and judgement. We have been making decisions, taking actions and assigning values that are leading us away from the world as it should be, away from the design of God for creation, away from all that is essential for a healthy planet and a healthy commonwealth of people. A new approach and a new culture are needed, based on the centrality of the human person within creation and inspired by environmentally ethical behavior stemming from our triple relationship to God, to self and to creation. Such an ethics fosters interdependence and stresses the principles of universal solidarity, social justice and responsibility, in order to promote a true culture of life.

Secondly, we must frankly admit that humankind is entitled to something better than what we see around us. We and, much more, our children and future generations are entitled to a better world, a world free from degradation, violence and bloodshed, a world of generosity and love.

Thirdly, aware of the value of prayer, we must implore God the Creator to enlighten people everywhere regarding the duty to respect and carefully guard creation.

We therefore invite all men and women of good will to ponder the importance of the following ethical goals:

1. To think of the world's children when we reflect on and evaluate our options for action.

2. To be open to study the true values based on the natural law that sustain every human culture.

3. To use science and technology in a full and constructive way, while recognizing that the findings of science have always to be evaluated in the light of the centrality of the human person, of the common good and of the inner purpose of creation. Science may help us to correct the mistakes of the past, in order to enhance the spiritual and material well-being of the present and future generations. It is love for our children that will show us the path that we must follow into the future.

4. To be humble regarding the idea of ownership and to be open to the demands of solidarity. Our mortality and our weakness of judgement together warn us not to take irreversible actions with what we choose to regard as our property during our brief stay on this earth. We have not been entrusted with unlimited power over creation, we are only stewards of the common heritage.

5. To acknowledge the diversity of situations and responsibilities in the work for a better world environment. We do not expect every person and every institution to assume the same burden. Everyone has a part

to play, but for the demands of justice and charity to be respected the most affluent societies must carry the greater burden, and from them is demanded a sacrifice greater than can be offered by the poor. Religions, governments and institutions are faced by many different situations; but on the basis of the principle of subsidiarity all of them can take on some tasks, some part of the shared effort.

6. To promote a peaceful approach to disagreement about how to live on this earth, about how to share it and use it, about what to change and what to leave unchanged. It is not our desire to evade controversy about the environment, for we trust in the capacity of human reason and the path of dialogue to reach agreement. We commit ourselves to respect the views of all who disagree with us, seeking solutions through open exchange, without resorting to oppression and domination.

It is not too late. God's world has incredible healing powers. Within a single generation, we could steer the earth toward our children's future. Let that generation start now, with God's help and blessing.

Rome - Venice, 10 June 2002

Appendix B

Influence of Traditional Chinese Wisdom of Eco Care on Westerners[1]

More and more scholars have cast their eyes on China in recent years. Not long ago a professor from Yale University gave me several books entitled *Confucianism and Ecological Civilization, Taoism and Ecological Civilization* and *Buddhism and Ecological Civilization* [Harvard Series].

I was shocked by the fact that westerners have begun to study the traditions of Chinese civilization to solve ecological crises. What interests them most, to my surprise, is the way our ancestors deal with the relationship between man and nature. In those books, they translated *Tianrenheyi* (literally means syncretism of man and nature) into *universal resonance*. Why is the Chinese nation able to subsist on its own? This is because our culture contains more profound wisdom of eco care, which is seen everywhere in our ethics and systems, practiced in our way of life and kept on in our history.

Confucianism, Buddhism and Taoism have dominated Chinese culture for five thousand years. Their joint influence helps create the unique cultural system of the Chinese with the Doctrine of the Mean, Harmony and Tolerance as its core. It calls for order, balance, tolerance and harmony. That's the root cause for endless succession of the Chinese nation.

All these values can be boiled down to the practice of discretion in practical systems and daily life. *Discretion* means sense of propriety, balance and harmony. It leaves people room to maneuver with ease; it is an art

[1] Speech given by vice-minister Pan Yue of the Ministry of Environmental Protection of the People's Republic of China, June 4, 2011. Excerpted from the speech at the Environmental Forum Marking the Thirtieth Anniversary of Reform and Opening Up.

with which people may advance or retreat freely. Discretion teaches us to strike a balance through abstention and proportion. It is the wisdom for one to conduct and establish himself or herself in the society. In a word, discretion not only embodies the political wisdom of China but also living wisdom and even ecological wisdom of the Chinese.

Not only does the wisdom exist in the classics of the sages, it also takes roots among the commons through families and etiquette. The wisdom is practiced everywhere from national system and administrative policies, to scholars, farmers, handicraftsman and merchants, from music, chess to calligraphy and painting. Whether in the doctrines of sages such as the Four Books and Five Classics or in the minor principles observed by the worldly, the wisdom maintains coherent and supplements one another, forming a flourishing tree reaching the sky.

Eco care connects the law of nature and human relations. By seeking the beauty and significance of life instead of enjoying material comforts to the maximum, it enables the daily life to excel the pursuit of fame and wealth. A trickle as the practice seems to be, it constitutes a healthy way of life called ecological civilization. This leisurely yet abstinent living style curbs man's endless desire while it spurs him to lead a full life. This value allows us to see through and correct a bunch of errors of consumerism and nihilism brought about by western industrial civilization.

Within a short span of over a hundred years China has jumped from agricultural civilization into industrialization and it even went further to move into ecological civilization in advance. This is absolutely possible, for China has been equipped with economic, political and culture foundations at one time to achieve this strategy. The modernization drive has immensely liberated and developed productivity, resulting in soaring national wealth and national power. This is the economic foundation for China to build ecological civilization. The modernization drive has accomplished the mission to save the nation from doom and strive for its survival and a political nation that carries several thousand years of traditions has after all stood erect in the east of the world. This is the political foundation for China to build ecological civilization. Chinese traditions brimming with ecological wisdom have gone through creative transformation in modern society. This is the cultural foundation of ecological civilization. Therefore, China has the conditions and capabilities for sure to realize the leapfrogging development across the three stages of human civilization.

Appendix C

Selections from the United Nations Declaration on the Rights of Indigenous Peoples, 2007[1]

Annex

The General Assembly,

Guided by the purposes and principles of the Charter of the United Nations, and good faith in the fulfillment of the obligations assumed by States in accordance with the Charter,

Affirming that indigenous peoples are equal to all other peoples, while recognizing the right of all peoples to be different, to consider themselves different, and to be respected as such,

Affirming also that all peoples contribute to the diversity and richness of civilizations and cultures, which constitute the common heritage of humankind,

Affirming further that all doctrines, policies and practices based on or advocating superiority of peoples or individuals on the basis of national origin or racial, religious, ethnic or cultural differences are racist, scientifically false, legally invalid, morally condemnable and socially unjust,

Reaffirming that indigenous peoples, in the exercise of their rights, should be free from discrimination of any kind,

Concerned that indigenous peoples have suffered from historic injustices as a result of, inter alia, their colonization and dispossession of their lands, territories and resources, thus preventing them from exercising, in particular, their right to development in accordance with their own needs and interests,

Recognizing the urgent need to respect and promote the inherent rights of indigenous peoples which derive from their political, economic and social structures and from their cultures, spiritual traditions, histories and philosophies, especially their rights to their lands, territories and resources,

Recognizing also the urgent need to respect and promote the rights of indigenous peoples affirmed in treaties, agreements and other constructive arrangements with States,

Welcoming the fact that indigenous peoples are organizing themselves for political, economic, social and cultural enhancement and in order to bring to an end all forms of discrimination and oppression wherever they occur,

Convinced that control by indigenous peoples over developments affecting them and their lands, territories and resources will enable them to maintain and strengthen their institutions, cultures and traditions, and to promote their development in accordance with their aspirations and needs,

Recognizing that respect for indigenous knowledge, cultures and traditional practices contributes to sustainable and equitable development and proper management of the environment,

Emphasizing the contribution of the demilitarization of the lands and territories of indigenous peoples to peace, economic and social progress and development, understanding and friendly relations among nations and peoples of the world,

Recognizing in particular the right of indigenous families and communities to retain shared responsibility for the upbringing, training, education and well-being of their children, consistent with the rights of the child,

Considering that the rights affirmed in treaties, agreements and other constructive arrangements between States and indigenous peoples are, in some situations, matters of international concern, interest, responsibility and character,

Considering also that treaties, agreements and other constructive arrangements, and the relationship they represent, are the basis for a strengthened partnership between indigenous peoples and States,

Acknowledging that the Charter of the United Nations, the International Covenant on Economic, Social and Cultural Rights and the International Covenant on Civil and Political Rights, as well as the Vienna Declaration and Programme of Action, affirm the fundamental importance of the right to self-determination of all peoples, by virtue of which they freely determine their political status and freely pursue their economic, social and cultural development,

Bearing in mind that nothing in this Declaration may be used to deny any peoples their right to self-determination, exercised in conformity with international law,

Convinced that the recognition of the rights of indigenous peoples in this

Declaration will enhance harmonious and cooperative relations between the State and indigenous peoples, based on principles of justice, democracy, respect for human rights, non-discrimination and good faith,

Encouraging States to comply with and effectively implement all their obligations as they apply to indigenous peoples under international instruments, in particular those related to human rights, in consultation and cooperation with the peoples concerned,

Emphasizing that the United Nations has an important and continuing role to play in promoting and protecting the rights of indigenous peoples,

Believing that this Declaration is a further important step forward for the recognition, promotion and protection of the rights and freedoms of indigenous peoples and in the development of relevant activities of the United Nations system in this field,

Recognizing and reaffirming that indigenous individuals are entitled without discrimination to all human rights recognized in international law, and that indigenous peoples possess collective rights which are indispensable for their existence, well-being and integral development as peoples,

Recognizing that the situation of indigenous peoples varies from region to region and from country to country and that the significance of national and regional particularities and various historical and cultural backgrounds should be taken into consideration,

Solemnly proclaims the following United Nations Declaration on the Rights of Indigenous Peoples as a standard of achievement to be pursued in a spirit of partnership and mutual respect:

Article 11

1. Indigenous peoples have the right to practise and revitalize their cultural traditions and customs. This includes the right to maintain, protect and develop the past, present and future manifestations of their cultures, such as archaeological and historical sites, artefacts, designs, ceremonies, technologies and visual and performing arts and literature.
2. States shall provide redress through effective mechanisms, which may include restitution, developed in conjunction with indigenous peoples, with respect to their cultural, intellectual, religious and spiritual property taken without their free, prior and informed consent or in violation of their laws, traditions and customs.

Article 12

1. Indigenous peoples have the right to manifest, practise, develop and teach their spiritual and religious traditions, customs and ceremonies; the right

to maintain, protect, and have access in privacy to their religious and cultural sites; the right to the use and control of their ceremonial objects; and the right to the repatriation of their human remains.

2. States shall seek to enable the access and/or repatriation of ceremonial objects and human remains in their possession through fair, transparent and effective mechanisms developed in conjunction with indigenous peoples concerned.

3. Indigenous peoples have the right to revitalize, use, develop and transmit to future generations their histories, languages, oral traditions, philosophies, writing systems and literatures, and to designate and retain their own names for communities, places and persons.

4. States shall take effective measures to ensure that this right is protected and also to ensure that indigenous peoples can understand and be understood in political, legal and administrative proceedings, where necessary through the provision of interpretation or by other appropriate means.

Article 13

1. Indigenous peoples have the right to revitalize, use, develop and transmit to future generations their histories, languages, oral traditions, philosophies, writing systems and literatures, and to designate and retain their own names for communities, places and persons.

2. States shall take effective measures to ensure that this right is protected and also to ensure that indigenous peoples can understand and be understood in political, legal and administrative proceedings, where necessary through the provision of interpretation or by other appropriate means.

Article 14

1. Indigenous peoples have the right to establish and control their educational systems and institutions providing education in their own languages, in a manner appropriate to their cultural methods of teaching and learning.

2. Indigenous individuals, particularly children, have the right to all levels and forms of education of the State without discrimination.

3. States shall, in conjunction with indigenous peoples, take effective measures, in order for indigenous individuals, particularly children, including those living outside their communities, to have access, when possible, to an education in their own culture and provided in their own language.

Appendix D

Save the Fraser Declaration[1]

We the undersigned indigenous nations of the Fraser River Watershed declare: We governed our territories within the Fraser watershed, according to our laws and traditions, since time immemorial. Our relationship with the watershed is ancient and profound, and our inherent Title and Rights and legal authority over these lands and waters have never been relinquished through treaty or war.

Water is life, for our peoples and for all living things that depend on it. The Fraser River and its tributaries are our lifeline.

A threat to the Fraser and its headwaters is a threat to all who depend on its health. We will not allow our fish, animals, plants, people and ways of life to be placed at risk.

We have come together to defend these lands and waters from a grave threat: the Enbridge Northern Gateway Pipelines project. This project which would link the Tar Sands to Asia through our territories and the headwaters of this great river, and the federal process to approve it, violate our laws, traditions, values and our inherent rights as Indigenous Peoples under international law. We are united to exercise our inherent Title, Rights, and responsibility to ourselves, our ancestors, our descendants and to the people of the world, to defend these lands and waters. Our laws require that we do this.

Therefore, in upholding our ancestral laws, Title, Rights and responsibilities, we declare:

We will not allow the proposed Enbridge Northern Gateway Pipelines, or similar Tar Sands projects, to cross our lands, territories and watersheds, or the ocean migration routes of Fraser River salmon.

We are adamant and resolved in this declaration, made according to our Indigenous laws and authority. We call on all who would place our lands and waters at risk—we have suffered enough, we will protect our watersheds, and we will not tolerate this great threat to us all and to all future generations.

Declared at T'exelc (Williams Lake), Secwepemc Territory, and Vancouver, Coast Salish Territories, and Affirmed by the Following Indigenous Nations[2]

Adams Lake; Alexis Creek First Nation; Bonaparte; Boston Bar First Nation; Bridge River Indian Band; Burns Lake Band; Chawathil First Nation; Coldwater Band; Cook's Ferry Band; Esketemc; Kwantlen; Lake Babine Nation; Lhoosk'uz Dene Nation; Lhatko (Red Bluff); Mt. Currie Band/Lil'wat Nation; Musqueam Indian Band; Nadleh Whut'en; Nak'azdli; Nicomen Indian Band; Nooaitch Indian Band; N'Quatqua; Saik'uz; Shackan Indian Band; Siska Indian Band; Skatsin/Neskonlith; Skeetchestn; Soowahlie; Splatsin; St'át'imc; Stswecem'c/Xgat'tem (Canoe Creek); Sumas; Takla Lake First Nation; T'exelc (Williams Lake Band); T'ít'q'et; Tl'esqox/Toosey; Tsq'escen First Nation (Canim Lake Band); Tzeachten; Ulkatcho Band; Upper Nicola; Wet'suwet'en; Xat'sull (Soda Creek); Xaxli'p; Xeni Gwet'in First Nations Government; Yakweakwioose

Supporting Nations

Cape Mudge Band; Campbell River; Da'naxda'xw Nation; Fort Nelson; Ktunaxa Nation; Kwakiutl; Lyackson; Okanagan Indian Band; Penticon Indian Band, Okanagan Nation; Quatsino; Tseshaht First Nation

Appendix E

Yamuna River Declaration Resulting from the Workshop "Yamuna River: A Confluence of Waters, a Crisis of Need"[1]

Coming together as scientists, religious scholars, religious leaders, and concerned participants we acknowledge the current state of the Yamuna River as severely degraded and in need of attention through collaborative research, focused action, and shared compassion. Several calls for central planning and professional engineering have been articulated at various times and at diverse forums that have preceded this workshop. However, we have consciously opted to explore the utility of interdisciplinary knowledge as well as the sense of religiosity and moral responsibility in restoring and protecting the river. We acknowledge the long history of work on the river, especially as related to the Yamuna Action Plan. Nonetheless, we hope to make our own modest contribution beginning with our interdisciplinary workshop held at TERI University in Delhi.

By focusing on the Yamuna River we do not intend to turn away from the problems of other rivers in India or stress the spiritual and cultural significance of one river over others. Rather, we have gathered as an interdisciplinary group committed to conservation of the precious resource of water, especially in north India where some 60 million people live near and thus depend on the Yamuna. In this workshop we have explored current conditions of the Yamuna River, the roles of interdisciplinary and values-based approaches in water management, conservation, and preservation, as well as what research projects and educational and conservation projects might be of

[1] Held at TERI University, Delhi, January 3–5, 2011, sponsored by TERI University with the support of Chancellor Rajendra Pachauri; Yale School of Forestry and Environmental Studies; and Sri Radha Raman Temple, Vrindaban, India.

197

assistance as we go forward. We have also reflected on the shared perspective of concern for the river that provides a common ground for dialogue among scientists, religious leaders, and humanists.

In our discussions we have come to realize that a segmented view of the Yamuna River, whether in analysis of the problems or in suggested solutions, may be insufficient inasmuch as it lacks a holistic and integrated framework that explicitly recognizes the intimate linkages between ecosystems and human communities.

A way toward more interdisciplinary, environmental action may be found in integrating cultural and religious perspectives with scientific analysis. Thus we can speak of different cultural communities along with distinct biotic communities along the river. At the same time we acknowledge the utilitarian agendas of damming and channeling the river for agriculture and waste management. Each of these differences has historical significance, but they all relate to one river whose life is now imperiled throughout.

Simultaneously, we especially ponder the paradoxical question of how a sacred river of love could become so defiled over several decades since the 1980s. No doubt the rapid industrialization and urbanization of north India has overwhelmed the ability of the river to purify itself, as its flow is diminished in so many sections. Concomitant with such analysis is an inquiry into the process that is commonly recognized as "development" so as to understand the historical and political forces shaping the course of the river.

Unique among world rivers, the Yamuna and several other Indian rivers are revered as Goddesses in the living Hindu tradition. We wonder, therefore, if there might be a way for devotees of the river to integrate a deeper sense of environmental awareness and conservation into their religiosity. Thus, pollution could be mitigated through environmental engagement as a loving and respectful relationship with the river. Are there not new and creative ways to bring scientific research on the river together with the transformational power of religious devotion? The life of the river may depend on such a synergy of efforts.

Recognizing that water is essential for life, that agricultural production is crucial for India, and that Mother Yamuna is more than a resource to be misused, we have entered into this interdisciplinary dialogue with the hope that the Yamuna River can be restored and sustained. With this in mind we are committed to:

1. **Fostering ongoing scientific research** at TERI and Yale Universities that increase our understanding of the hydrological, biological, and ecological dynamics of the Yamuna River. This information

should be shared across interdisciplinary boundaries to promote an understanding of the inherent value of the river.

For example:

- How can scientific research assist agricultural water usage to increase the amount of flow in the Yamuna River, and decrease the pesticide, insecticide, and fertilizer load returned to the river?
- What are the implications of climate change on the Yamuna River for the human and non-human communities that depend on it in many ways?
- How can scientific information regarding water quality be made available in an intelligible form to a larger public?

2. **Promoting local educational and conservation projects** in religious settings that would deepen particular communities' understandings of the relationships between human waste, industrial pollution, and reduced river flow. What religious practices and concepts can educate practitioners to store rainwater, conserve water, and restore the river?

3. **Continuing this process of dialogue** that brings together diverse communities along the Yamuna River so that voices, projects, and aspirations might be articulated regarding scientific research and religious education concerning water usage and water ethics. We should consider how we might draw into future gatherings the regulatory and water law communities so that these interdisciplinary and values-based discussions might have policy implications. We hope to engage the business community and developers along the river, especially in the pilgrimage city of Vrindaban where apartment construction is occurring at a feverish pace.

We remain convinced that interdisciplinary discussions bringing together scientific, policy, religious, and economic perspectives may help to move discussions beyond stagnation and reach out toward creative possibilities of restoration.

Appendix F

The Earth Charter, 2000[1]

Preamble

We stand at a critical moment in Earth's history, a time when humanity must choose its future. As the world becomes increasingly interdependent and fragile, the future at once holds great peril and great promise. To move forward we must recognize that in the midst of a magnificent diversity of cultures and life forms we are one human family and one Earth community with a common destiny. We must join together to bring forth a sustainable global society founded on respect for nature, universal human rights, economic justice, and a culture of peace. Towards this end, it is imperative that we, the peoples of Earth, declare our responsibility to one another, to the greater community of life, and to future generations.

Earth, Our Home

Humanity is part of a vast evolving universe. Earth, our home, is alive with a unique community of life. The forces of nature make existence a demanding and uncertain adventure, but Earth has provided the conditions essential to life's evolution. The resilience of the community of life and the well-being of humanity depend upon preserving a healthy biosphere with all its ecological systems, a rich variety of plants and animals, fertile soils, pure waters, and clean air. The global environment with its finite resources is a common concern of all peoples. The protection of Earth's vitality, diversity, and beauty is a sacred trust.

The Global Situation

The dominant patterns of production and consumption are causing environmental devastation, the depletion of resources, and a massive extinction of species. Communities are being undermined. The benefits of development are not shared equitably and the gap between rich and poor is widening. Injustice, poverty, ignorance, and violent conflict are widespread and the cause of great suffering. An unprecedented rise in human population has overburdened ecological and social systems. The foundations of global security are threatened. These trends are perilous—but not inevitable.

The Challenges Ahead

The choice is ours: form a global partnership to care for Earth and one another or risk the destruction of ourselves and the diversity of life. Fundamental changes are needed in our values, institutions, and ways of living. We must realize that when basic needs have been met, human development is primarily about being more, not having more. We have the knowledge and technology to provide for all and to reduce our impacts on the environment. The emergence of a global civil society is creating new opportunities to build a democratic and humane world. Our environmental, economic, political, social, and spiritual challenges are interconnected, and together we can forge inclusive solutions.

Universal Responsibility

To realize these aspirations, we must decide to live with a sense of universal responsibility, identifying ourselves with the whole Earth community as well as our local communities. We are at once citizens of different nations and of one world in which the local and global are linked. Everyone shares responsibility for the present and future well-being of the human family and the larger living world. The spirit of human solidarity and kinship with all life is strengthened when we live with reverence for the mystery of being, gratitude for the gift of life, and humility regarding the human place in nature.

We urgently need a shared vision of basic values to provide an ethical foundation for the emerging world community. Therefore, together in hope we affirm the following interdependent principles for a sustainable way of life as a common standard by which the conduct of all individuals, organizations, businesses, governments, and transnational institutions is to be guided and assessed.

Principles

I.   Respect and Care for the Community of Life
    1.   Respect Earth and life in all its diversity.
        a.   Recognize that all beings are interdependent and every form of life has value regardless of its worth to human beings.

      b.   Affirm faith in the inherent dignity of all human beings and in the intellectual, artistic, ethical, and spiritual potential of humanity.

2.   Care for the community of life with understanding, compassion, and love.

      a.   Accept that with the right to own, manage, and use natural resources comes the duty to prevent environmental harm and to protect the rights of people.

      b.   Affirm that with increased freedom, knowledge, and power comes increased responsibility to promote the common good.

3.   Build democratic societies that are just, participatory, sustainable, and peaceful.

      a.   Ensure that communities at all levels guarantee human rights and fundamental freedoms and provide everyone an opportunity to realize his or her full potential.

      b.   Promote social and economic justice, enabling all to achieve a secure and meaningful livelihood that is ecologically responsible.

4.   Secure Earth's bounty and beauty for present and future generations.

      a.   Recognize that the freedom of action of each generation is qualified by the needs of future generations.

      b.   Transmit to future generations values, traditions, and institutions that support the long-term flourishing of Earth's human and ecological communities. In order to fulfill these four broad commitments, it is necessary to:

II. Ecological Integrity

5.   Protect and restore the integrity of Earth's ecological systems, with special concern for biological diversity and the natural processes that sustain life.

      a.   Adopt at all levels sustainable development plans and regulations that make environmental conservation and rehabilitation integral to all development initiatives.

      b.   Establish and safeguard viable nature and biosphere reserves, including wild lands and marine areas, to protect Earth's life support systems, maintain biodiversity, and preserve our natural heritage.

      c.   Promote the recovery of endangered species and ecosystems.

      d.   Control and eradicate non-native or genetically modified organisms harmful to native species and the environment, and prevent introduction of such harmful organisms.

      e.   Manage the use of renewable resources such as water, soil, forest products, and marine life in ways that do not exceed rates of regeneration and that protect the health of ecosystems.

    f.   Manage the extraction and use of non-renewable resources such as minerals and fossil fuels in ways that minimize depletion and cause no serious environmental damage.

6. Prevent harm as the best method of environmental protection and, when knowledge is limited, apply a precautionary approach.

    a.   Take action to avoid the possibility of serious or irreversible environmental harm even when scientific knowledge is incomplete or inconclusive.

    b.   Place the burden of proof on those who argue that a proposed activity will not cause significant harm, and make the responsible parties liable for environmental harm.

    c.   Ensure that decision making addresses the cumulative, long-term, indirect, long distance, and global consequences of human activities.

    d.   Prevent pollution of any part of the environment and allow no build-up of radioactive, toxic, or other hazardous substances.

    e.   Avoid military activities damaging to the environment.

7. Adopt patterns of production, consumption, and reproduction that safeguard Earth's regenerative capacities, human rights, and community well-being.

    a.   Reduce, reuse, and recycle the materials used in production and consumption systems, and ensure that residual waste can be assimilated by ecological systems.

    b.   Act with restraint and efficiency when using energy, and rely increasingly on renewable energy sources such as solar and wind.

    c.   Promote the development, adoption, and equitable transfer of environmentally sound technologies.

    d.   Internalize the full environmental and social costs of goods and services in the selling price, and enable consumers to identify products that meet the highest social and environmental standards.

    e.   Ensure universal access to health care that fosters reproductive health and responsible reproduction.

    f.   Adopt lifestyles that emphasize the quality of life and material sufficiency in a finite world.

8. Advance the study of ecological sustainability and promote the open exchange and wide application of the knowledge acquired.

    a.   Support international scientific and technical cooperation on sustainability, with special attention to the needs of developing nations.

    b.   Recognize and preserve the traditional knowledge and spiritual wisdom in all cultures that contribute to environmental protection and human well-being.

    c.   Ensure that information of vital importance to human health and environmental protection, including genetic information, remains available in the public domain.

III. Social and Economic Justice

  9. Eradicate poverty as an ethical, social, and environmental imperative.

    a.   Guarantee the right to potable water, clean air, food security, uncontaminated soil, shelter, and safe sanitation, allocating the national and international resources required.

    b.   Empower every human being with the education and resources to secure a sustainable livelihood, and provide social security and safety nets for those who are unable to support themselves.

    c.   Recognize the ignored, protect the vulnerable, serve those who suffer, and enable them to develop their capacities and to pursue their aspirations.

 10. Ensure that economic activities and institutions at all levels promote human development in an equitable and sustainable manner.

    a.   Promote the equitable distribution of wealth within nations and among nations.

    b.   Enhance the intellectual, financial, technical, and social resources of developing nations, and relieve them of onerous international debt.

    c.   Ensure that all trade supports sustainable resource use, environmental protection, and progressive labor standards.

    d.   Require multinational corporations and international financial organizations to act transparently in the public good, and hold them accountable for the consequences of their activities.

 11. Affirm gender equality and equity as prerequisites to sustainable development and ensure universal access to education, health care, and economic opportunity.

    a.   Secure the human rights of women and girls and end all violence against them.

    b.   Promote the active participation of women in all aspects of economic, political, civil, social, and cultural life as full and equal partners, decision makers, leaders, and beneficiaries.

    c. Strengthen families and ensure the safety and loving nurture of all family members.

12. Uphold the right of all, without discrimination, to a natural and social environment supportive of human dignity, bodily health, and spiritual well-being, with special attention to the rights of indigenous peoples and minorities.

    a. Eliminate discrimination in all its forms, such as that based on race, color, sex, sexual orientation, religion, language, and national, ethnic or social origin.

    b. Affirm the right of indigenous peoples to their spirituality, knowledge, lands and resources and to their related practice of sustainable livelihoods.

    c. Honor and support the young people of our communities, enabling them to fulfill their essential role in creating sustainable societies.

    d. Protect and restore outstanding places of cultural and spiritual significance.

IV. Democracy, Nonviolence, and Peace

13. Strengthen democratic institutions at all levels, and provide transparency and accountability in governance, inclusive participation in decision making, and access to justice.

    a. Uphold the right of everyone to receive clear and timely information on environmental matters and all development plans and activities which are likely to affect them or in which they have an interest.

    b. Support local, regional and global civil society, and promote the meaningful participation of all interested individuals and organizations in decision making.

    c. Protect the rights to freedom of opinion, expression, peaceful assembly, association, and dissent.

    d. Institute effective and efficient access to administrative and independent judicial procedures, including remedies and redress for environmental harm and the threat of such harm.

    e. Eliminate corruption in all public and private institutions.

    f. Strengthen local communities, enabling them to care for their environments, and assign environmental responsibilities to the levels of government where they can be carried out most effectively.

14. Integrate into formal education and life-long learning the knowledge, values, and skills needed for a sustainable way of life.

    a.   Provide all, especially children and youth, with educational opportunities that empower them to contribute actively to sustainable development.

    b.   Promote the contribution of the arts and humanities as well as the sciences in sustainability education.

    c.   Enhance the role of the mass media in raising awareness of ecological and social challenges.

    d.   Recognize the importance of moral and spiritual education for sustainable living.

15. Treat all living beings with respect and consideration.

    a.   Prevent cruelty to animals kept in human societies and protect them from suffering.

    b.   Protect wild animals from methods of hunting, trapping, and fishing that cause extreme, prolonged, or avoidable suffering.

    c.   Avoid or eliminate to the full extent possible the taking or destruction of non-targeted species.

16. Promote a culture of tolerance, nonviolence, and peace.

    a.   Encourage and support mutual understanding, solidarity, and cooperation among all peoples and within and among nations.

    b.   Implement comprehensive strategies to prevent violent conflict and use collaborative problem solving to manage and resolve environmental conflicts and other disputes.

    c.   Demilitarize national security systems to the level of a non-provocative defense posture, and convert military resources to peaceful purposes, including ecological restoration.

    d.   Eliminate nuclear, biological, and toxic weapons and other weapons of mass destruction.

    e.   Ensure that the use of orbital and outer space supports environmental protection and peace.

    f.   Recognize that peace is the wholeness created by right relationships with oneself, other persons, other cultures, other life, Earth, and the larger whole of which all are a part.

The Way Forward

As never before in history, common destiny beckons us to seek a new beginning. Such renewal is the promise of these Earth Charter principles. To fulfill this promise, we must commit ourselves to adopt and promote the values and objectives of the Charter.

This requires a change of mind and heart. It requires a new sense of global interdependence and universal responsibility. We must imaginatively develop and apply the vision of a sustainable way of life locally, nationally, regionally, and globally. Our cultural diversity is a precious heritage and different cultures will find their own distinctive ways to realize the vision. We must deepen and expand the global dialogue that generated the Earth Charter, for we have much to learn from the ongoing collaborative search for truth and wisdom.

Life often involves tensions between important values. This can mean difficult choices. However, we must find ways to harmonize diversity with unity, the exercise of freedom with the common good, short-term objectives with long-term goals. Every individual, family, organization, and community has a vital role to play. The arts, sciences, religions, educational institutions, media, businesses, nongovernmental organizations, and governments are all called to offer creative leadership. The partnership of government, civil society, and business is essential for effective governance.

In order to build a sustainable global community, the nations of the world must renew their commitment to the United Nations, fulfill their obligations under existing international agreements, and support the implementation of Earth Charter principles with an international legally binding instrument on environment and development.

Let ours be a time remembered for the awakening of a new reverence for life, the firm resolve to achieve sustainability, the quickening of the struggle for justice and peace, and the joyful celebration of life.

Appendix G

Online Resources for Religious Ecology

International

Forum on Religion and Ecology at Yale: http://fore.research.yale.edu

World Wildlife Fund: http://worldwildlife.org/about/history

Assisi Declarations: http://www.arcworld.org/downloads/THE%20ASSISI %20DECLARATIONS.pdf

World Council of Churches: http://www.oikoumene.org/en/programmes /justice-diakonia-and-responsibility-for-creation/eco-justice.html

Religion, Science, and Environment Initiative: http://www.rsesymposia .org/index.php

International Society for the Study of Religion, Nature and Culture: http://www.religionandnature.com

Alliance of Religions and Conservation: http://www.arcworld.org/

Indigenous Environmental Network: http://www.ienearth.org/about.html

Islamic Foundation for Ecology and Environmental Sciences: http://www .ifees.org.uk/

EcoSikh: http://www.ecosikh.org/

Spiritual Ecology: http://spiritualecology.info

Regional

Friends of the Earth Middle East: http://foeme.org/www/?module = projects&record_id=23

Southern African Faith Communities' Environment Institute: http://safcei .org/about/

Forum on Religion and Ecology at Monash: http://artsonline.monash.edu .au/fore/

United States

National Religious Partnership for the Environment: http://www.nrpe
.org/
EPA Faith-Based Neighborhood Partnerships Initiative: http://www.epa
.gov/fbnpartnerships/
Earth Ministry: http://earthministry.org/about
Faith in Place: http://www.faithinplace.org/about/history
Au Sable Institute: http://ausable.org/
GreenFaith: http://greenfaith.org/
Green Seminary Initiative: http://www.greenseminaries.org/
National Council of Churches of Christ Eco-Justice Program: http://
nccecojustice.org/
U.S. Conference of Catholic Bishops: http://www.usccb.org/issues-and
-action/human-life-and-dignity/environment/environmental-justice
-program/
Evangelical Environmental Network: http://creationcare.org/blank.php
?id=35
Coalition on the Environment and Jewish Life: http://coejl.org/aboutus/
Alliance for Jewish Renewal: http://www.aleph.org/about.htm
Shomrei Adamah: http://ellenbernstein.org/about_ellen.htm#shomrei
_adamah
Teva Learning Center: http://tevacenter.readyhosting.com/programs_sa.asp
Interfaith Power & Light: http://interfaithpowerandlight.org/about/
Statements and activities of the religious communities on climate change:
http://fore.research.yale.edu/climate-change/

Bibliography

Grim, John et. al., eds. "Religion and Ecology." *Oxford Bibliographies Online.*
http://www.oxfordbibliographies.com/obo/page/ecology

Articles

Tucker, Mary Evelyn, and John Grim, eds. "Religion and Ecology: Can the
Climate Change?" *Daedalus* 130, no. 4 (Fall 2001). https://www.amacad
.org/content/publications/publication.aspx?i=845
Hitzhusen, Gregory and Mary Evelyn Tucker. "The potential of religion
for Earth Stewardship." *Frontiers in Ecology and the Environment* 11,
no. 7 (September 2013): 368-76. http://www.esajournals.org/doi
/full/10.1890/120322

Journals

Worldviews: Global Religions, Culture, and Ecology. http://booksandjournals
.brillonline.com/content/15685357

Journal for the Study of Religion, Nature and Culture. https://www
.equinoxpub.com/journals/index.php/JSRNC

Notes

Introduction

1. The population issue is a crucial part of our environmental challenges, and it is clearly necessary to address it for a sustainable future. Our work here is not focused specifically on this issue but recognizes its importance. The United Nations Population Fund has been working on this for decades (see http://www.unfpa.org/public/). With the education and empowerment of women, population growth has slowed, but this remains an ongoing issue. The role of world religions is an important component of population reduction. Some traditions have conservative policies regarding birth control and women's reproductive rights. These include certain groups of Islam, Orthodox Judaism, and Roman Catholicism. The majority of world religions are not opposed to birth control. There have been conferences on this issue led by Daniel Maguire, who wrote *Sacred Choices* (Minneapolis, MN: Fortress, 2001). See also Harold Coward and Daniel Maguire, *Visions of a New Earth: Religious Perspectives on Population, Consumption, and Ecology* (Albany: State University of New York, 1999); and Daniel Maguire and Larry Rasmussen, *Ethics for a Small Planet: New Horizons on Population, Consumption, and Ecology* (Albany: State University of New York, 1998).

2. See, for example, the op-ed article by Thomas E. Lovejoy, "The Climate Change Endgame," *New York Times*, January 21, 2013.

3. See Kay Milton, ed., *Environmentalism: The View from Anthropology* (London: Routledge, 1993); Thomas Dunlap, *Faith in Nature: Environmentalism as Religious Quest* (Seattle: University of Washington Press, 2004); Bronislaw Szerszynski, *Nature, Technology and the Sacred* (Oxford, England: Blackwell, 2005); Targei Ronnow, *Saving Nature: Religion as Environmentalism, Environmentalism as Religion* (New Brunswick, NJ: Transaction Publishers, 2006); Corinne Dempsey, *Bringing the Sacred Down to Earth: Adventures in Comparative Religion* (Oxford, England: Oxford University Press, 2012); and Robert Nelson, *The New Holy Wars: Economic Religion versus Environmental Religion in Contemporary America* (University Park, PA: Penn State University Press, 2010).

4. For example, the Princeton Environmental Institute has the Barron Visiting Professorship in environmental humanities that has included religion and ecology. Many environmental studies programs offer courses in religion and ecology. In

addition, professional associations in the sciences have included participation in their annual meetings by scholars of religion and ecology. This includes the American Association for the Advancement of Science (AAAS), the Ecological Society of America (ESA), the Geological Society of America (GSA), and the Cary Institute of Ecosystems Studies. In addition, environmental groups such as the Sierra Club and the World Wildlife Fund have had a strong interest in religious perspectives on the environment. The Society for Conservation Biology (SCB) has a working group on Religion and Conservation Biology.

5. See Mary Evelyn Tucker, *Moral and Spiritual Cultivation in Japanese Neo-Confucianism* (Albany: State University of New York, 1989); and also *The Philosophy of Qi* (New York: Columbia University Press, 2007).

6. This contestation has dominated international politics since the United Nations Conference on Environment and Development in Rio in 1992. We are still pondering the question: What are viable ways forward for genuine human flourishing? To this end the Rio+20 conference in June 2012 focused on improving global governance and creating a green economy. There is still a long way to go to integrate ethics, religion, and culture into these discussions.

7. See John Grim, *The Shaman: Patterns of Religious Healing among the Ojibway Indians* (Norman: University of Oklahoma Press, 1983); and also *Indigenous Traditions and Ecology: The Interbeing of Cosmology and Community* (Cambridge, MA: Harvard Center for the Study of World Religions, 2001).

8. An emphasis on place-based knowledge is evident but muted in his early work, *The Shaman: Patterns of Religious Healing among the Ojibway Indians* (Norman: University of Oklahoma Press, 1983). Parallels with place-based knowledge in early American writings can be found in Belden Lane, *Landscapes of the Sacred: Geography and Narrative in American Spirituality* (Baltimore, MD: Johns Hopkins University Press, 1988).

9. The Crow/Apsaalooka, an Indigenous people located in the state of Montana, relate to nature, animals, and the local bioregion in a religious setting outsiders call "Sundance" but which the Crow call *Ashkisshelissua*, or "Dancing in the Big Lodge." See (as told to) Michael Oren Fitzgerald, *Yellowtail: Crow Medicine Man and Sun Dance Chief* (Norman: University of Oklahoma Press, 1991); and Fred Voget, *The Shoshoni–Crow Sun Dance* (Norman: University of Oklahoma Press, 1984).

10. *Lifeway* is a descriptive term describing religious ecologies on the ground rather than an abstract imposition of notions of holism. *Lifeway* emphasizes both cultural continuity and dynamic change rather than an ahistorical static view often associated with "tradition."

11. William Theodore de Bary's knowledge of Asian religions was extensive, and he was instrumental in organizing translations of the Asian classics and publishing them in the *Sources of Indian Tradition*, *Sources of Chinese Tradition*, *Sources of Japanese Tradition*, and *Sources of Korean Tradition* from Columbia University Press.

12. Tu Weiming taught at Berkeley, Princeton, and Harvard and directed the Harvard–Yenching Institute for a decade. He then returned to China in 2010 to head the first Institute for the Humanities at Beijing University.

13. Tu Weiming, "Beyond the Enlightenment Mentality," in *Worldviews and Ecology: Religion, Philosophy, and the Environment*, ed. Mary Evelyn Tucker and John Grim (Maryknoll, NY: Orbis, 2006), 19–29.

14. They built on the work of Steven Rockefeller at Middlebury College, who in

1990 convened one of the first conferences in academia on religion and ecology. This was titled "Spirit and Nature" and resulted in a film and a book: Steven Rockefeller and John Elder, eds., *Spirit and Nature: Why the Environment Is a Religious Issue—An Interfaith Dialogue* (Boston: Beacon, 1992). An earlier conference on Faith and Nature took place at the Massachusetts Institute of Technology in the 1970s, organized by Christian theologians. This was part of a larger effort within the World Council of Churches to address environmental issues. The North American Conference on Christianity and Ecology was held in Indiana in August 1987.

15. We worked closely with specialists in each of these traditions who were generous in their time and commitment as editors of particular volumes. Kathryn Dodgson at the Center for the Study of World Religions and Eric Edstam were painstaking editors in this series. In addition, Stephanie Snyder at Bucknell University and Malgorzata Radziszewska-Hedderick and Don Kunkel at the Center for the Study of World Religions played key supportive roles in the conferences. The conference series was supported by foundations that included the V. Kann Rasmussen Foundation, the Germeshausen Foundation, and the Kendeda Sustainability Fund.

16. The Canadian Forum on Religion and Ecology was established in 2004 by Heather Eaton of St. Paul's University and James Miller of Queens University. Now there are similar groups in Europe and Australia, including the European Forum for the Study of Religion and the Environment, directed by Sigurd Bergmann, and the Forum on Religion and Ecology at Monash University in Australia.

17. In May 1999 the Forum convened a conference at the Harvard–Yenching Institute on Religion and Animals that was later published as *A Communion of Subjects* by Columbia University Press. Tu Weiming, director of the Harvard–Yenching Institute, hosted the conference. See Paul Waldau and Kimberley Patton, eds., *A Communion of Subjects: Animals in Religion, Science, and Ethics* (New York: Columbia University Press, 2006). Paul Waldau went on to found the Religion and Animals group in 2003 at the American Academy of Religion along with Laura Hobgood-Oster. The Humane Society of the United States (HSUS) was instrumental in this and in assisting the conference series as a whole. This was due to the leadership of Rick Clugston, who directed the Center for Respect of Life and Environment at HSUS and led Earth Charter US. We also convened several conferences at the American Academy of Arts and Sciences in Cambridge, Massachusetts. These included one in collaboration with the Orion Society, with major American nature writers and religious thinkers, in autumn 1999. Two other conferences were held to prepare a *Daedalus* volume focusing on world religions and climate change in 2000 and 2001. This was the first *Daedalus* issue to be published both in print and online. See Mary Evelyn Tucker and John Grim, eds., "Religion and Ecology: Can the Climate Change?" *Daedalus* (Fall 2001), http://www.amacad.org/publications/fall2001/fall2001.aspx.

18. Although retrieval, reevaluation, and reconstruction bear similarities to some methods in feminist theologies, they are not derived from those approaches.

19. For example, see Mark Elvin, *The Retreat of the Elephants: An Environmental History of China* (New Haven, CT: Yale University Press, 2004).

20. See http://fore.research.yale.edu. The website contains detailed information on the religious traditions of the world and their ecological contributions, including introductory essays, annotated bibliographies, selections from sacred texts, environmental statements from religious communities, and descriptions of engaged projects

of religious grassroots environmental movements. There is also a section focusing on religion and climate change: http://fore.research.yale.edu/climate-change/. To facilitate interdisciplinary dialogue, there are resources that address environmental issues related to ethics, economics, policy, gender, and evolutionary and ecological sciences. To enhance teaching, the website includes syllabi, lists of educational videos and CDs, links to programs and institutions related to environmental education, and a variety of other resources for educators. There is a monthly online newsletter that provides current information to more than twelve thousand people around the world on conferences, publications, and events related to religion and ecology. Related articles from the United Nations Environment Programme are also sent out each month. Those who have helped to establish and maintain the website include Anne Custer, Whitney Bauman, Elizabeth McAnally, Sam Mickey, Tara Trapani, Donald Lehr, Matthew T. and Christina Riley, Matt Garrett, and other graduate students.

21. See http://www.brill.com/worldviews-global-religions-culture-and-ecology.

22. See Bron Taylor and Jeffrey Kaplan, eds., *Encyclopedia of Religion and Nature*, 2 vols. (New York: Continuum International, 2005). In 2006 the *Journal for the Study of Religion, Nature and Culture* was launched. In the revised edition of the *Encyclopedia of Religion* in 2005 the Forum contributed a dozen articles marking the coming of age of religion and ecology as a recognized field within religious studies. See Lindsay Jones, ed., *Encyclopedia of Religion*, 2nd ed. (New York: Macmillan/Thompson and Gale, 2005). A comprehensive bibliography on "Religion and Ecology" was published online by Oxford University Press in 2013: Mary Evelyn Tucker, John Grim, Matthew T. Riley, Tara C. Trapani, and Russell C. Powell, "Religion and Ecology," in *Oxford Bibliographies in Ecology*, ed. David Gibson (New York: Oxford University Press, forthcoming).

For many years Leslie Sponsel, at the University of Hawaii, has directed a program in the area of spiritual ecology and in 2012 published a book with this title. See Leslie Sponsel, *Spiritual Ecology: A Quiet Revolution* (Santa Barbara, CA: ABC-CLIO, 2012). See http://www.spiritualecology.info. With the Forum's active involvement, the *Berkshire Encyclopedia of Sustainability* volume on "The Spirit of Sustainability" appeared in 2010. See Willis Jenkins and Whitney Bauman, eds., *The Berkshire Encyclopedia of Sustainability*, Vol. 1, *The Spirit of Sustainability* (Great Barrington, MA: Berkshire Publishing Group, 2010). Also see Roger Gottlieb, ed., *The Oxford Handbook on Religion and Ecology* (New York: Oxford University Press, 2006).

23. David Barnhill and Eugene Bianchi were the founders of this group, and for some 15 years the Forum on Religion and Ecology has sponsored a luncheon meeting at AAR to share new research and teaching.

24. See http://fore.research.yale.edu/information/Yale_MA_Program.html. This is the only program of its kind between science-based and religiously oriented schools and now includes the Porter Chair in Religion and Environmental Stewardship. There is also a PhD program in religion and nature at the University of Florida and in religion and environmental studies at Drew Theological School. St. Michael's College at the University of Toronto also has graduate studies in this area through the Elliott Allen Institute of Theology and Ecology. A master's program in religion and the environment was established at Sewanee University in 2013. Earlier, there was a concentration in spiritual ecology under ecological anthropology at the University of Hawaii. The California Institute of Integral Studies established a program in ecology,

spirituality, and religion, offering master's and doctoral degrees, in the Department of Philosophy and Religion in 2013.

25. We assisted with the film titled *Renewal* and developed a conference at Yale celebrating its premiere in 2008. For *Renewal* film, see http://www.renewalproject .net, and for the conference, see http://www.yale.edu/divinity/news/071128_news _renewing.shtml. This film features eight engaged projects of religious grassroots environmentalism in the United States. We also helped organize several other Yale conferences: in Aspen, Colorado in 2007 titled "Toward a New Consciousness: Creating a Society in Harmony with Nature" (see http://environment.research.yale.edu/publi cation-series/5952), at Yale Divinity School in 2009 titled "Environmental (Dis)Locations: Exploring Environmental Justice and Climate Change" (see http://www.yale.edu /divinity/dislocations/), at the School of Forestry and Environmental Studies in 2011 on "Journey of the Universe" (see http://www.journeyoftheuniverse.org/conference -at-yale/), and "Religion and Environmental Stewardship" in 2012 (see http://fore .research.yale.edu/yale-summer-symposium-religion-and-environmental-stewardship).

26. See http://www.journeyoftheuniverse.org.

27. See "The New Story," in Thomas Berry, *The Dream of the Earth* (San Francisco, CA: Sierra Club Books, 1998), 123–137.

28. Lawrence Buell, *The Environmental Imagination: Thoreau, Nature Writing, and the Formation of American Culture* (Cambridge, MA: Harvard University Press, 1995); Scott Slovic, *Seeking Awareness in American Nature Writing: Henry Thoreau, Annie Dillard, Edward Abbey, Wendell Berry, Barry Lopez* (Salt Lake City: University of Utah Press, 1992); Cheryll Glotfelty and Harold Fromm, eds., *The Ecocriticism Reader: Landmarks in Literary Ecology* (Athens: University of Georgia, 1996); Stephanie LeMenager, Tess Shewry, and Ken Hiltner, eds., *Environmental Criticism for the Twenty-First Century* (New York: Routledge, 2011).

29. See Donald Worster, *The Wealth of Nature: Environmental History and the Ecological Imagination* (Oxford, England: Oxford University Press, 1994); also J. Donald Hughes, ed., *The Face of the Earth: Environment and World History* (Armonk, NY: M.E. Sharpe, 2000), which contains two articles by the editor, "Ecological Process and World History," 3–21, and "Biodiversity and World History," 22–46; William Cronin, "The Uses of Environmental History," Presidential Address, American Society for Environmental History, *Environmental History Review* 17(3) (Fall 1993):1–22; and Patricia Limerick, *Something in the Soil: Legacies and Reckonings in the New West* (New York: W.W. Norton, 2000).

30. This intersects with the rich discussions in environmental ethics, where debates over utilitarian uses of nature versus the intrinsic value of nature have taken place for the last 40 years. This has resulted in a new field of pragmatism in environmental ethics that concentrates on interdisciplinary approaches to particular case studies. In addition, the field of environmental ethics has expanded to include comparative ethics drawing on diverse cultural and religious traditions beyond the West. Thus, questions posed by these new forms of environmental ethics not only bring traditional religious perspectives into the discussions but also present novel challenges for the religions. See, for example, Roderick Nash, *The Rights of Nature: A History of Environmental Ethics* (Madison: University of Wisconsin Press, 1989).

31. The first such texts were David Kinsley, *Ecology and Religion: Ecological Spirituality in Cross-Cultural Perspective* (Englewood Cliffs, NJ: Prentice Hall, 1995); Peter

Marshall, *Nature's Web: Rethinking Our Place on Earth* (New York: M.E. Sharpe, 1996); Edward Goldsmith, *The Way: An Ecological Worldview* (Athens: University of Georgia, 1998); Mary Evelyn Tucker, *Worldly Wonder: Religions Enter Their Ecological Phase* (LaSalle, IL: Open Court, 2003); and more recently Leslie Sponsel, *Spiritual Ecology: A Quiet Revolution* (Santa Barbara, CA: Praeger, 2012). Other edited collections are Mary Evelyn Tucker and John Grim, eds., *Worldviews and Ecology: Religion, Philosophy and the Environment* (Maryknoll, NY: Orbis, 1996); Richard Foltz, ed., *Worldviews, Religion, and the Environment: A Global Anthology* (Belmont, CA: Wadsworth, 2002); Roger Gottlieb, ed., *This Sacred Earth: Religion, Nature, Environment* (New York: Routledge, rev. ed. 2006); Whitney Bauman, Richard Bohannon, and Kevin O'Brien, eds., *Grounding Religion: A Field Guide to the Study of Religion and Ecology* (London: Taylor & Francis, 2010); Eugene Hargrove, ed., *Religion and Environmental Crisis* (Athens: University of Georgia, 1986); David and Eileen Spring, eds., *Ecology and Religion in History* (New York: Harper and Row, 1974). Three edited volumes concentrating on non-Western religions are Roger Ames and J. Baird Callicott, eds., *Nature in Asian Traditions of Thought* (Albany, NY: SUNY, 1989); Helain Selin, ed., *Nature Across Cultures: Views of Nature and the Environment in Non-Western Cultures* (Dordrecht, the Netherlands: Kluwer, 2003); and Fritz Hull, ed., *Earth and Spirit: The Spiritual Dimension of the Environmental Crisis* (New York: Continuum, 1993). See also Susan Power Bratton, "Ecology and Religion," in Philip Clayton, ed., *The Oxford Handbook of Religion and Science* (New York: Oxford University Press, 2006), 207–25.

32. See "Joint Appeal in Religion and Science," 1991; and The Union of Concerned Scientists, "Warning to Humanity," 1992, in Mary Evelyn Tucker, *Worldly Wonder: Religions Enter Their Ecological Phase* (Chicago: Open Court, 2004).

Chapter 1

1. For the *Millennium Ecosystems Assessment Report*, see http://www.maweb.org/en/index.aspx; for the *Stern Review*, see http://webarchive.nationalarchives.gov.uk/+/http://www.hm-treasury.gov.uk/independent_reviews/stern_review_economics_climate_change/sternreview_index.cfm; and for the *Convention on Biodiversity*, see http://www.cbd.int/.

2. See Paul J. Crutzen and E. F. Stoermer, "The Anthropocene," in *Global Change Newsletter* 41 (2000):17–18.

3. See Thomas Berry, *The Sacred Universe* (New York: Columbia University Press, 2009); and Corrine Dempsey, *Bringing the Sacred Down to Earth: Adventures in Comparative Religion* (New York: Oxford University Press, 2011).

4. Some fundamentalisms also advocate future forms of political freedom; for example, eschatological drives in the Abrahamic traditions have led to political visions of apocalyptic futures promising freedom and relief from oppression. In Buddhism some fundamentalisms focus on a future of political liberation and personal salvation associated with Maitreya, the future Buddha.

5. For Religions for Peace, see http://www.religionsforpeace.org/; and for the Temple of Understanding, see http://templeofunderstanding.org/.

6. Yet these claims of exclusivity or of a unity of religions can mask vast differences between people and their Indigenous religions, as in Indonesia and the policy

of Pancasilla. These examples reinforce the social and collective character of unitive efforts in religion, which is to erase differences so as to have a united whole.

7. An apt example of this idea is James G. Watt, Ronald Reagan's secretary of the interior from 1981 to 1983, who was a Dispensationalist Christian, believing environmental management to be immaterial in light of Christ's impending second coming.

8. See Mary Evelyn Tucker, *The Philosophy of Qi: The Record of Great Doubts* (New York: Columbia University Press, 2007).

9. Randall Balmer, *Mine Eyes Have Seen the Glory: A Journey into the Evangelical Subculture in America* (New York: Oxford University Press, 2006); Katharine Wilkinson, *Between God and Green: How Evangelicals Are Cultivating a Middle Ground on Climate Change* (New York: Oxford University Press, 2012).

10. See the Columbia University series on *Religion and Politics*, edited by Gaston Espinosa and Chester Gillis, of which five books have been published since 2007.

11. See http://www.ucc.org/about-us/archives/pdfs/toxwrace87.pdf.

12. http://www.sierraclub.org/ej/partnerships/faith/.

13. Stephen Kellert and E. O. Wilson, eds., *The Biophilia Hypothesis* (Washington, DC: Island Press, 1995). See also Stephen Kellert, *Birthright: People and Nature in the Modern World* (New Haven, CT: Yale University Press, 2012). Others speak of the evolutionary character of religious sensibilities and drives as in alignment with evolutionary processes themselves, e.g., Robert Bellah, *Religion in Human Evolution* (Cambridge, MA: Harvard University Press, 2011).

14. Peter Berger, *The Sacred Canopy: Elements of a Sociological Theory of Religion* (New York: Anchor Books, 1990), originally published in 1967.

15. Thomas Altizer and William Hamilton, *Radical Theology and the Death of God* (Indianapolis, IN: Bobbs-Merrill, 1966).

16. This secularization thesis followed from social theories of Ludwig Feuerbach (1804–1872) and Karl Marx (1818–1883) on the "withering of religions."

17. Jose Cassanova, *Public Religions in the Modern World* (Chicago: University of Chicago Press, 1994).

18. See the book series edited by Martin E. Marty and R. Scott Appleby, *The Fundamentalism Project* (Chicago: University of Chicago Press, 1991–1995).

19. For Barth's neo-orthodoxy, see his *Church Dogmatics*, 14 vols. It is important to note Barth's strong aversion to anything being revelatory about the natural world. For instance, when Emil Brunner wrote a brief treatise on the revelatory importance of nature in Christian theology, Barth responded with a treatise of his own, titled "Nein!," or "No!" See Emil Brunner and Karl Barth, *Natural Theology: Comprising "Nature and Grace" by Professor Dr. Emil Brunner and the Reply "No!" by Dr. Karl Barth* (Eugene, OR: Wipf and Stock, 2002).

20. See Charles Taylor, *A Secular Age* (Cambridge, MA: Harvard University Press, 2007).

21. Jurgen Habermas et al., *An Awareness of What Is Missing: Faith and Reason in a Post-Secular Age* (Cambridge, MA: Polity Press, 2010), 18–19.

22. In this work the phrase *world religions* refers to the location of religions in the surrounding world. This complements the claims of transcendence in religious traditions. Rather than a reference to the universalizing character of a religion, *world religions* situates the religious phenomenon as engaged with the natural world.

23. For orientalism, see Edward Said, *Orientalism* (New York: Vintage, 1978). Regarding a critique of the history of religions and world religions, see Tim Murphy, *The Politics of Spirit: Phenomenology, Genealogy, Religion* (Albany: State University of New York Press, 2010); and Tomoko Masuzawa, *The Invention of World Religions: Or, How European Universalism Was Preserved in the Language of Pluralism* (Chicago: University of Chicago Press, 2005).

24. This robust syncretism between Shinto and Buddhism in Japan is well documented as an intellectual and ritual movement called *honji suijaku*. See Mark Teeuwen and Fabio Rambelli, eds., *Buddhas and Kami in Japan: Honji Suijaku as a Combinatory Paradigm* (London: RoutledgeCurzon, 2002).

25. See Belden Lane, *Landscapes of the Sacred: Geography and Narrative in American Spirituality* (Baltimore, MD: Johns Hopkins University Press, 1988).

26. See James Miller, *Daoism: A Short Introduction* (London: Oneworld, 2003); and James Miller, *The Way of Highest Clarity: Nature, Vision, and Revelation in Medieval China* (Magdalena, NM: Three Pines Press, 2008).

27. For yogic meditation and ecology, see Christopher Chapple, *Yoga and Ecology: Dharma for the Earth* (Hampton, VA: Deepak Publishing, 2009).

28. Daniel Hillel, *Natural History of the Bible* (New York: Columbia University Press, 2005).

29. See Thomas Buckley, *Standing Ground: Yurok Indian Spirituality, 1850–1990* (Berkeley: University of California Press, 2002).

30. See *The Green Bible* (New York: Harper, 2010).

31. See Hava Tirosh-Samuelson, ed., *Judaism and Ecology: Created World and Revealed Word* (Cambridge, MA: Harvard Center for the Study of World Religions, 2002).

32. See Dieter Hessel and Rosemary Radford Ruether, eds., *Christianity and Ecology: Seeking the Well-Being of Earth and Humans* (Cambridge, MA: Harvard Center for the Study of World Religions, 2000).

33. See Richard Foltz, Frederick Denny, and Azizan Baharuddin, eds., *Islam and Ecology: A Bestowed Trust* (Cambridge, MA: Harvard Center for the Study of World Religions, 2003).

34. For socially engaged Buddhism, see especially the work of Sulak Sivaraksa, *Seeds of Peace: A Buddhist Vision for Renewing Society* (Berkeley, CA: Parallax Press, 1992). Also see http://www.sulak-sivaraksa.org; Johanna Macy, *Mutual Causality in Buddhism and General Systems Theory: The Dharma of Natural System* (Albany: State University of New York Press, 1991); Joanna R. Macy and Molly Young Brown, eds., *Coming Back to Life: Practices to Reconnect Our Lives, Our World* (Gabriola Island, BC: New Society Publishers, 1998); Ken Kraft and Stephanie Kaza, eds., *Dharma Rain: Sources of Buddhist Environmentalism* (Boulder, CO: Shambhala, 2000); and Christopher Queen, *Engaged Buddhism in the West* (Somerville, MA: Wisdom Publications, 2000).

35. See Norman Giardot and James Miller, eds., *Daoism and Ecology: Ways within a Cosmic Landscape* (Cambridge, MA: Harvard Center for the Study of World Religions, 2001); and Mary Evelyn Tucker and John Berthrong, eds., *Confucianism and Ecology: The Interrelation of Heaven, Earth, and Human* (Cambridge, MA: Harvard Center for the Study of World Religions, 1998).

36. See Tu Weiming, *Centrality and Commonality: An Essay on Confucian Religiousness* (Albany: State University of New York Press, 1989).

37. See Roger Ames and David Hall, eds., *Thinking from the Han: Self, Truth, and*

Transcendence in Chinese and Western Culture (Albany: State University of New York Press, 1998).

38. For Confucianism, see Tu Weiming, *Confucian Thought: Selfhood as Creative Transformation* (Albany: State University of New York, 1985); and for Daoism, see Livia Kohn, *Sitting in Oblivion: The Heart of Daoist Meditation* (Magdalena, NM: Three Pines Press, 2010).

39. Commonly known as slash-and-burn agriculture.

40. For an alternative and related term, *lifeworld*, see Tim Ingold, "Globes and Spheres: The Topology of Environmentalism," in *The Perception of the Environment: Essays in Livelihood, Dwelling and Skill* (London: Routledge, 2000), 209–18. "What I hope to have established, at least in outline, is that the lifeworld, imaged from an experiential centre, is spherical in form, whereas a world divorced from life, then, is a matter not of sensory attunement but of cognitive reconstruction. . . . In the global outlook . . . the world does not surround us, it lies beneath our feet. . . . [The] world . . . becomes an object of human interest and concern. But it is not a world of which humans themselves are conceived to be a part. . . . They [humans] may observe it, reconstruct it, protect it, tamper with it or destroy it, but they do not dwell in it."

41. For example, see Stephen Feld, *Sound and Sentiment: Birds, Weeping, Poetics, and Song in Kaluli Expression* (Philadelphia: University of Pennsylvania Press, 1982). For a critical perspective, see Shepard Krech III, *The Ecological Indian: Myth and History* (New York: W.W. Norton, 2000).

42. http://fore.research.yale.edu.

43. See Mary Evelyn Tucker and John Grim, eds., "Religion and Ecology: Can the Climate Change?" *Daedalus* (2001), http://www.amacad.org/publications/fall2001 /fall2001.aspx. In addition, there are several articles on religion and climate change on the Forum on Religion and Ecology website at http://fore.research.yale.edu /climate-change/articles-on-religion-and-climate-change/.

44. See Katharine Wilkinson, *Between God and Green: How Evangelicals Are Cultivating a Middle Ground on Climate Change* (Oxford, England: Oxford University Press, 2012). It is important to note that the Evangelical community is not uniform in its response to climate change. For example, some Evangelicals do not think climate change is human caused. See Laurel Kearns, "Christian Environmentalism and Its Opponents in the United States," in *Religion in Environmental and Climate Change*, ed. Dieter Gerten and Sigurd Bergmann (New York: Continuum, 2012).

45. http://old.usccb.org/sdwp/international/globalclimate.shtml.

46. See the Forum on Religion and Ecology listing at http://fore.research.yale .edu/climate-change/statements-from-world-religions/christianity/.

47. For Interfaith Power and Light, see http://interfaithpowerandlight.org/.

48. For the "Fraser River Declaration" see appendix D; see also the "Idle No More" movement at http://idlenomore.ca/.

49. These documents available at http://fore.research.yale.edu/publications /statements/preserve/, http://fore.research.yale.edu/publications/statements/joint -appeal/, and http://fore.research.yale.edu/publications/statements/union/.

50. One of the more promising meetings about cooperation on environmental issues resulted in the 2007 declaration of U.S. Evangelical leaders and scientists signed in Georgia. See http://www.pbs.org/now/shows/343/letter.pdf.

51. See Libby Bassett, John Brinkman, and Kusumita Pedersen, eds., *Earth and*

Faith: A Book of Reflection for Action (New York: United Nations Environment Programme, 2000). This was a project of the Forum on Religion and Ecology.

52. As Gary Gardner suggests, religions create communities of cohesion and trust that can assist integrated, appropriate, and just forms of social, economic, and ecological development. See chapter 3 in Gary Gardner, *Inspiring Progress: Religions' Contributions to Sustainable Development* (Washington, DC: Worldwatch Institute, 2006), 41–53.

Chapter 2

1. Mark Johnston, *Saving God: Religion after Idolatry* (Princeton, NJ: Princeton University Press, 2009); and Ronald Dworkin's Einstein Lectures, *Religion without God* (Cambridge, MA: Harvard University Press, 2013).

2. See, for example, the extensive series *Classics of Western Spirituality* from Paulist Press, which present Jewish, Christian, and Islamic spiritual texts, as well as the twenty-five-volume series by Ewert Cousins, ed., *World Spirituality: An Encyclopedic History of the Religious Quest* (New York: Crossroad Publishing, 1985–2004).

3. Douglas Christie, *The Blue Sapphire of the Mind: Notes for a Contemplative Ecology* (Oxford, England: Oxford University Press, 2012).

4. See Roger Gottlieb, *Spirituality: What It Is and Why It Matters* (Oxford, England: Oxford University Press, 2012).

5. Bron Taylor, *Dark Green Religion: Nature Spirituality and the Planetary Future* (Berkeley: University of California Press, 2009).

6. Leslie Sponsel, *Spiritual Ecology: A Quiet Revolution* (Santa Barbara, CA: ABC-CLIO Praeger, 2012); also see http://www.spiritualecology.info. Religious ecology is an emerging field of academic study as well as an engaged social force for religious environmentalism focusing primarily on the world religions. Spiritual ecology is broadly attentive to nature as a source of interior meaning and inspiration in a variety of sources, usually beyond the religious traditions. It can be noted that religious traditions also have robust spiritualities that draw on nature as a source of ecological imagination. Religious ecology emphasizes the history, texts, rituals, and symbols of particular religions as living and vital placing of humans in the natural world. As a new discipline within the environmental humanities, religious ecology draws extensively on literature, history, and philosophy to understand the larger contexts of a particular religion's relationships with nature and the larger cosmos.

7. See Nancy Frankenberry, ed., *The Faith of Scientists in Their Own Words* (Princeton, NJ: Princeton University Press, 2008). Later scientific worldviews of the natural world led to seeing the universe through the lens of a mechanistic metaphysics, which, it has been argued, stripped the world of its sacred character.

8. Ibid., 124.

9. Ronald Dworkin's 2011 Einstein Lectures at https://cast.switch.ch/vod/channels/1gcfvlebil. See also William James, *The Varieties of Religious Experience* (Rockville, MD: Arc Manor, 2008), 31, originally published in 1902. He says, "Religion . . . shall mean for us the *feelings, acts, and experiences of individual men in their solitude, so far as they apprehend themselves in relation to whatever they may consider the divine.* . . . There are systems of thought which the world usually calls religious, and which do not positively assume a God."

10. Ronald Dworkin's 2011 Einstein Lectures at https://cast.switch.ch/vod

/channels/1gcfvlebil. See also Chet Raymo, *When God Is Gone, Everything Is Holy: The Making of a Religious Naturalist* (Notre Dame, IN: Sorin Books, 2008).

11. See Tu Weiming and Mary Evelyn Tucker, eds., *Confucian Spirituality*, 2 vols. (New York: Crossroad Publishing, 2004); Mary Evelyn Tucker and John Berthrong, eds., *Confucianism and Ecology: The Interrelation of Heaven, Earth, and Humans* (Cambridge, MA: Center for the Study of World Religions, 1998); and Norman Girardot and James Miller, eds., *Daoism and Ecology: Ways within a Cosmic Landscape* (Cambridge, MA: Center for the Study of World Religions, 2001).

12. As Robert Bellah observes, "I have also argued that practice is prior to belief and that belief is best understood as an expression of practice," in *Religion in Human Evolution: From the Paleolithic to the Axial Age* (Cambridge, MA: Harvard University Press, 2011), 115.

13. See Robert Bellah, *Religion in Human Evolution: From the Paleolithic to the Axial Age* (Cambridge, MA: Harvard University Press, 2011).

14. Clifford Geertz, *The Interpretation of Cultures* (New York: Basic Books, 1973), 90.

15. Some neuroscientists call this "deep enculturation," or ways in which cultures help shape brain architecture through symbolic knowing. See Merlin Donald, *A Mind So Rare: The Evolution of Human Consciousness* (New York: W.W. Norton, 2002), 213–15.

16. Marc Bekoff, *Minding Animals: Awareness, Emotions and Heart* (Oxford, England: Oxford University Press, 2003); Frans DeWaal, *The Age of Empathy: Nature's Lessons for a Kinder Society* (New York: Broadway, 2010).

17. Terrence Deacon and Tyrone Cashman, "The Role of Symbolic Capacity in the Origin of Religion," *Journal for the Study of Religion, Nature and Culture* 3 (2009):490–517; see also Ursula Goodenough and Terrence Deacon, "Sacred Emergence of Nature," in *The Oxford Handbook of Religion and Science*, ed. Philip Clayton (New York: Oxford University Press, 2006), 853–71.

18. For a visual presentation of these paintings at Chauvet cave in southern France, see Werner Herzog's 2010 film *The Cave of Forgotten Dreams*.

19. See Giambattista Vico, *The New Science of Giambattista Vico* (Ithaca, NY: Cornell University Press, 1984), originally published in 1725.

20. Recent neurological research by Antonio Damasio provides evidence of the multiple roles of feeling and the emotions in the generation of mental activity associated with cognition and knowing. See Antonio Damasio, *The Feeling of What Happens: Body and Emotion in the Making of Consciousness* (New York: Harcourt, 1999).

21. Peter Crane, *Ginkgo: The Tree That Time Forgot* (New Haven, CT: Yale University Press, 2013).

22. Steve Pacala, director of Princeton Environmental Institute, shared this observation with us in Spring 2013.

23. Examples of such cultural objects are national flags, which elicit a broad range of sentiments associated with symbolic knowing. The stripes on the American flag represent the original thirteen colonies, and the stars represent the individual states. This symbolism contributes to love of country and a sense of belonging to something larger than oneself. Singing the national anthem, observing parades, and celebrating national holidays may amplify this sense. This kind of participatory patriotism is sometimes described

as civil religion. See, for example, Robert Bellah, *Broken Covenant: American Civil Religion in a Time of Trial* (Chicago: University of Chicago Press, 1992).

24. On economism, see Herman Daly and John Cobb, *For the Common Good: Redirecting the Economy Towards Community, the Environment, and a Sustainable Future* (Boston: Beacon Press, 1989); see also David Loy, "The Religion of the Market," in *Visions of the New Earth: Religious Perspectives on Population, Consumption, and Ecology*, ed. Harold Coward (Albany: State University of New York Press, 2000), 15–28.

25. Lynn White, "The Historical Roots of Our Ecologic Crisis," *Science* 155(3767) (March 10, 1967):1203–7.

26. See Max Weber, *The Protestant Ethic and the Spirit of Capitalism*, trans. Talcott Parsons (London: Routledge, 1992).

27. An example of this is the Nazis' use of the saying *Blut und Boden*, or "blood and soil," which tapped into symbolic concepts of the German nation and its people, thereby valorizing a state and people who, nourished by their mythic homeland, would take up arms to extend their geopolitical power.

28. Terrence Deacon, *The Symbolic Species: The Co-Evolution of Language and the Brain* (New York: W.W. Norton, 1998).

29. Early social science contributions to the study of religion and ecology emerged from the field of geography. David Soper's study *The Geography of Religions* (Englewood Cliffs, NJ: Prentice Hall, 1967) outlined a range of topics, modes of investigation, and examples of interactions between religious systems and landscapes. The geography of religions explored religions as material, social, and cultural expressions that evolved in relation to environments. Religions were understood as molding environmental space in such diverse ways as ritualization of ecology, spatial and organizational structures, political processes, and interactions with other religions.

Geographer Yi-Fu Tuan provides an example of the creative possibilities of this approach. His book *Topophilia: A Study of Environmental Perception, Attitudes, and Values* (Englewood Cliffs, NJ: Prentice Hall, 1974) explored ways in which individuals' affective ties with the environment result from their being simultaneously biological organisms, social beings, and unique individuals with perceptions, attitudes, and values. For Tuan the neologism *topophilia* described this coupling of sentiment with multiple connections to place evident in human cultures. Thus, environments stimulate sensory commitments, giving rise to emotions and ideals expressed in religion. In this context, the many religious symbols are secondary manifestations of the deeper ecological connections described as *topophilia*.

30. Religion has immense diversity of expression, including cosmological stories, symbol systems, ritual practices, spiritual insights, ethical norms, historical processes, cultural contexts, scriptural texts, and institutional structures.

31. These limitations, transmitted in Indigenous religious ecologies, can be compared with such modern forms of critical restraint as the precautionary principle. Applied in various fields of ecological concern, the precautionary principle seeks to curtail unmonitored development that may have unknown deleterious effects on biodiversity and ecosystems, including humans.

32. For the Lakota concept of "all my relations," see William Powers, *Oglala Religion* (Lincoln: University of Nebraska Press, 1977); and Raymond J. Demallie and Douglas Parks, eds., *Sioux Indian Religion: Tradition and Innovation* (Norman: University of Oklahoma Press, 1989).

33. See, for example, Gary Witherspoon, *Language and Art in the Navajo Universe* (Ann Arbor: University of Michigan Press, 1977).

34. See Anthony Aveni, *World Archaeoastronomy* (Cambridge, England: Cambridge University Press, 1989).

35. See, for example, Malcolm Miller, *Chartres Cathedral* (Andover, NH: Pitkin Guide, 1996); and George Mitchell, *The Hindu Temple: An Introduction to Its Meaning and Forms* (Chicago: University of Chicago Press, 1988), originally published in 1977.

36. See, for example, John Miksic, *Borobudur: Golden Tales of the Buddhas*, Photographs by Marcello Tranchini (Berkeley, CA: Periplus Editions, 1990).

37. See, for example, Peter Nabokov, *Native American Architecture* (Oxford, England: Oxford University Press, 1990).

38. See David Carrasco, *Religions of MesoAmerica* (San Francisco, CA: Harper, 1990).

39. These correspondences are at the heart of Han cosmology (second century BCE to second century CE). See William Theodore de Bary and Irene Bloom, eds., *Sources of Chinese Tradition* (New York: Columbia University Press, 1999), 292–310.

40. Sarah Queen, *From Chronicle to Canon: The Hermeneutics of the Spring and Autumn Annals according to Tung Chung-shu* (Cambridge, England: Cambridge University Press, 1996).

41. *Mahapurusha*, the cosmic "great person" in the Rig Veda hymn 10, see chapter 1 "Cosmic and Ritual Order in Vedic Literature," in Ainslie Embree, ed., *Sources of Indian Tradition*, Vol. 1 (New York: Columbia University Press, 1988), 7–28.

42. Rudolf Otto, *Idea of the Holy* (Oxford, England: Oxford University Press, 1923), first published in 1917 as *Das Heilige*.

43. Religious cosmologies continue to be transmitted, and in many instances they are attempting to respond to the scientific theory of evolution and social movements of secularization.

44. Tu Weiming, "Continuity of Being: Chinese Visions of Nature," in *Confucianism and Ecology*, ed. Mary Evelyn Tucker and John Berthrong (Cambridge, MA: Harvard Center for the Study of World Religions, 1998), 105–21.

45. See Belden Lane, *The Solace of Fierce Landscapes: Exploring Desert and Mountain Spirituality* (Oxford, England: Oxford University Press, 2007).

46. Thich Nhat Hanh, *The Heart of Understanding: Commentaries on the Prajnaparamita Heart Sutra* (Berkeley, CA: Parallax Press, 1995).

47. See Thomas Berry, *The Sacred Universe*, ed. Mary Evelyn Tucker (New York: Columbia University Press, 2009); and Thomas Berry, *Evening Thoughts*, ed. Mary Evelyn Tucker (San Francisco, CA: Sierra Club Books, 2006).

Chapter 3

1. Complex views of human–nature relations have also emerged in South Asia regarding *rita* (cosmological order), *dharma* (natural law), and *deva* (natural forces). Similarly, in East Asia the concepts of *Dao* (the Way) and *ch'i* (material force) signal a continuity of being between Heaven, Earth, and human. Buddhist understandings of *pratityasamutpada* (dependent origination) and *buddhacitta* (Buddha mind) also indicate the interrelationship of all reality. In addition, Indigenous traditions provide rich examples of a kinship with nature that is widely experienced in the lifeways of native peoples around the world.

2. The classic source on this discussion is Clarence J. Glacken, *Traces on the Rhodian Shore: Nature and Culture in Western Thought from Ancient Times to the End of the Eighteenth Century* (Berkeley: University of California Press, 1967). This chapter is indebted to Glacken's pathbreaking book. See also the important work of Peter Coates, who notes how paradoxes pervade these discussions in his book *Nature: Western Attitudes since Ancient Times* (Berkeley: University of California Press, 2004). For example, the conservation of parklands in the United States masks the dispossession of those lands from native peoples. Moreover, the widespread changes in the land made by those diverse Indigenous communities belie any simplistic view of wilderness as untouched by humans. Also see Anna Bramwell, *Ecology in the 20th Century: A History* (New Haven, CT: Yale University Press, 1990). For a country-specific study see Keith Thomas, *Man and the Natural World: Changing Attitudes in England, 1500–1800* (Harmondsworth, England: Penguin, 1984); and Raymond Williams, *Keywords: A Vocabulary of Culture and Society* (Oxford: Oxford University Press, 1985).

3. Nurit Bird-David, "'Animism' Revisited: Personhood, Environment, and Relational Epistemology," *Current Anthropology* 40(Supplement) (February 1999):S67–91.

4. Because none of Pythagoras's writings endured, many details of his thought are lost. See, for example, Walter Burkert, *Lore and Science in Ancient Pythagoreanism*, trans. Edwin Minar Jr. (Cambridge, MA: Harvard University Press, 1972).

5. See Pierre Hadot, *Philosophy as a Way of Life: Spiritual Exercises from Socrates to Foucault* (New York: Wiley-Blackwell, 1995). Many of the later Hellenistic philosophers reformulated the ideas of Pythagoras and other pre-Socratic thinkers who are credited with reflecting on the natural world and its relationships with humans. These Greek philosophers critiqued the tendencies of folk religions toward personification of forces (animism), favoring instead a more empirical investigation of the relation of the natural world to humans. *Airs, Waters, and Places* of Hippocrates (460–370 BCE) is the first known work in the West to do this, focusing on the formative influences of environments on people, culture, and health. Concepts regarding the environment were further explored in third-century BCE Hellenistic thought under the holistic idea of *oikumene*, or the human inhabited world. These philosophical developments went beyond, but also complemented, ancient notions of animism in the landscape.

Hellenic thinkers were also concerned with empirical studies and ecological investigations. For example, Eratosthenes (276–195 BCE) not only calculated the circumference of the Earth but also commented on the deforestation of Cyprus and the adverse effects that government policies were having on the environment. Most importantly, these early thinkers gave new philosophical expression to older, traditional ways of thinking about the inhabited world (*oikumene*) by resituating humans in the broader horizon of nature and the cosmos.

6. See Martha Nussbaum, "Kant and Stoic Cosmopolitanism," *Journal of Political Philosophy* 5(1) (1997):1–25.

7. Arthur Lovejoy, *The Great Chain of Being: A Study of the History of an Idea* (Cambridge, MA: Harvard University Press, 1936).

8. Clarence Glacken, *Traces on the Rhodian Shore* (Berkeley: University of California, 1967), 140; see also Stephen Greenblatt, *The Swerve: How the World Became Modern* (New York: W.W. Norton, 2011).

9. These two views of the "good," the Platonic articulation of the One as good and the foundational biblical description of the divine view of creation as good, were

transmitted into Judaism and Christianity as they emerged in the later Hellenistic era. These views of the "good," though historically and culturally different in each tradition, began to overlap and merge in medieval Judaism and Christianity.

10. For *harmonia*, see Tad Brennan, *Stoic Life: Emotions, Duty and Fate* (Oxford, England: Oxford University Press, 2005); for *harmonia* in Abrahamic traditions, see Marcia Colish, *Stoic Traditions from Antiquity to the Early Middle Ages* (Leiden, the Netherlands: E.J. Brill, 1990).

11. See Glacken, *Traces on the Rhodian Shore*, 17.

12. For example, Genesis 1:26–28, Job 26:8–13, and Psalms 65 and 104.

13 Wilderness is sometimes recognized in the Hebrew and Christian scriptures as a wasteland, that is, a place from which no good things can come.

14. Daniel Hillel, *The Natural History of the Bible: An Environmental Exploration of the Hebrew Scriptures* (New York: Columbia University Press, 2005).

15. See, for example, the argument of Ramon Gutierrez, *When Jesus Came, the Corn Mothers Went Away: Marriage, Sexuality, and Power in New Mexico 1500–1846* (Stanford, CA: Stanford University Press, 1991).

16. This is the purpose of the 6-day, or *hexaemeron*, biblical account of Creation in Genesis chapter 1. References to the *hexaemeron* literature can be found in the writings of Philo (20–50 CE), Origen (185–254 CE), and such early church fathers as Basil (330–379 CE), Gregory of Nazianzus (329–390 CE), Gregory of Nyssa (ca. 335–386 CE), and Augustine (354–430 CE). See Frank Robbins, *The Hexaemeral Literature: A Study of the Greek and Latin Commentaries on Genesis* (Chicago: University of Chicago Press, 1912); and A. J. Maas, "Hexaemeron," in *Original Catholic Encyclopedia*, Vol. 7 of 16 volumes (New York: Encyclopedia Press, 1914). Many of the church fathers explored values inherent in that orderly, patterned creation in 6 days that supported particular political and religious worldviews emerging in the Mediterranean region. The "good" with which God greeted his work of creation was conceptualized as a philosophical value connecting the separate worlds of humans, biodiversity, and bioregions.

17. Cf. Genesis 1:26–28; See also Rita Nakashima Brock and Rebeccah Parker, *Saving Paradise: How Christianity Traded Love of This World for Crucifixion and Empire* (Boston: Beacon Press, 2008).

18. See Sachiko Murata and William Chittick, *The Vision of Islam* (London: I.B. Tauris, 2000). In the passages in the Qur'an evoking *ihsan*, this term is translated primarily as "excellence" or "perfection," but some translators render *ihsan* as "love," "care," or "beauty."

19. Consider, for example, Tertullian (160–240 CE), an early Christian writer who extrapolated from the dominion theme in Genesis to the expansion of population as having negative effects on landscapes. See Glacken, *Traces on The Rhodian Shore*, 296–297.

20. Cf. Paul's *Epistle to the Romans* 5:12–14. See Glacken, *Traces on the Rhodian Shore*, 198.

21. See Russell C. Powell, "A Brief Exposition of Augustine's Thought on Creation's Goodness," in *Reformed Perspectives Magazine* 13(40) (2011).

22. See an annotated translation of *Summa Contra Gentiles*, trans. Joseph Rickaby (London: Burns & Oates, 1905), especially Book 1, chapters 45–51; online at http://www2.nd.edu/Departments/Maritain/etext/gc.htm.

23. See Giovanni Pico della Mirandola, *Oration on the Dignity of Man*, trans. Robert Caponigri and Russell Kirk (Chicago: Henry Regnery Co., 1956), available online at http://vserver1.cscs.lsa.umich.edu/~crshalizi/Mirandola/.

24. Ibid., 7.

25. See Paul Santmire, *The Travail of Nature: The Ambiguous Ecological Promise of Christian Theology* (Minneapolis, MN: Fortress, 1985); and also Mark Stoll, *Nature in the Colors of the Spirit: Religion and the Making of American Environmentalism* (Oxford, England: Oxford University Press, forthcoming).

26. See Belden Lane, *Ravished by Beauty:The Surprising Legacy of Reformed Spirituality* (Oxford: Oxford University Press, 2011), 17–46.

27. The question of Bacon's use of *torture* in describing experimental method regarding a feminine nature is discussed in Carolyn Merchant, *The Death of Nature: Women, Ecology, and the Scientific Revolution* (New York: HarperOne, 1990); and "The Violence of Impediments: Francis Bacon and the Origins of Experimentation," online at http://leopold.asu.edu/sustainability/sites/default/files/Warren,%20Violence%20of%20Impediments,%20Merchant_2.pdf.

28. See the records of Portuguese explorers to Brazil as the colony grew in Fernand Braudel, *Civilization and Capitalism: 15th–18th Centuries*,Vol. 3, *The Perspective of the World* (Berkeley: University of California Press, 1992); and the observations recorded by John Smith in Helen Rountree,Wayne Clark, and Kent Mountford, *John Smith's Chesapeake Voyages, 1607–1609* (Charlottesville: University ofVirginia Press, 2007).

29. Spinoza both influenced and challenged the rational orientations of René Descartes (1596–1650). The concept of *natura naturata* was developed in his *Ethics*. See *The Collected Works of Spinoza*,Vol. 1, ed. and trans. Edwin Curley (Princeton, NJ: Princeton University Press, 1985).

30. For John Ray as first to use the term *species*, see Charles Raven, *John Ray: Naturalist: His Life and Works*, 2nd ed. (Cambridge, England: Cambridge University Press, 1986); and *The Wisdom of God Manifested in the Works of the Creation*, Google Books version of 1717 edition at http://www.jri.org.uk/ray/wisdom/.

31. See Gerard Helfrich, *Humboldt's Cosmos: Alexander Humboldt and the Latin American Journey That Changed the Way We See the World* (Los Angeles: Gotham Press, 2004); and Aaron Sachs, *The Humboldt Current: A European Explorer and His American Disciples* (Oxford, England: Oxford University Press, 2007).

32. See Donald Worster, *Nature's Economy*, 2nd ed. (Cambridge, England: Cambridge University Press, 1994), 17; and Anne Rowthorn, *The Wisdom of John Muir* (Birmingham, AL:Wilderness Press, 2012).

33. See Thomas Berry, *The Christian Future and the Fate of Earth*, ed. Mary Evelyn Tucker and John Grim (Maryknoll, NY: Orbis, 2009).

34. See David Ehrenfeld, *The Arrogance of Humanism* (Oxford, England: Oxford University Press, 1981).

35. Lynn White,"The Historical Roots of Our Ecologic Crisis," *Science* 155(3767) (March 10, 1967):1203–7.

36. Matthew T. Riley, "Rethinking Lynn White: Christianity, Creatures, and Democracy," speech given at *Yale Summer Symposium: Religion and Environmental Stewardship Conference* (Yale University, June 6, 2012).

37. See Bill Devall and George Sessions, *Deep Ecology: Living as if Nature Mattered* (Salt Lake City, UT: Gibbs Smith, 1985).

38. See David Barnhill and Roger Gottlieb, eds., *Deep Ecology and World Religions* (Albany: State University of New York Press, 2001).

39. Alfred North Whitehead, *Science and the Modern World* (New York: Free Press–Simon & Schuster, 1997), originally published in 1925.

40. See Jeff Malpas, *Heidegger's Topology: Being, Place, World* (Cambridge, MA: MIT Press, 2008); and Ladelle McWhorter and Gail Stenstad, *Heidegger and the Earth: Essays in Environmental Philosophy* (Toronto: University of Toronto Press, 2009).

41. This inspiration has drawn largely on his major books *The Structure of Behavior* (1942), *The Phenomenology of Perception* (1962), and his posthumously published work *The Visible and the Invisible* (1968).

42. James Gibson writes, "The *affordances* of the environment are what it offers to the animal, what it *provides* or *furnishes*, either for good or ill. The verb to *afford* is found in the dictionary, but the noun *affordance* is not. I have made it up. I mean by it something that refers both to the environment and the animal in a way that no existing term does. It implies the complementarity of the animal and the environment." See *Ecological Approach to Visual Perception* (Hillsdale, NJ: Erlbaum, 1986), 127.

43. David Abram, *Spell of the Sensuous* (New York: Vintage, 1997) and *Becoming Animal* (New York: Vintage, 2011).

44. Pierre Teilhard de Chardin, *The Human Phenomenon*, trans. Sarah Appleton-Weber (Eastbourne, UK: Sussex Academic Press, 1999). It should be noted that Teilhard situated the human as a culminating dimension of the evolutionary process. See also Arthur Fabel and Donald St. John, eds., *Teilhard in the 21st Century: The Emerging Spirit of Earth* (Maryknoll, NY: Orbis, 2003); and Philip Hefner, *The Human Factor* (Minneapolis, MN: Augsburg Fortress, 2000).

45. Thomas Berry, "The New Story," in *The Dream of the Earth* (San Francisco, CA: Sierra Club Books, 1988), 123–37. This article was first published in 1978 as a *Teilhard Study* by the American Teilhard Association.

46. Brian Swimme and Thomas Berry, *The Universe Story: From the Primordial Flaring Forth to the Ecozoic Era, a Celebration of the Unfolding of the Cosmos* (San Francisco, CA: HarperSanFrancisco, 1992).

47. See Ilya Prigogine and Isabelle Stengers, *The End of Certainty: Time, Chaos and the New Laws of Nature* (New York: Free Press, 1997).

48. See Terrence Deacon, *Incomplete Nature: How Mind Emerged from Matter* (New York: W.W. Norton, 2011).

49. Stuart Kauffman, *At Home in the Universe: The Search for Laws of Self-Organization and Complexity* (Oxford, England: Oxford University Press, 1995).

50. See Simon Levin, "Cooperation and Sustainability," in *Practicing Sustainability*, ed. G. Madhavan et al. (New York: Springer, 2013), 39–43.

51. Ursula Goodenough, *The Sacred Depths of Nature* (New York: Oxford University Press, 2000).

52. See http://www.journeyoftheuniverse.org.

Chapter 4

1. The debate about whether humans are part of nature or apart from nature is an ongoing one, especially in the social sciences. Even the uniqueness of humans with regard to language and the creation of culture is contested by some animal behaviorists.

See also William Cronon, ed., *Uncommon Ground: Rethinking the Human Place in Nature* (New York: W.W. Norton, 1996).

2. A text that provides an overview of the study of ecology is Kevin deLaplante, Bryson Brown, and Kent A. Peacock, eds., *Philosophy of Ecology* (Waltham, MA: North Holland/Elsevier, 2011).

3. See Edward L. McCord, *The Value of Species* (New Haven, CT: Yale University Press, 2012).

4. From Aldo Leopold, "The Round River," in *A Sand County Almanac* (New York: Ballantine, 1986), 190, originally published by Oxford University Press in 1949.

5. See Eugene Odum, *Ecology and Our Endangered Life-Support Systems* (Stanford, CT: Sinauer, 1989). See also Loren Eiseley, *The Immense Journey* (New York: Vintage, 1959); and John Stanley Rowe, *Earth Alive: Essays on Ecology*, ed. Don Kerr (Edmonton, AB: NeWest Press, 2006).

6. Donald Worster, *Nature's Economy: A History of Ecological Ideas* (Cambridge, England: Cambridge University Press, 1994), originally published 1977. This chapter is indebted to Worster's work.

7. For an overview of ecology and ecosystems, see Oswald Schmidt, *Ecology and Ecosystem Conservation* (Washington, DC: Island Press, 2007).

8. This is the thesis of Donald Worster's book *Nature's Economy: A History of Ecological Ideas*, where he develops the term *bioeconomics*. The International Society for Bioeconomics and the *Journal of Bioeconomics* provide settings for these interdisciplinary discussions between biologists and economists.

9. Behind these two approaches is the question of whether ecology is a science that gives rise to predictive laws. If this is so, what sort of facts prove those laws, or can they describe only localized cases? There is some discussion in ecology over whether and why it is a "hard" science, which shows up in some of the tensions between holists and bioeconomists.

10. See Jan Smuts, *Holism and Evolution* (London: Macmillan, 1927). Available online at http://archive.org/details/holismandevoluti032439mbp. Reference to Smuts's work on holism is incomplete without mention of his support for the separation of ethnic and racial groups leading to apartheid in South Africa.

11. Worster, *Nature's Economy*, 192. Worster notes that Haeckel's term was largely ignored in favor of the older phrase "the economy of nature" until after the International Botanical Congress of 1893, when the modern spelling, *ecology*, came into usage.

12. Humboldt's synthesis of his early travels with Aimé Bonpland can be found in *Personal Narrative of Travels to the Equinoctial Regions of the New Continent during the Years 1799–1804* (London: Longman, Rees, Orme, Brown, Green, Paternoster and Row, 1827). This view of the unity of the organisms continued with philosophers such as Alfred North Whitehead (1861–1947) and scientists such as David Bohm (1917–1992).

13. Ernst Haeckel, *Monism as Connecting Religion and Science: The Confessions of Faith of a Man of Science*, trans. J. Gilchrist (London: Adam and Charles Black, 1895). Reprinted as *O-P Book* (Ann Arbor, MI: Microfilm Xerography/University Microfilms, 1963); and *Wonder of Life: A Popular Study of Biological Philosophy*, trans. Joseph McCabe (London: Watts, 1904). Haeckel's understanding of nature has been taken up by some Christian ecotheologians, who appropriate it for romantic visions of nature.

However, Lisa Sideris demonstrates that in stressing the theme of harmony, such views of ecology are often blind to nature's profligate inefficiencies and excessive wastes of life forms. See Lisa Sideris, *Environmental Ethics, Ecological Theology, and the Natural Sciences* (New York: Columbia University Press, 2003).

14. See Henri Bortoft, *The Wholeness of Nature* (Hudson, NY: Lindisfarne Press, 1996); and the article by Timothy Lenoir, "The Eternal Laws of Form: Morphotypes and the Conditions of Existence in Goethe's Biological Thought," in the *Journal of Social Biological Structures* 7 (1984):307–24 and 345–56, available online at http://www.stanford.edu/dept/HPST/TimLenoir/Publications/Lenoir_LawsOfForm.pdf.

15. Thus, instead of "survival of the fittest" as strictly species competitiveness, fitness orients an investigator to a sense of genetic representation in future generations.

16. John Stanley Rowe, *Earth Alive: Essays on Ecology*, ed. Don Kerr (Edmonton, AB: NeWest Press, 2006).

17. Ibid., 61.

18. Ibid., 76.

19. For reading selections from American environmentalists, see Bill McKibben, ed., *American Earth: Environmental Writings since Thoreau* (New York: Library of America, 2008).

20. George Perkins Marsh, *Man and Nature, or Physical Geography as Modified by Human Action* (New York: Charles Scribner, 1865), iii.

21. See Donald Worster, *A Passion for Nature: The Life of John Muir* (New York: Oxford University Press, 2008).

22. *Atlantic Monthly* (January 1869). See http://www.sierraclub.org/john_muir _exhibit/writings/favorite_quotations.aspx.

23. Gifford Pinchot, *Breaking New Ground* (Washington, DC: Island Press, 1998), 505.

24. See Char Miller, *Gifford Pinchot and the Making of Modern Environmentalism* (Washington, DC: Island Press, 2001).

25. This paragraph was formulated in a comment from Warren Abrahamson, emeritus professor of biology at Bucknell University.

26. It was not until the 1960s and 1970s that ecologists such as John Harper led plant ecologists to demographic studies of individual plants. John Harper, "The Individual in the Population," *Journal of Ecology* 52 (1964):149–158.

27. See Robert H. MacArthur and E. O. Wilson, *The Theory of Island Biogeography* (Princeton, NJ: Princeton University Press, 1967); see also the discussion in Worster, *Nature's Economy*, 374–77.

28. Arthur Tansley had a keen interest in Sigmund Freud. In 1920 he published *The New Psychology and Its Relation to Life*, a bestseller that helped introduce Freud to England. In 1923 Tansley went to Vienna to study with Freud for a year. Three years before he died, he published *Mind and Life: An Essay in Simplification* (London: Allen & Unwin, 1952). There he said that humans are not just biological beings but also spiritual beings (170–71).

29. Arthur Tansley, "The Use and Abuse of Vegetational Concepts and Terms," *Ecology* 16(3) (July 1935):284–307; quoted in Worster, *Nature's Economy*, 301.

30. Tansley, "The Use and Abuse of Vegetational Concepts and Terms," 284–307.

31. See *Ecology and Field Biology* at http://v-polhem.ita.mdh.se/polopoly _fs/1.16332!ws6smithetal.pdf.

32. Donald Worster, *Nature's Economy*, 304.

33. Julianne Warren, *Aldo Leopold's Odyssey: Rediscovering the Author of* A Sand County Almanac (Washington, DC: Island Press, 2006); Curt Meine, *Aldo Leopold: His Life and Work* (Madison: University of Wisconsin Press, 2010); J. Baird Callicott, *In Defense of the Land Ethic: Essays in Environmental Philosophy* (Albany: State University of New York Press, 1989).

34. See J. Baird Callicott, *In Defense of the Land Ethic: Essays in Environmental Philosophy* (Albany: State University of New York Press, 1989); and J. Baird Callicott and Susan Flader, eds., *The River of the Mother of God and Other Essays by Aldo Leopold* (Madison: University of Wisconsin Press, 1991).

35. Aldo Leopold, "The Land Ethic," in *A Sand County Almanac* (New York: Oxford University Press, 1966), 240, originally published in 1949.

36. Ibid., 246.

37. For further discussion of the founding of the Wilderness Society in 1935, see Paul Sutter, *Driven Wild: How the Fight against Automobiles Launched the Modern Wilderness Movement* (Seattle: University of Washington, 2002).

38. From the Ecological Society of America website at http://www.esa.org /history/.

39. Restoration ecology (the science) and ecological restoration (the practice) have emerged as an important discipline and field. The "guild" is the Society for Ecological Restoration International (http://www.ser.org/), and the SER Primer is an excellent resource on ecological restoration (http://www.ser.org/resources /resources-detail-view/ser-international-primer-on-ecological-restoration). See also Eric Higgs, *Nature by Design: People, Natural Processes, and Ecological Restoration* (Cambridge, MA: MIT Press, 2003); Donald A. Falk, Margaret A. Palmer, and Joy B. Zedler, eds., *Foundations of Restoration Ecology* (Washington, DC: Island Press, 2006); and Dave Egan, Even E. Hjerpe, and Jesse Abrams, eds., *Human Dimensions of Ecological Restoration: Integrating Science, Nature, and Culture* (Washington, DC: Island Press, 2011).

40. See Fred van Dyke, *Conservation Biology: Foundations, Concepts, Applications*, 2nd ed. (Amsterdam: Springer Verlag, 2008).

41. It is important to acknowledge Fairfield Osborn's racist positions on eugenics. See Walter Hines Page and Arthur Wilson Page, *The World's Work: A History of Our Time* (New York: Doubleday, 1924), 253; also Henry Fairfield Osborn Jr., *Man Rises to Parnassus* (Princeton, NJ: Princeton University Press, 1928), 220–21.

42. Donald Worster, *Nature's Economy*, 355; the conference proceedings for "Man's Role in Changing the Face of the Earth" were published in 1956 by the University of Chicago Press.

43. See Douglas Helms, "Walter Lowdermilk's Journey: Forester to Land Conservationist," *Environmental Review* 8 (1984):132–45.

44. Walter Lowdermilk, "Lessons from the Old World to the Americas in Land Use," in *Annual Report of the Board of Regents of the Smithsonian Institution* (Washington, DC: Government Printing Office, 1944), 413–27.

45. For Walter Lowdermilk's "Eleventh Commandment," written in Jerusalem in 1939, see http://www.watershed.org/?q=node/202.

46. For 10 years *Fundamentals of Ecology* was the only textbook in this field, and it was revised many times. See Eugene Odum, *Fundamentals of Ecology* (Philadelphia: Wm. Saunders, 1953).

47. Eugene Odum, "Introduction," in *Ecosystems Theory and Applications*, ed. Nicholas Polunin (New York: Wiley, 1986), 1–11; cited in Donald Worster, *Nature's Economy*, 363, who observed that these two brothers "did more than anyone else to define the science [of ecology] in the post-war period," 362.

48. Worster, *Nature's Economy*, 366.

49. See William Drury and Ian Nisbet, "Succession," *Journal of the Arnold Arboretum* 54 (1973):331–68; and S. T. A. Pickett and P. S. White, "Patch Dynamics: A Synthesis," in *The Ecology of Natural Disturbance and Patch Dynamics* (New York: Academic Press, 1985), 371–84.

50. Daniel Botkin, *Discordant Harmonies: A New Ecology for the Twenty-First Century* (New York: Oxford University Press, 1992); and *The Moon in the Nautilus Shell: Discordant Harmonies Reconsidered* (Oxford, England: Oxford University Press, 2012).

51. See Stephen H. Kellert, *In the Wake of Chaos: Unpredictable Order in Dynamical Systems* (Chicago: University of Chicago Press, 1993).

52. See Albert Schweitzer, "The Ethics of Reverence for Life," in *Christendom* 1 (1936):225–39; also reprinted in Henry Clark, *The Ethical Mysticism of Albert Schweitzer* (Boston: Beacon, 1962), 180–94.

53. Rachel Carson, *Silent Spring* (New York: Houghton Mifflin, 1962).

54. See http://www.edf.org/.

55. J. E. de Steiguer, *The Origins of Modern Environmental Thought* (Tucson: University of Arizona Press, 2006).

56. See Adam Rome, *The Genius of Earth Day: How a 1970 Teach-in Unexpectedly Made the First Green Generation* (New York: Hill & Wang, 2013).

57. Holmes Rolston III, "Environmental Ethics," in *Ecology, Economics, Ethics: The Broken Circle*, ed. F. Herbert Bormann and Stephen R. Kellert (New Haven, CT: Yale University Press, 1991), 73–96.

58. J. Baird Callicott, *In Defense of the Land Ethic: Essays in Environmental Philosophy* (Albany: State University of New York Press, 1987). Callicott has been a participant in the Forum on Religion and Ecology project since the Harvard conferences on world religions.

59. See Hilary Putnam, *The Collapse of the Fact/Value Dichotomy and Other Essays* (Cambridge, MA: Harvard University Press, 2004). Putnam argues against the dichotomy of fact as objective and values as subjective.

60. Holmes Rolston III, "Environmental Ethics," 95–96; see also J. Baird Callicott, "Hume's Is/Ought Dichotomy and the Relation of Ecology to Leopold's Land Ethic," *Environmental Ethics* 4 (1982):311–28.

61. Ibid., 10.

62. See Joseph DesJardins, *Environmental Ethics: An Introduction to Environmental Philosophy* (Independence, KY: Cengage Learning, 2012).

63. See Gretchen Daly, ed., *Nature's Services: Societal Dependence on Natural Ecosystems* (Washington, DC: Island Press, 1997).

64. For TEEB, see http://www.teebweb.org/.

65. TEEB is being directed by Pavan Sukdev, who is the author of *Corporation 2020: Transforming Business for Tomorrow's World* (Washington, DC: Island Press, 2012).

66. See Helaine Selin, ed., *Encyclopaedia of the History of Science, Technology, and Medicine in Non-Western Cultures* (New York: Springer, 2008); also Gregory Cajete, *Native Science: Natural Laws of Interdependence* (Santa Fe, NM: Clear Light Publishers, 1999).

Chapter 5

1. Michael Dove and Carol Carpenter, *Environmental Anthropology: A Historical Reader* (Indianapolis, IN: Wiley-Black, 2007); and Patricia Townsend, *Environmental Anthropology* (Long Grove, IL: Waveland, 2008).

2. Historian William Cronin underscored this idea in his groundbreaking study *Changes in the Land: Indians, Colonists, and the Ecology of New England* (New York: Hill & Wang, 1983).

3. See Eleanor Sterling's work at the Center for Biodiversity and Conservation at the American Museum of Natural History: http://www.amnh.org/science/bios/bio.php?scientist=sterling.

4. Jared Diamond, *Collapse: How Societies Choose to Fail or Succeed* (New York: Penguin, 2005).

5. Eco-justice is concerned with bringing together justice for humans and justice for the Earth community. See http://fore.research.yale.edu/publications/books/ecology-and-justice-series/.

6. See Joseph Sittler, *Care of the Earth* (Minneapolis, MN: Fortress, 2004); and Peter Bakken and Steven Bouma-Prediger, eds., *Evocations of Grace: Writings on Ecology, Theology, and Ethics* (Grand Rapids, MI: Eerdmans, 2000), http://www.josephsittler.org/.

7. See Donald Worster, *Nature's Economy*, 326–28.

8. John Cobb, *Is It Too Late? A Theology of Ecology*, revised ed. (Denton, TX: Environmental Ethics Books, 1995). See also Philip N. Joranson, *Cry of the Environment: Rebuilding the Christian Creation Tradition*, ed. Ken Butigan (Santa Fe, NM: Bear & Co, 1984).

9. *Harvard Theological Review*, 65 (1972):337–66.

10. One of the first publications from the Evangelical community about the environment was edited by Loren Wilkenson, *Earthkeeping: Christian Stewardship of Natural Resources* (Grand Rapids, MI: Eerdmans, 1980). This arose from a meeting on science and religion at Calvin College in 1978. A new edition appeared in 1991 with the subtitle *Stewardship of Creation*, indicating the broadening of environmental concerns among Evangelicals. Cal DeWitt also was instrumental in several other meetings, including the Windsor Castle Consultation (2000), the Sandy Cove Covenant (2004), and the Evangelical Climate Initiative (2006), which issued *An Urgent Call to Action*. Also see Calvin DeWitt, *Earthwise: A Guide to Hopeful Creation* (Grand Rapids, MI: Faith Alive, 2011). For Au Sable Institute, see http://ausable.org/.

11. See http://fore.research.yale.edu/publications/books/ecology-and-justice-series/.

12. George Tinker, *American Indian Liberation: A Theology of Sovereignty* (Maryknoll, NY: Orbis, 2008); and Jace Weaver, *Defending Mother Earth: Native American Perspectives on Environmental Justice* (Maryknoll, NY: Orbis, 1996).

13. Chung Hyun Kyung, *Struggle to Be the Sun Again: Introducing Asian Women's Theology* (Maryknoll, NY: Orbis, 1990); and Kwok Pui-lan, *Introducing Asian Feminist Theology* (Berea, OH: Pilgrim Press, 2000).

14. After many years of studying world religions and cultures, Berry published a sequence of books that elaborated these ideas: *The Dream of the Earth* (1988), *The Great Work* (1999), *Evening Thoughts* (2006), *Sacred Universe* (2009), and *The Christian Future and the Fate of Earth* (2009).

15. Berry was indebted to the cosmological thinking of Jesuit paleontologist Pierre Teilhard de Chardin (1881–1955). This led to a radical revisioning of the scientific discoveries of universe emergence as a new cosmological story of our times. He first expressed these ideas in 1978 in his seminal essay "The New Story," published in the *Teilhard Study* series and later in *The Dream of the Earth* (San Francisco, CA: Sierra Club Books, 1998), 123–37. With Brian Swimme he then published *The Universe Story* in 1992.

16. See *Journey of the Universe* film and book along with an educational series: http://www.journeyoftheuniverse.org.

17. Thomas Berry, *Sacred Universe* (New York: Columbia University Press, 2009), 100.

18. Sarah Taylor, *Green Sisters: A Spiritual Ecology* (Cambridge, MA: Harvard University Press, 2009).

19. For Genesis Farm, see http://www.genesisfarm.org/. Crystal Spring is located in Plainville, Massachusetts with the Kentucky Dominican Sisters.

20. See http://www.greenmountainmonastery.org/.

21. See Sean McDonagh, *To Care for the Earth: A Call to a New Theology* (Rochester, VT: Bear & Co., 1987).

22. See the Very Reverend James Parks Morton, "Environment and Religion: The Evolution of a New Vision," in *Earth and Spirit: The Spiritual Dimension of the Environmental Crisis*, ed. Fritz Hull (New York: Continuum, 1993), 119–32.

23. For Global Forum, see http://akiomatsumura.com/akio/global-forums. Preserving and Cherishing the Earth: An Appeal for Joint Commitment in Science and Religion, 1990.

24. For this Vesper liturgy, see http://www.goarch.org/chapel/liturgical_texts/vespers_creation/.

25. See the *Great Learning*: "Those in antiquity who wish to illuminate luminous virtue throughout the world would first govern their states; wishing to govern their states, they would first bring order to their families; wishing to bring order to their families, they would first cultivate their own person; wishing to cultivate their own person, they would first rectify their minds; wishing to rectify their minds, they would first make their thoughts sincere; wishing to make their thoughts sincere, they would first extend their knowledge. The extension of knowledge lies in the investigation of things." William Theodore de Bary and Irene Bloom, eds., *Sources of Chinese Tradition*, Vol. 1 (New York: Columbia University Press, 1999), 330–31.

26. Ibid., 338.

27. Ibid., 338.

28. Chung-ying Cheng, "The Trinity of Cosmology, Ecology, and Ethics in the Confucian Personhood," in *Confucianism and Ecology: The Interrelation of Heaven, Earth, and Humans*, ed. Mary Evelyn Tucker and John Berthrong (Cambridge, MA: Harvard Center for the Study of World Religion, 1998), 211–25.

29. The complex religious nature of this ceremony is evident in the spiritual motivations of outsiders attending a Winter Dance who may not have been as immediately connected to that local lifeway of subsistence practices, social hierarchies, and cultural values. Nonetheless, even visitors would have appreciated and entered into this ceremonial by singing their vision songs or dancing around the centering tree in imitation of the animals moving at that time of year as others sang. See John Grim,

"Cosmogony and the Winter Dance: Native American Ethics in Transition," *Journal of Religious Ethics* (Fall 1992), 389–413.

30. John Grim's Winter Dance field notes (1986).

31. Clearly, other practices are also transformative, such as *yoga* as body meditation and movement, *jnana* as intellectual discipline and study, *karma* as performance of action, and *dharma* as one's duty in life. These groupings of religious ideas and practices have a rich scriptural history, beginning with the Vedic hymns. The Vedas were initially transmitted orally in northwestern India from at least 1500 BCE and later written in Sanskrit from approximately 900 BCE.

32. Vedic religion focused on sacrifice as mediating between humans, nature, and the gods. By the end of the Vedas, or *Upanishads*, a new religious emphasis emerged, namely, an ultimate monism. That is, the sages posited an undifferentiated unity of the Absolute (*Brahman*) and the interior self of the human (*atman*). This Oneness, or identity of all reality, became a seminal religious idea in Hinduism. Gradually, another form of religious expression emerged affirming a difference between self and divine, human and god. The Sanskrit term for this difference is *bheda* as in *bheda-abedha*, "difference in nondifference." Among *bhakti* religious thinkers, the use of *dualism* to describe this difference is viewed negatively. Our thanks to David Haberman for bringing this point regarding difference to our attention.

33. This major text of Hinduism is generally dated to the last centuries BCE and placed in the Gangetic River plain of northern India. The *Gita* is set in the struggles of the Bharata family narrated by the sage Vyasa in the epic *Mahabharata*.

34. Before the fighting begins, Arjuna, seeing his close relatives on the opposing side, is filled with doubt and unable to fight. While urging him to accept his duty (*dharma*) as a warrior, Krishna also recommends the devotion of *bhakti* as a meditational concentration upon Ultimate Oneness in the form of himself as a deity. The *Bhagavad Gita* is one of the most widely recited texts in Hinduism and has had a profound influence on many thinkers into the present, including Mahatma Gandhi, who drew on it to develop his ideas of nonviolence.

35. From Shri Vallabhacharya, *Yamunashtakam*, trans. David Haberman, in *River of Love in an Age of Pollution: The Yamuna River in Northern India* (Berkeley: University of California Press, 2006), 106.

Chapter 6

1. This watery chaos, formless and void, *tohu wabohu*, תֹהוּ וָבֹהוּ, occurs three times in the Bible (Genesis 1:2, Jeremiah 4:23, Isaiah 34:11). For an interpretive perspective that opens questions rather than boxes answers, see Catherine Keller, *Apocalypse Now and Then: A Feminist Guide to the End of the World* (Minneapolis, MN: Fortress Press, 2005). In her work, Keller suggests a collaborative creation of God with "this matrix of relations." Keller writes, "I am here presupposing a certain cosmology according to which everything to which language could conceivably refer, that is, anything which exists and most of which is non-human and 'natural,' is ipso facto a hermeneutical event, an 'interpretive process.' Anything to which language points is actively interpreting itself and therefore that which stands in relation to it. Transcendence is a process of transformation immanent within the relationships constituting the discursive field within what is biblically referred to as 'the deep'" (301).

2. See Jaroslav Pelikan, *The Christian Tradition: A History of the Development of Doctrine*, 5 vols. (Chicago: University of Chicago Press, 1973–1990).

3. For Christian Orthodox theology, see Vladimir Lossky, *Orthodox Theology: An Introduction* (Yonkers, NY: St.Vladimir Seminary Press, 2001); Bishop Kallistos of Diokleia, *Through the Creation to the Creator* (London: Friends of the Centre Papers, 1997).

4. Consider, for example, the significance of the text of the writer known as Pseudo-Dionysius for the history of mystical thought in all of Christian history. See *Pseudo-Dionysius: The Complete Works*, trans. C. Luibheid and P. Rorem (London: Society for the Promotion of Christian Knowledge, 1987).

5. This emphasis on religious art in Orthodoxy is not an attempt to pass by the historical controversies such a position can provoke. This is evident in the icon controversies of Byzantine Christianity. See, for example, Charles Barber, *Figure and Likeness: On the Limits of Representation in Byzantine Iconoclasm* (Princeton, NJ: Princeton University Press, 2002); Moshe Barasch, *Icon: Studies in the History of an Idea* (New York: New York University Press, 1992); and Kurt Weitzmann, ed., *Age of Spirituality: Late Antique and Early Christian Art, Third to Seventh Century*, Exhibition catalogue (New York: Metropolitan Museum of Art, 1979).

6. Some of the differences between the two churches included theological interpretations of the Trinity, original sin, and free will. See, for example, Pelikan, *The Christian Tradition*.

7. Prayers for the environment sung by the Greek Byzantine Choir, directed by Lykourgos Angelopoulos at Basilica San Marco. Also see Barbara Rossing, *The Rapture Exposed: The Message in the Book of Revelation* (Boulder, CO: Westview, 2004).

8. Styled the "Green Patriarch," he is known in the Greek Orthodox tradition as the All-Holiness Ecumenical Patriarch of Constantinople. Born as Demetrios Archontonis in 1940, he became the Ecumenical Patriarch in October 1991. Located in Istanbul, Turkey, the Ecumenical Patriarch is the center, or first among the independent unity, of Christian Orthodoxy. See John Chryssavgis, ed., *Cosmic Grace, Humble Prayer: The Ecological Vision of the Greek Orthodox Patriarch Bartholomew I* (Grand Rapids, MI: Wm. B. Eerdmans, 2003).

9. In Ravenna such ancient Christian examples of cosmological themes, imaged as the blue sky with stars, can be found in the vaulted dome in the mausoleum of Galla Placidia, the dome in the Archiepiscopal Chapel, the top of the chancel vault in the Church of San Vitale, and the hand reaching from the clouds in the apse of the Church of St. Apollinare in Classe. For Christian art, see Diane Apostolos-Cappadona, *Dictionary of Christian Art* (New York: Continuum Press, 1995).

10. See, for example, Derek Kreuger, ed., *Byzantine Christianity: A People's History of Christianity* (Minneapolis, MN: Fortress Press, 2006), particularly Vol. 3; Peter Brown, *The Rise of Western Christendom: Triumph and Diversity A.D. 200–1000* (Malden, MA: Blackwell, 2003); Thomas Matthews, *The Clash of the Gods: A Reinterpretation of Early Christian Art* (Princeton, NJ: Princeton University Press, 1993); Rita Nakashima Brock and Rebecca Parker, *Saving Paradise: How Christianity Traded Love of This World for Crucifixion and Empire* (Boston: Beacon Press, 2008); Gerard Lutikhuizen, ed., *Paradise Interpreted: Representations of Biblical Paradise in Judaism and Christianity* (Leiden, the Netherlands: Brill, 1999); and Jean Delumeau, *History of Paradise: The Garden of Eden in Myth and Tradition* (New York: Continuum Press, 1995).

11. In Patriarch Bartholomew's closing address to the symposium titled "Sacrifice: The Missing Dimension," he observes, "The cross is our guiding symbol in the supreme sacrifice to which we are all called. It sanctifies the waters and, through them, transforms the entire world. Who can forget the imposing symbol of the cross in the splendid mosaic of the Basilica of Saint Apollinare in Classe? As we celebrated the Divine Liturgy in Ravenna, our attention was focused on the cross, which stood at the center of our heavenly vision, at the center of the natural beauty that surrounds it, and at the center of our celebration of heaven on earth. Such is the model of our ecological endeavors. Such is the foundation of any environmental ethic. . . . The cross *must* be at the very center of our vision. Without the cross, without sacrifice, there can be no blessing and no cosmic transfiguration." In Chryssavgis, ed., *Cosmic Grace, Humble Prayer*, 13.

12. Lynn White, "The Historical Roots of Our Ecologic Crisis," *Science* 155(3767) (March 10, 1967):1203–7.

13. John Chryssavgis, *On Earth as in Heaven: Ecological Vision and Initiatives of Ecumenical Patriarch Bartholomew* (New York: Fordham University Press, 2012).

14. Other prominent religious leaders who have made public statements voicing environmental concern beyond simple rhetoric are the Tibetan Buddhist Dalai Lama and Vietnamese Buddhist monk Thich Nhat Hahn, the Roman Catholic popes John Paul II and Benedict XVI, Rowan Williams, the former Anglican Archbishop of Canterbury, and Katharine Jefferts Schori, presiding bishop of the Episcopal Church in the United States.

15. See http://www.halkisummit.org.

16. Chryssavgis, *Cosmic Grace, Humble Prayer*, 221.

17. John Zizoulas (Metropolitan John of Pergamon), *Remembering the Future: An Eschatological Ontology* (London: T&T Clark, 2012); John Chryssavgis, *Beyond the Shattered Image: Orthodox Insights into the Environment* (Minneapolis, MN: Light and Life, 1999); and John Chryssavgis and Bruce Foltz, eds., *Toward an Ecology of Transfiguration: Orthodox Christian Perspectives on Environment, Nature, and Creation* (New York: Fordham University Press, 2013).

18. For Metropolitan John of Pergamon, "Towards an Environmental Ethic," see http://www.rsesymposia.org/themedia/File/1151678281-Ethic.pdf.

19. Ibid.

20. Chryssavgis, *Cosmic Grace, Humble Prayer*, 299.

21. Ibid., 24; here the Patriarch cites major Orthodox theologian Gregory Palamas.

22. Ibid., 91.

23. Ibid., 147.

24. Ibid., 41, 269, and 313.

25. *On the Cosmic Mystery of Jesus Christ: Selected Writings from Maximus the Confessor*, trans. Paul Blowers and Robert Wilken (New York: St. Vladimir's Seminary Press, 2003), 55.

26. See Willis Jenkins, *Ecologies of Grace: Environmental Ethics and Christian Theology* (New York: Oxford University Press, 2008); and Donald St. John, "Contemplation and Cosmos: Merton on Maximus and Teilhard," *Teilhard Study #62*, American Teilhard Association (Spring 2011).

27. "The Word becomes thickened . . . concealing Himself mysteriously for our sakes within the *logoi* of creatures and thus He reveals Himself accordingly/analogously through the visible things as through some written signatures as a whole in

His fullness from the whole of nature and undiminished in each part, in the varieties of natures as one who has no variation and is always the same, in composites, as One who is simple, without parts, in things which have their beginning in time, as the One without beginning, as the Invisible in the visible, the ungraspable in tangible things. For our sake He received flesh to embody Himself and to incarnate within letters and deigned to be expressed in syllables and sounds [Holy Scriptures]. The purpose of all this is to draw us after Him and to gather us together in His presence within a short space of time having become one in spirit, we, who are thickened in mind." *On the Cosmic Mystery of Jesus Christ*, 58.

28. See Dragos Bahrim, "The Anthropic Cosmology of St. Maximus the Confessor," in *Journal for Interdisciplinary Research on Religion and Science* 3 (July 2008):11–37.

29. It is significant that both Pope Benedict XVI and the Ecumenical Patriarch cite Maximus the Confessor's emphasis on reality as "the cosmic liturgy" from his *Mystagogia*. For Pope Benedict, see his June 25, 2008 remarks in St. Peter's Square, and for the Patriarch, ibid., 315.

30. Chryssavgis, *Cosmic Grace, Humble Prayer*, 57.

31. Ibid., 55 and 313.

Chapter 7

1. Air pollution has increased, see http://www.nytimes.com/2013/01/13/science/earth/beijing-air-pollution-off-the-charts.html.

2. For a history of the Institute, see Wu Yungui, "The History of the Institute for World Religions, Chinese Academy of Social Sciences," at http://www.iop.or.jp/0010/yungui.pdf.

3. Pan Yue, "Green China and Young China," in *China Dialogue* (July 2007), http://www.chinadialogue.net/article/show/single/en/1168-Green-China-and-young-China-part-two-. China Dialogue is one of the best Internet sites for information on China (www.chinadialogue.net).

4. Mark Elvin, *The Retreat of the Elephants: An Environmental History of China* (New Haven, CT: Yale University Press, 2004).

5. It might also be observed that Daoism and Buddhism have important perspectives on these issues. See Mary Evelyn Tucker and Duncan Ryuken Williams, eds., *Buddhism and Ecology: The Interconnection of Dharma and Deeds* (Cambridge, MA: Harvard Center for the Study of World Religions, 1997). See also Norman Girardot, James Miller, and Liu Xiaogan, eds., *Daoism and Ecology: Ways within a Cosmic Landscape* (Cambridge, MA: Harvard Center for the Study of World Religions, 2001).

6. Tu Weiming and Mary Evelyn Tucker, eds., *Confucian Spirituality*, 2 vols. (New York: Crossroads, 2003–2004). These volumes illustrate the religious and spiritual dimensions of the Confucian traditions from the classical period to the present. See also Stephen Angle, *Sagehood: The Contemporary Significance of Neo-Confucian Philosophy* (New York: Oxford University Press, 2009); Anna Sun, *Confucianism as a World Religion: Contested Histories and Contemporary Realities* (Princeton, NJ: Princeton University Press, 2013); John and Evelyn Berthrong, *Confucianism: A Short Introduction* (London: Oneworld, 2000); John Makeham, "*Rujiao* [Confucianism] as Religion," in *Lost Soul: "Confucianism" in Contemporary Academic Discourse* (Cambridge, MA: Harvard University Asia Center, 2008), 277–309; William Theodore de Bary, *The Great Civilized Conversation: Education for a World Community* (New York: Columbia University Press, 2013).

7. Mary Evelyn Tucker and John Berthrong, eds., *Confucianism and Ecology* (Cambridge, MA: Harvard Center for the Study of World Religions, 1998).

8. This term was first used by historian of religion Mircea Eliade and then by Confucian scholar Tu Weiming. See Tu Weiming, *Confucian Thought: Selfhood as Creative Transformation* (Albany: State University of New York Press, 1985).

9. William Theodore de Bary and Irene Bloom, eds., *Sources of Chinese Tradition*, Vol. 1 (New York: Columbia University Press, 1999), 330–31.

10. Chang Tsai's *Western Inscription* continues as follows: "The great ruler [the emperor] is the eldest son of my parents [Heaven and Earth], and the great ministers are his stewards. Respect the aged—this is the way to treat them as elders should be treated. Show affection toward the elder and weak. . . . The sage identifies his virtue with that of Heaven and Earth, and the worthy is the best [among the children of Heaven and Earth]. Even those who are tired and infirm, crippled and sick, those who have no brothers or children, wives or husbands, all are my brothers who are in distress and have no one to turn to." de Bary and Bloom, *Sources of Chinese Tradition*, 683.

11. This generation of New Confucians kept alive the tradition in Taiwan and Hong Kong. They include Xiong Shili (1885–1968), Fang Dong Mei (1899–1977), Tang Junyi (1909–1978), and Mou Jongsan (1909–1995).

12. From Makeham, *Lost Soul*, 43.

13. Makeham, *Lost Soul*; Daniel Bell, *China's New Confucianism: Politics and Everyday Life in a Changing Society* (Princeton, NJ: Princeton University Press, 2008).

14. Liu Zongchao, *An Outlook on Ecological Civilization* (Xianmen, China: Xianmen University Press, 2010).

15. President Hu Jintao first mentioned ecological civilization at the seventeenth Party Congress on October 24, 2007. At the eighteenth Party Congress, held November 8–14, 2012, President Hu mentioned ecological civilization fifteen times in his report. In the same Party Congress, the new president, Xi, also mentioned ecological civilization as benefitting contemporary and future generations.

16. See professor of philosophy at Beijing University Tang Yijie, "The Enlightenment and Its Difficult Journey in China," in *Wen Hui Bao* (Shanghai newspaper), November 14, 2011.

17. Yang Fubin, "The Influence of Whitehead's Process Thought on the Chinese Academy," *Process Studies* 39(2) (Fall–Winter 2010):342–49.

18. *The Analects of Confucius: A Philosophical Translation*, trans. Roger Ames and Henry Rosemont (New York: Ballantine, 1999).

19. Mary Evelyn Tucker, *Moral and Spiritual Cultivation in Japanese Neo-Confucianism* (Albany: State University of New York Press, 1989); and Mary Evelyn Tucker, *The Philosophy of Qi* (New York: Columbia University Press, 2007).

20. See Irene Bloom, *Mencius* (New York: Columbia University Press, 2009).

21. de Bary and Bloom, *Sources of Chinese Tradition*, Vol. 1, 129.

22. Sarah Allan, *The Way of Water and Sprouts of Virtue* (Albany: State University of New York, 1997).

23. Burton Watson, *Xunzi: Basic Writings* (New York: Columbia University Press, 2003).

24. de Bary and Bloom, *Sources of Chinese Tradition*, Vol. 1, 171.

25. *Reflections on Things at Hand: The Neo-Confucian Anthology Compiled by Chu Hsi and Lü Tsu-Ch'ien*, trans. Wing-tsit Chan (New York: Columbia University Press,

1967); see also Wing-tsit Chan, *Chu Hsi and Neo-Confucianism* (Honolulu: University of Hawaii Press, 1986).

26. Julia Ching, *The Religious Thought of Chu Hsi* (Oxford, England: Oxford University Press, 2000).

27. de Bary and Bloom, *Sources of Chinese Tradition*, Vol. 1, 338.

28. These ideas of the organismic process of Chinese thought as marked by continuity, wholeness, and dynamism are developed by Tu Weiming, "The Continuity of Being: Chinese Visions of Nature," in *Confucianism and Ecology*, ed. Mary Evelyn Tucker and John Berthrong (Cambridge, MA: Harvard Center for the Study of World Religions, 1998), 105–21.

29. For a commentary on the *Doctrine of the Mean*, see Tu Weiming, *Commonality and Centrality: An Essay on Confucian Religiousness* (Albany: State University of New York Press, 1989).

30. Daniel Gardner, *The Four Books: The Basic Teachings of the Later Confucian Tradition* (Boston: Hackett, 2007).

31. de Bary and Bloom, *Sources of Chinese Tradition*, Vol. 1, 346–48.

32. See David Hall and Roger Ames, "Chinese Philosophy," in *Routledge Encyclopedia of Philosophy* (London: Routledge, 1998, revised 2013). From http://www.rep .routledge.com/article/G001.

Chapter 8

1. On ritual and ritualization, see Tom Driver, *The Magic of Ritual: The Need for Liberating Rites That Transform Our Lives and Our Communities* (San Francisco, CA: HarperSanFrancisco, 1993).

2. My thanks to Father Pat Twohy, SJ for that early conversation at the American Academy of Religion in 1984. Some of Pat Twohy's reflections on his experiences at Inchelium and among the Colville Confederated Tribes from 1973 to 1984 are available in his book *Finding a Way Home: Indian and Catholic Spiritual Paths of the Plateau Tribes* (Inchelium, WA: St. Michael's Mission, 1983). Mary Evelyn and I were also assisted by my nephew, Ed Grim, who teaches at the secondary school in Inchelium. Ed graciously asked permission of Martin Louie for permission to attend the Louie family Winter Dance. He and his wife, Karen, gave me hospitality over those years before and after the Winter Dance, for which I thank them.

3. The language designation *syilx* is more appropriate for Salish. However, because *Salish* is a more familiar term it is used here to refer to a number of Interior Plateau Indigenous peoples who transmit the Winter Dance ceremonial. *Okanagan* could also be used to designate this central grouping of Indigenous peoples. See the Okanagan Nation Alliance's website at http://www.syilx.org. The Winter Dance, *snyxwám*, sometimes called "Spirit Dance," or "Jump Dance," refers here to the major winter ceremonial also practiced by peoples other than Okanagan in this Columbia River region.

4. See Harry Robinson, *Nature Power: In the Spirit of an Okanagan Storyteller*, compiled and edited by Wendy Wickwire (Vancouver: Talonbooks, 1992); for a historical overview see Larry Cebula, *Plateau Indians and the Quest for Spiritual Power 1700–1850* (Lincoln: University of Nebraska, 2003); and Douglas Hudson, "The Okanagan Indians of British Columbia," in *Okanagan Sources*, ed. Jean Webber (Penticton, BC: Theytus, 1990), 54–89.

5. My thanks again to all the Louie family for their permission to attend those many years, to teach students about the Winter Dance, and to write about it. See John Grim, "Cosmogony and the Winter Dance: Native American Ethics in Transition," *Journal of Religious Ethics* (Fall 1992):389–413.

6. This is a complex and sensitive topic that native elders and scholars have addressed. See, for example, the work of American Indian theologian George Tinker, who speaks of "Indian dysfunctionality" in his *American Indian Liberation: A Theology of Sovereignty* (Maryknoll, NY: Orbis, 2008); see also his *Spirit and Resistance: Political Theology and American Indian Liberation* (Minneapolis, MN: Fortress Press, 2004). Also see Robert H. Ruby and John A. Brown, *Dreamer-Prophets of the Columbia Plateau* (Norman, OK: University of Oklahoma Press, 1989).

7. One insight into traditional environmental knowledge about plants is provided in Nancy J. Turner, Randy Bouchard, and Dorothy I. D. Kennedy, *Ethnobotany of the Okanagan–Colville Indians of British Columbia and Washington*, Occasional Papers Series, No. 21 (Victoria: British Columbia Provincial Museum, 1980).

8. See Tim Ingold, *Bring Alive: Essays on Movement, Knowledge, and Description* (London: Routledge, 2011); and especially his earlier work *The Perception of the Environment: Essays in Livelihood, Dwelling and Skill* (London: Routledge, 2000).

9. For an overview of the mythic narratives among the Salish, see Susan Staiger Gooding, "Interior Salishan Stories: Historical Ethics in the Making," *Journal of Religious Ethics* (Fall 1992):353–87.

10. See Andrew Fisher, *Shadow Tribe: The Making of Columbia River Identity* (Seattle: University of Washington Press, 2010).

11. The loss of salmon fishing by the indigenous village peoples along the Columbia River has been ameliorated to some extent by the exchange with other native peoples in the region who continue to fish salmon. Snpakchin/Martin Louie was especially troubled by the case of David Sohappy, a Yakama elder who was arrested for fishing salmon and distributing to other native peoples. See the website "Salmon and the Columbia River: Continuities and Challenges" for an overview at http://www.webpages.uidaho.edu/~rfrey/422salmon.htm.

12. Cf. Verne Ray, "The Sanpoil and Nespelem Salishan Peoples of Northeastern Washington," *University of Washington Publications in Anthropology* 5 (December 1932):182–211; V. Ray, "Native Villages and Groupings of the Columbia Basin," *Pacific Northwest Quarterly* 27 (1936); V. Ray, "Religious Life: The Guardian Spirit Complex," in *Cultural Relations in the Plateau of Northwestern America* (Frederick Webb Hodge Anniversary Publication Fund, 1939), 68–131; Walter Cline, "Religion and World View," in *Sinkaietk or Southern Okanagon of Washington*, General Series in Anthropology, no. 6, ed. Lellie Spier (Menasha, WI: George Banta, 1938); and Joyce Wike, *Modern Spirit Dancing of North Puget Sound*, MA thesis, Department of Anthropology, University of Washington, 1941.

13. Norman Lerman, "Fieldnotes Collected at Riverside, Washington, February 1954," in *Indians of British Columbia*, ed. Jill A. Willmott (Vancouver: University of British Columbia Press, 1963), 35.

14. For *sumix* in relation to an earthquake, see Danielle Metcalfe-Chenail, *Unsettling Times: Interior Salish Responses to the 1872 Earthquake in the Inland Northwest*, MA thesis, McGill University, 2005.

15. See Harry Robinson, "The Indians, They Got the Power," in *Nature Power: In the Spirit of an Okanagan Storyteller*, compiled and edited by Wendy Wickwire (Vancouver: Talonbooks, 1992); also see Harry Robinson, *Write It on Your Heart: The Epic World of an Okanagan Storyteller* (Vancouver: Talonbooks, 2004).

16. John Grim's field notes, 1986.

17. See Mourning Dove, *Mourning Dove: A Salishan Autobiography*, ed. Jay Miller (Lincoln: University of Nebraska Press, 1990), 125; also Walter Cline, "Religion and World View," 186; and Verne Ray, "The Sanpoil and Nespelem Salishan Peoples of Northeastern Washington," 186.

18. For an overview of the mythic narratives among the Salish, see Christopher L. Miller, *Prophetic Worlds: Indians and Whites on the Columbia Plateau* (New Brunswick, NJ: Rutgers University Press, 1985).

19. Howard Harrod, *The Animals Came Dancing: Native American Sacred Ecology and Animal Kinship* (Tucson: University of Arizona Press, 2000), 58–59.

20. Many current elders have reflected on the estrangement and anomie resulting from Salish interactions over the centuries with dominant Euro-American cultures as a form of spirit sickness that can also be relieved at the Winter Dance. See Wolfgang Jilek, *Indian Healing: Shamanic Ceremonialism in the Pacific Northwest Today* (Blaine, WA: Hancock House Publishers, 1982).

21. Walter Cline, "Religion and World View," in *Sinkaietk or Southern Okanogon of Washington*, General Series in Anthropology, no. 6, ed. Lellie Spier (Menasha, WI: George Banta, 1938), 152.

Chapter 9

1. For information on the conference "Yamuna River: A Confluence of Waters, a Crisis of Need," held January 3–5, 2011 at TERI University in Delhi and at Radha Raman Temple in Vrindaban, see http://fore.research.yale.edu/information /Yamuna_River_Conference.html; see also Richard Conniff, "The Yamuna River: India's Dying Goddess," in *Environment Yale* (Spring 2011):4–13; see http://environ ment.yale.edu/magazine/spring2011/the-yamuna-river-indias-dying-goddess/.

2. See Kelly Alley, "Separate Domains: Hinduism, Politics, and Environmental Pollution," in *Hinduism and Ecology: The Intersection of Earth, Sky, and Water*, ed. Christopher Chapple and Mary Evelyn Tucker (Cambridge, MA: Center for the Study of World Religions, 2000), 355–87; also see Kelly Alley, *On the Banks of the Ganga: When Wastewater Meets a Sacred River* (Ann Arbor: University of Michigan Press, 2002).

3. David Haberman, *River of Love in an Age of Pollution: The Yamuna River of Northern India* (Berkeley: University of California Press, 2006), 55–56. Haberman has studied the Yamuna for several decades and was key in the planning of the conference in Vrindaban in January 2011.

4. See http://www.india-angling.com/yamuna.html.

5. For policy approaches to the Narmada River, another sacred river in India, see Harry Blair, "Social Movements & Saving Rivers: What Can Be Learned from the Narmada?" published online at the Forum on Religion and Ecology website: http:// fore.research.yale.edu/information/Yamuna/HBlair_NarmadaLessons.pdf.

6. Debate over the relationships of *technai*, arts and crafts, with *episteme*, knowledge, reaches back into both classical Sanskrit (*Dharmashastras*) and Greek (Plato and

Aristotle) philosophical thought. A twentieth-century critic of technology was Martin Heidegger. He saw technology as a new transcendent axis that was intensified by the Protestant Reformation. Heidegger was deeply concerned with the linkage of science and technology as a way of perceiving the world. See Martin Heidegger, "The Question Concerning Technology," in *Philosophy of Technology: The Technological Condition: An Anthology*, ed. Robert Scharff and Val Dusek (Oxford, England: Blackwell, 2003), 252–64.

7. Thomas Berry wrote, "Once the scientific–technological period established itself . . . the intensity of its own dedication to its objectives took on the characteristics of a religious attitude and of a spiritual discipline parallel with the religious dedication and spiritual discipline of the classical religious cultures that preceded it. This included a new sense of orthodoxy, a new dogmatic integrity not to be challenged by reasonable persons. Yet . . . neither the creators of this new situation nor the spiritual personalities of the period have known how to read the change that has taken place." From "Christian Spirituality and the American Experience," in *The Dream of the Earth* (San Francisco, CA: Sierra Club Books, 1988), 118; Berry also observed that "scientific and social ideals have both become substitute mysticisms. Technology is the sacrament of our new birth. With their inner mystical dimensions and outer efficacy, science and technology provide an analysis of the human condition and a transforming remedy." From "Traditional Religions in the Modern World," in *The Sacred Universe: Earth, Spirituality, and Religion in the Twenty-First Century*, ed. Mary Evelyn Tucker (New York: Columbia University Press, 2009), 11–12.

8. Thus, one of the first new, modern dams was planned on the Yamuna River at Dakpathar at the time of India's independence in 1947 and was completed in the 1960s. See C. V. J. Sharma, ed., *Modern Temples of India: Selected Speeches of Jawaharlal Nehru at Irrigation and Power Projects* (New Delhi: Central Board of Irrigation and Power, 1989).

9. See Central Pollution Control Board, *Water Quality Status of Yamuna River* (Delhi: Central Pollution Control Board, 2000); also Central Pollution Control Board, *Quality and Trend of River Yamuna (1977–1982)*, details at http://www.cpcb.nic.in /index.php.

10. For civil advocacy see Harry Blair, "Gauging Civil Society Advocacy: Charting Pluralist Pathways," in *Evaluating Democracy Support: Methods and Experiences*, ed. Peter Burnell (Stockholm: International Institute for Democracy and Electoral Assistance, and Swedish International Development Cooperation Agency, 2007), 171–92 and 228–39. See http://www.idea.int/publications/evaluating_democracy_support /upload/evaluating_democracy_support_cropped.pdf; see also Blair, "Social Movements & Saving Rivers."

In this article, Blair observes that *civil advocacy* can be defined as organized activity not part of the state, the private sector, or the family, in which people act to promote mutual interests. In turn, *advocacy* can be defined as the process through which individuals or organizations endeavor to influence public policy making and implementation. Thus, *civil society advocacy* would mean efforts on the part of civil society organizations to influence state behavior.

11. When the Yamuna arrives on the northern plains of India from its origins in a Himalayan glacier, barrages and dams are the first set of controls imposed on the river. Barrages are simply lower dams used to direct the flow of the river. The Assan barrage at Dakpathar, finished in 1965, now redirects much of the water into utility

canals for hydroelectric power and agricultural irrigation. Some would say that the river as a goddess ends here because for the remainder of its flow into the city of Delhi and beyond, the Yamuna is so diminished as to be no more than a managed canal.

The Yamuna is further impeded at Tajewala by the massive Hathnikund barrage, where the river is broken into two canals that date from the Mughal dynasty of the fourteenth century CE. Often silted and cleared over the centuries, the Western canal now flows through the industrial cities of Yamunagar, Karnal, Panipat, and Sonepat. Industrial wastewater is pumped into the canals to replace the water extracted for irrigation of the large agricultural areas north of Delhi. The Eastern canal also supplies irrigation water for the "green revolution" agriculture area in the Doab between the Yamuna and Ganges Rivers. So much water is taken out of the Yamuna at Tajewala and directed into these two canals that in the dry season the main channel of the river is dry en route to Delhi.

12. The predominance of a managerial and engineering mindset in modern India gives little attention to sustainability of natural ecological processes. Rather, global economic development is mostly evident in websites and publications focused on human resource management among younger generations in India. See Pawan Budhwar and Jyotsna Bhatnagar, eds., *The Changing Faces of People Management in India* (New York: Routledge, 2009).

13. See Roy Rappaport, *Ecology, Meaning, and Religion* (Berkeley, CA: North Atlantic Books, 1979).

14. This devotion to the Yamuna River is also found in religions other than Hinduism, such as the respect shown by Muslim Mughal ruler Shahjahan, who built the magnificent Taj Mahal beside the river. This reverence appears in the poems of Muslim writer Mirza Ghalib and eclectic poet Kabir Das, and in the religious shrine along the river built by Sikh guru Gobind Singh. It was evident in fishing villages that are now long gone from the Yamuna River between Delhi and Vrindaban. There fish populations ceased flourishing in the 1980s, with deoxygenation and methane buildup resulting from urban waste flushed into the river.

15. This form of religiosity associated with the Mathura region of Uttar Pradesh (often called *Braj*) is practiced widely in northern India, including in Delhi, and in the states of Rajasthan and Haryana. The Vaishnava tradition of Hinduism also flourishes in southern India, and the relationships between the different regions are historically complex and intensely interactive. See William Sax, ed., *The Gods at Play: Lila in South Asia* (New York: Oxford University Press, 1995).

16. In Hinduism more than one deity can occupy the status of supreme being. That is, for the Vaishnava traditions, Vishnu is supreme, whereas for the Saivite tradition, Siva is supreme. These two positions need not be in conflict in Hindu theology, which allows multiple understandings of the unity of reality as expressed in the *Upanishads*.

17. See Milton Singer, ed., *Krishna: Myths, Rites and Attitudes* (Chicago: University of Chicago Press, 1966); John Hawley, *At Play with Krishna: Pilgrimage Dramas at Brindaban* (Princeton, NJ: Princeton University Press, 1981); *Songs of the Saints of India*, texts and notes by John Hawley, trans. John Hawley and Mark Juergensmeyer (New York: Oxford University Press, 1988); and Daniel Sheridan, *The Advaitic Theism of the Bhagavata Purana* (Delhi: Motilal Banarsidas, 1986).

18. *Bhagavata Purana*, canto 10, chapter 3 from *Srimad Bhagavatam*, online at http://www.srimadbhagavatam.org/.

19. This story is narrated in the *Bhagavata Purana*, canto 10, chapter 16 from *Srimad Bhagavatam*, online at http://www.srimadbhagavatam.org/.

20. See Haberman, *River of Love in an Age of Pollution*, 150ff.

21. Scholars have long noted the interweaving of *bhakti* dimensions in such texts as the *Isha Upanishad*. See *Upanishads*, trans. Patrick Olivelle (New York: Oxford University Press, 1996); and *The Thirteen Principal Upanishads*, trans. Robert Ernest Hume (Oxford, England: Oxford University Press, 1921).

22. Most importantly, social and economic divisions so crucial to the hierarchical society of India are subtly transformed in the heat of devotion. The mythic story describes the break from strict caste divisions by having all the wives of Prahlad, who are low-caste cow-herders, become the Gopi maidens who play (*lila*) with Krishna. These lower-caste women are the paradigmatic devotees.

23. See "A Tale of Two Rivers: Only One Happy Ending," *The Times of India*, July 8, 2012, http://timesofindia.indiatimes.com//articleshow/14738489.cms? intenttarget=no; "Delhi's Yamuna River: A Catastrophe in the Making," *The Hindu*, March 6, 2010, http://www.thehindu.com/sci-tech/energy-and-environment /article246228.ece; Rajar Banerji and Max Martin, "Yamuna: The River of Death," in *Homicide by Pesticides*, ed. Anil Agarwal (New Delhi: Centre for Science and Environment, 1997); and the Centre for Science and Environment website at http://cseindia .org/. See also http://indiatoday.intoday.in/story/yamuna-bachao-yatra-to-protest -at-jantar-mantar/1/257364.html.

24. It should be noted that in secular contexts this same kind of denial can be found about levels of pollution in rivers, wetlands, and oceans around the world, but rarely is the natural world set in the context of religion as clearly as it is in India. For example, the Po River, Italy's longest river, has experienced staggering industrial pollution and sewage from its urban centers, such as Milan. Only when the European Environmental Agency fined Milan was a treatment facility considered. The industrial and commercial benefits of using the Po as a dumping canal continued until environmental monitoring raised an alarm.

Chapter 10

1. For a similar argument about the decrease in violence over the last century, see Steven Pinker, *The Better Angels of Our Nature* (New York: Viking, 2011).

2. For the Universal Declaration of Human Rights, see http://www.un.org/en /documents/udhr/index.shtml.

3. See, for example, William Theodore de Bary and Tu Weiming, eds., *Confucianism and Human Rights* (New York: Columbia University Press, 1999).

4. The term *anthropocene* is attributed to Edward Stoemer and popularized by Paul Crutzen in *International Geophysics–Biosphere Program Newsletter* 41 (2000); for a Smithsonian conference on the anthropocene, see http://www.si.edu/content/consortia /Anthropocene-symposium-program-11_Oct_2012.pdf.

5. See the Global Ethic Foundation, founded by Hans Küng at Tübingen University in Germany, at http://www.weltethos.org/data-en/c-10-stiftung/10a-definition .php; and the Center for Global Ethics, founded by Leonard Swidler at Temple University in the United States, at http://globalethic.org/.

For publications in this area, see Hans Kung and Karl-Josef Kuschel, eds., *A Global Ethic: The Declaration of the Parliament of the World's Religions* (New York: Continuum,

1993). See also Leonard Swidler, *Toward a Universal Declaration of a Global Ethic*, presented at the 1993 American Academy of Religion Annual Meeting, available at http://globalethic.org/Center/intro.htm; Marcus Braybrooke, ed., *Stepping Stones to a Global Ethic* (London: SCM Press, 1992); and Sumner Twiss and Bruce Grelle, eds., *Explorations in Global Ethics* (Boulder, CO: Westview, 1998), 118–40.

6. See Earth Charter at http://www.earthcharter.org. Each of the world religions contributed its perspective to the principles of the Earth Charter through the drafting stage during the Harvard conferences on religion and ecology.

7. Mary Evelyn Tucker was a member of the International Drafting Committee of the Earth Charter that met during 1997–2000 and a member of the Earth Charter International Council during 2000–2012.

8. See Laura Westra, Klaus Bosselman, and Colin Soskoine, eds., *Globalisation and Ecological Integrity in Science and International Law* (Cambridge, England: Cambridge Scholars Publishing, 2011).

9. See Peter Blaze Corcoran, Mirian Vilela, and Alide Roerink, eds., *Earth Charter in Action: Toward a Sustainable World* (Amsterdam: Royal Tropical Institute, 2005); http://www.earthcharterinaction.org/invent/details.php?id=251.

10. See the Faith Meets Faith series at Orbis Books, edited by Paul Knitter.

11. See http://www.society-buddhist-christian-studies.org/. For many years there was an important Buddhist–Christian dialogue chaired by Masao Abe and John Cobb. See John B. Cobb Jr. and Christopher Ives, eds., *The Emptying God: A Buddhist–Jewish–Christian Conversation* (Maryknoll, NY: Orbis, 1990).

12. See Friends of the Earth, Middle East, at http://www.foeme.org/www/?module=home.

13. It must be noted that the Parliament took place in the context of the Chicago World's Fair, which was marked by a colonialist worldview. The Parliament excluded some groups such as American Indians and Sikhs.

14. Carlton J. H. Hayes, *A Generation of Materialism: 1871–1900* (New York: Harper Torchbooks, 1963).

15. See http://www.parliamentofreligions.org.

16. For Assisi Declarations, see http://www.arcworld.org/downloads/THE%20ASSISI%20DECLARATIONS.pdf.

17. From the Preamble of the Earth Charter; see appendix F.

Epilogue

1. This numinous feeling in the presence of such grandeur often calls forth responses of joy and gratitude as well as awe and praise. Such sentiments are at the heart of religious experience that often occurs in natural settings. Indeed, our human inclination toward *biophilia*, love of nature, may be seen as fundamentally a spiritual instinct. We embrace the natural world as that which gives us life and from which we have arisen, recognizing that it has creative and destructive powers far greater than ours.

2. See the Encyclical of September 2012, http://www.patriarchate.org/documents/encyclical-of-his-all-holiness-for-the-church-new-year.

3. See John Zizoulas, Metropolitan John of Pergamon, "Towards an Environmental Ethic," http://www.rsesymposia.org/themedia/File/1151678281-Ethic.pdf.

4. For engaged Buddhism, see http://www.dharmanet.org/lcengaged.htm; for

Hindu service, see http://bhumiproject.org/; for Indigenous resurgence, see http://www.ienearth.org/ and the "Idle No More" movement at http://idlenomore.ca/.

5. Stephen Kellert and James Gustave Speth, eds., *The Coming Transformation: Values to Sustain Human and Natural Communities* (New Haven, CT:Yale School of Forestry and Environmental Studies, 2009), a publication that came out of the Aspen conference in Fall 2007.

6. In the United States groups such as the National Resources Defense Council, Environmental Defense Fund, and Earthjustice have been at the forefront of environmental legislation.

7. Donald Worster, *Nature's Economy: A History of Ecological Ideas* (Cambridge, England: Cambridge University Press, 1994), 257, originally published in 1977.

8. Ecological economics has been led by such thinkers as Herman Daly, Richard Norgaard, Gretchen Daily, Robert Costanza, Juliet Schor, Peter Brown, and Gus Speth.

9. Juliet Schor, *Plenitude: The New Economics of True Wealth* (New York: Penguin, 2010).

10. For the New Economics Institute, see http://neweconomicsinstitute.org/; and for the New Economics Foundation, see http://www.neweconomics.org/.

11. For the Bhutanese United Nations high-level meeting on Happiness Indicators on April 2, 2012, see http://www.un.org/apps/news/story.asp?NewsID=41685#.USADQ44rz0c.

12. See Thomas Berry, *The Great Work: Our Way into the Future* (New York: Bell Tower, 1999).

Appendix A

1. Available at http://www.vatican.va/holy_father/john_paul_ii/speeches/2002/june/documents/hf_jp-ii_spe_20020610_venice-declaration_en.html.

Appendix B

1. Available at http://english.mep.gov.cn/Ministers/Speeches/201107/t20110704_214385.htm.

Appendix C

1. Full text available at http://www.un.org/esa/socdev/unpfii/documents/DRIPS_en.pdf.

Appendix D

1. Available at http://savethefraser.ca/fraser_declaration.pdf.

2. In addition to the original signing nations listed here, seventy-six nations signed the declaration in 2011 and 2012, for a total of 130.

Appendix E

1. Available at http://fore.research.yale.edu/files/Yamuna_River_Declaration.pdf

Appendix F

1. Available at http://www.earthcharterinaction.org/content/pages/read-the-charter.html.

Bibliography

Abrecht, Paul, ed. *Faith, Science, and the Future.* Geneva: World Council of Churches, 1978.

Albanese, Catherine. *Nature Religion in America: From the Algonkian Indians to the New Age.* Chicago: University of Chicago Press, 1990.

Anderson, Eugene N. *Ecologies of the Heart: Emotion, Belief, and the Environment.* New York: Oxford University Press, 1996.

Aveni, Anthony. *World Archaeoastronomy.* Cambridge, England: Cambridge University Press, 1989.

Ball, James. *Global Warming and the Risen Lord: Christian Discipleship and Climate Change.* Washington, DC: Evangelical Environmental Network, 2010.

Ban, Ki-moon. Speech given at the Celebration of Faiths and the Environment, Windsor Castle, UK, November 3, 2009, transcript. http://www.windsor2009 .org/ARC-UNDPWindsor2009-SpeechBanKi-moon.pdf.

Barbour, Ian, ed. *Earth Might Be Fair: Reflections on Ethics, Religion and Ecology.* Englewood Cliffs, NJ: Prentice Hall, 1972.

———. *Western Man and Environmental Ethics: Attitudes towards Nature and Technology.* Reading, MA: Addison-Wesley, 1973.

Barnhill, David, and Roger Gottlieb, eds. *Deep Ecology and World Religions: New Essays on Sacred Ground.* Albany: State University of New York Press, 2001.

Basso, Keith H. *Wisdom Sits in Places: Landscape and Language among the Western Apache.* Albuquerque: University of New Mexico Press, 1996.

Bauman, Whitney. *Theology, Creation, and Environmental Ethics.* New York: Routledge, 2009.

Bauman, Whitney, Richard Bohannon II, and Kevin O'Brien, eds. *Grounding Religion: A Field Guide to the Study of Religion and Ecology.* New York: Routledge, 2011.

Bekoff, Marc, and Jessica Pierce. *Wild Justice: Moral Lives of Animals.* Chicago: University of Chicago Press, 2009.

Berger, Peter. *The Sacred Canopy: Elements of a Sociological Theory of Religion.* New York: Anchor Books, 1990. Originally published in 1967.

Bergman, Sigurd. *Creation Set Free: The Spirit as Liberator of Nature.* Grand Rapids, MI: Eerdmans, 2005.

————, series ed. *Studies in Religion and the Environment / Studien zur Religion und Umwelt* (SiRE). Berlin: LIT Verlag.

Berry, Thomas. *The Christian Future and the Fate of Earth*, ed. Mary Evelyn Tucker and John Grim. Maryknoll, NY: Orbis, 2009.

————. *The Dream of the Earth*. San Francisco, CA: Sierra Club Books, 1988.

————. *The Great Work: Our Way into the Future*. New York: Bell Towers–Random House, 1999.

————. *The Sacred Universe: Earth, Spirituality, and Religion in the Twenty-First Century*, ed. Mary Evelyn Tucker. New York: Columbia University Press, 2009.

Bird-David, Nurit. "'Animism' Revisited: Personhood, Environment, and Relational Epistemology," *Current Anthropology* 40(Supplement), February 1999.

Boff, Leonardo. *Cry of the Earth, Cry of the Poor*. Maryknoll, NY: Orbis, 1997.

————. *Ecology and Liberation: A New Paradigm*, trans. J. Cumming. Maryknoll, NY: Orbis, 1995.

Botkin, Daniel. *Discordant Harmonies: A New Ecology for the Twenty-First Century*. New York: Oxford University Press, 1992.

Bramwell, Anna. *Ecology in the 20th Century: A History*. New Haven, CT: Yale University Press, 1990.

Bratton, Susan Power. "Ecology and Religion," in *The Oxford Handbook of Religion and Science*, ed. Philip Clayton. New York: Oxford University Press, 2006.

Brennan, Tad. *Stoic Life: Emotions, Duty and Fate*. Oxford, England: Oxford University Press, 2005.

Brock, Rita Nakashima, and Rebeccah Parker. *Saving Paradise: How Christianity Traded Love of This World for Crucifixion and Empire*. Boston: Beacon, 2008.

Brown, Lester. "Challenges of the New Century," in *State of the World 2000*, ed. Lester R. Brown, Christopher Flavin, and Hilary French. New York: Norton, 2000.

Brown, Peter. *Right Relationship: Building a Whole Earth Community*. San Francisco, CA: Berrett-Koehler, 2009.

Buckley, Thomas. *Standing Ground: Yurok Indian Spirituality, 1850–1990*. Berkeley: University of California Press, 2002.

Bullard, Robert, et al. *Toxic Wastes and Race at Twenty: Grassroots Struggles to Dismantle Environmental Racism in the United States*. Cleveland, OH: United Church of Christ Justice and Witness Ministry, 2007.

Burkert, Walter. *Lore and Science in Ancient Pythagoreanism*, trans. Edwin Minar Jr. Cambridge, MA: Harvard University Press, 1972.

Callicott, J. Baird. *Earth's Insights: A Survey of Ecological Insights from the Mediterranean Basin to the Australian Outback*. Berkeley: University of California Press, 1994.

————. *In Defense of the Land Ethic: Essays in Environmental Philosophy*. Albany: State University of New York Press, 1987.

Callicott, J. Baird, and Roger Ames. *Nature in Asian Traditions of Thought: Essays in Environmental Philosophy*. Albany: State University of New York Press, 1989.

Carrasco, David. *Religions of MesoAmerica: Cosmovision and Ceremonial Centers*. San Francisco, CA: Harper, 1990.

Carson, Rachel. *Silent Spring*. Boston: Houghton Mifflin; Cambridge, MA: Riverside, 1962.

Cassanova, Jose. *Public Religions in the Modern World*. Chicago: University of Chicago Press, 1994.

Chaisson, Eric. *Cosmic Evolution: The Rise of Complexity in Nature*. Cambridge, MA: Harvard University Press, 2002.

Chan, Wing-tsit. *Sources of Chinese Civilization*, 2 vols. New York: Columbia University Press, 1960.

Chapple, Christopher Key, ed. *Jainism and Ecology: Nonviolence in the Web of Life*. Cambridge, MA: Harvard Center for the Study of World Religions, 2003.

———. *Nonviolence to Animals, Earth, and Self in Asian Traditions*. Albany: State University of New York Press, 1993.

Chapple, Christopher Key, and Mary Evelyn Tucker, eds. *Hinduism and Ecology: The Intersection of Earth, Sky, and Water*. Cambridge, MA: Harvard Center for the Study of World Religions, 2000.

Chryssavgis, John, ed. *Cosmic Grace, Humble Prayer: The Ecological Vision of the Green Patriarch Bartholomew I*. Grand Rapids, MI: Wm. B. Eerdmans, 2000.

Coates, Peter. *Nature: Western Attitudes Since Ancient Times*. Berkeley: University of California Press, 1998.

Cobb, John. *Is it Too Late? A Theology of Ecology*. Denton, TX: Environmental Ethics Books, 1995. Originally published in 1972.

Cooper, David, and Joy Palmer. *Spirit of the Environment*. London: Routledge, 1998.

Costanza, Robert, et al. *An Introduction to Ecological Economics*. Boca Raton, FL: CRC Press, 1997.

Cronon, William. *Changes in the Land: Indians, Colonists, and the Ecology of New England*. New York: Hill & Wang, 1983.

———, ed. *Uncommon Ground: Rethinking the Human Place in Nature*. New York: W.W. Norton, 1996.

Curry, Patrick. *Ecological Ethics: An Introduction*. Malden, MA: Polity, 2006.

Dallmayr, Fred. *Return to Nature? An Ecological Counterhistory*. Lexington: University Press of Kentucky, 2011.

Daly, Herman, and John Cobb. *For the Common Good: Redirecting the Economy Toward Community, the Environment, and a Sustainable Future*. Boston: Beacon, 1989.

Damasio, Antonio. *The Feeling of What Happens: Body and Emotion in the Making of Consciousness*. New York: Harcourt, 1999.

Daneel, Marthinus. *African Earthkeepers: Holistic Interfaith Mission*. Maryknoll, NY: Orbis, 2001.

Deane-Drummond, Celia. *Eco-Theology*. Winona, MN: Anselm Academic, 2008.

de Bary, William Theodore, and Irene Bloom, eds. *Sources of Chinese Tradition*, Vol. 1: *From Earliest Times to 1600*. New York: Columbia University Press, 1999.

de Bary, William Theodore, Carol Gluck, and Arthur Tiedemann, eds. *Sources of Japanese Tradition*, Vol. 2: *1600 to 2000, Introduction to Asian Civilizations*. New York: Columbia University Press, 2005.

de Bary, William Theodore, Donald Keene, George Tanabe, and Paul Varley, eds. *Sources of Japanese Tradition*, Vol. 1: *From Earliest Times to 1600*. New York: Columbia University Press, 2002.

de Bary, William Theodore, and Richard Lufrano, eds. *Sources of Chinese Tradition*, Vol. 2: *From 1600 to the Twentieth Century*. New York: Columbia University Press, 2001.

Dempsey, Corinne. *Bringing the Sacred Down to Earth: Adventures in Comparative Religion*. New York: Oxford University Press, 2012.

Devall, Bill, and George Sessions. *Deep Ecology: Living as if Nature Mattered*. Salt Lake City, UT: Gibbs M. Smith, 1985.

DeWitt, Calvin B. *A Sustainable Earth: Religion and Ecology in the Western Hemisphere*. Marcelona, MI: AuSable Institute, 1987.

Diamond, Jared. *Collapse: How Societies Choose to Fail or Succeed*. New York: Penguin, 2005.

Donald, Merlin. *A Mind So Rare: The Evolution of Human Consciousness*. New York: W.W. Norton, 2002.

Dove, Michael, and Carol Carpenter. *Environmental Anthropology: A Historical Reader*. Malden, MA: Wiley-Blackwell, 2007.

Dunlap, Thomas. *Faith in Nature: Environmentalism as Religious Quest*. Seattle: University of Washington Press, 2005.

Dupré, Louis. *Passage to Modernity: An Essay in the Hermeneutics of Nature and Culture*. New Haven, CT: Yale University Press, 1993.

Eaton, Heather. *Introducing Ecofeminist Theologies*. London: T&T Clark, 2005.

Eaton, Heather, and Lois Lorentzen, eds. *Ecofeminism and Globalization: Exploring Culture, Context, and Religion*. Lanham, MD: Rowman & Littlefield, 2003.

Ecumenical Patriarch, Bartholomew. *Encountering the Mystery: Understanding Orthodox Christianity Today*. New York: Doubleday, 2008.

Eldredge, Niles. *Life in the Balance: Humanity and the Biodiversity Crisis*. Princeton, NJ: Princeton University Press, 1998.

Elvin, Mark. *The Retreat of the Elephants: An Environmental History of China*. New Haven, CT: Yale University Press, 2004.

Embree, Ainslee, ed. *Sources of Indian Tradition*, Vol. 1: *From the Beginning to 1800*. New York: Columbia University Press, 1988.

Engel, J. Ronald, and Joan Gibb Engel, eds. *Ethics of Environment and Development: Global Challenge, International Response*. Tucson: University of Arizona Press, 1990.

Erhlich, Paul. *Human Natures*. Washington, DC: Island Press, 2001.

Fabel, Arthur, and Donald St. John, eds. *Teilhard in the 21st Century: The Emerging Spirit of Earth*. Maryknoll. NY: Orbis, 2003.

Feld, Stephen. *Sound and Sentiment: Birds, Weeping, Poetics, and Song in Kaluli Expression*. Philadelphia: University of Pennsylvania Press, 1982.

Foltz, Richard, ed. *Environmentalism in the Muslim World*. New York: Nova Science Publishers, 2003.

———, ed. *Worldviews, Religion, and the Environment: A Global Anthology*. Belmont, CA: Wadsworth, 2003.

Foltz, Richard, Frederick M. Denny, and Azizan Baharuddin, eds. *Islam and Ecology: A Bestowed Trust*. Cambridge, MA: Harvard Center for the Study of World Religions, 2003.

Foster, George M., and Barbara Gallatin Anderson. *Medical Anthropology*. New York: Pergamon, 1978.

Fox, Matthew. *The Coming of the Cosmic Christ: The Healing of Mother Earth and the Birth of a Global Renaissance*. San Francisco, CA: Harper & Row, 1988.

———. *Original Blessing: A Primer in Creation Spirituality*. New York: Tarcher, 2000.

Frankenberry, Nancy, ed. *The Faith of Scientists in Their Own Words*. Princeton, NJ: Princeton University Press, 2008.

Funkenstein, Amos. *Theology and the Scientific Imagination from the Middle Ages to the Seventeenth Century*. Princeton, NJ: Princeton University Press, 1986.

Gardner, Gary. *Inspiring Progress: Religions' Contributions to Sustainable Development*. Washington, DC: Worldwatch Institute, 2006.

———. *Invoking the Spirit: Religion and Spirituality in the Quest for a Sustainable World*. Worldwatch Paper 164. Washington, DC: Worldwatch Institute, 2002.

Gatta, John. *Making Nature Sacred: Literature, Religion, and Environment in America from the Puritans to the Present*. New York: Oxford University Press, 2004.

Gebara, Ivone. *Longing for Running Water: Ecofeminism and Liberation*. Minneapolis, MN: Augsburg Fortress, 1999.

Geertz, Clifford. *The Interpretation of Cultures*. New York: Basic Books, 1973.

Giradot, N. J., James Miller, and Liu Xiaogan, eds. *Daoism and Ecology: Ways within a Cosmic Landscape*. Cambridge, MA: Harvard Center for the Study of World Religions, 2001.

Glacken, Clarence. *Traces on the Rhodian Shore: Nature and Culture in Western Thought from Ancient Times to the End of the Eighteenth Century*. Berkeley: University of California Press, 1969.

Goldsmith, Edward. *The Way: An Ecological Worldview*. Athens: University of Georgia, 1998.

Good, Byron. *Medicine, Rationality and Experience: An Anthropological Perspective*. New York: Cambridge University Press, 1994.

Goodenough, Ursula. *The Sacred Depths of Nature*. New York: Oxford University Press, 2000.

Gottlieb, Roger, ed. *A Greener Faith: Religious Environmentalism and Our Planet's Future*. Oxford, England: Oxford University Press, 2006.

———, ed. *Liberating Faith: Religious Values for Justice, Peace, and Ecological Wisdom*. Burlington, VT: Rowan & Littlefield, 2003.

———, ed. *The Oxford Handbook on Religion and Ecology*. New York: Oxford University Press, 2006.

———, ed. *The Sacred Earth*. New York: Routledge, 2003.

Gould, Rebecca. *At Home in Nature: Modern Homesteading and Spiritual Practice in America*. Berkeley: University of California Press, 2005.

Granberg-Michaelson, Wesley. *Redeeming the Creation*. Geneva: World Council of Churches Publication, 1992.

Grim, John A., ed. *Indigenous Traditions and Ecology: The Interbeing of Cosmology and Community*. Cambridge, MA: Harvard Center for the Study of World Religions, 2001.

———. *The Shaman: Patterns of Religious Healing among the Ojibway Indians*. Norman: Oklahoma University Press, 1983.

Haberman, David. *River of Love in an Age of Pollution: The Yamuna River in Northern India*. Berkeley: University of California Press, 2006.

Habermas, Jürgen, et al. *An Awareness of What Is Missing: Faith and Reason in a Post-Secular Age*. Cambridge, MA: Polity, 2010.

Hadot, Pierre. *Philosophy as a Way of Life: Spiritual Exercises from Socrates to Foucault*. New York: Wiley-Blackwell, 1995.

Haeckel, Ernst. *Monism as Connecting Religion and Science: The Confessions of Faith of a Man of Science*, trans. J. Gilchrist. London: Adam and Charles Black, 1895. Reprinted as *O-P Book*. Ann Arbor, MI: Microfilm Xerography: University Microfilms, 1963.

————. *Wonder of Life: A Popular Study of Biological Philosophy*, trans. Joseph McCabe. London: Watts, 1904.

Hallman, D. *Ecotheology: Voices from the South and North*. Maryknoll, NY: Orbis, 1994.

Hargrove, Eugene, ed. *Religion and Environmental Crisis*. Athens: University of Georgia Press, 1986.

Harvey, David. *Justice, Nature, and the Geography of Difference*. Cambridge, MA: Blackwell, 1996.

Hathaway, Mark, and Leonardo Boff. *The Tao and Liberation: Exploring the Ecology of Transformation*. Maryknoll, NY: Orbis, 2009.

Hay, Stephen, ed. *Sources of Indian Tradition*, Vol. 2: *Modern India and Pakistan*. New York: Columbia University Press, 1988.

Hayes, Carlton J. H. *A Generation of Materialism: 1871–1900*. New York: Harper Torchbooks, 1963.

Hefner, Philip. *The Human Factor*. Minneapolis, MN: Augsburg Fortress, 2000.

Hessel, Dieter. *Theology for Earth Community: A Field Guide*. Maryknoll, NY: Orbis, 2003.

Hessel, Dieter, and Rosemary Radford Ruether, eds. *Christianity and Ecology: Seeking the Well-Being of Earth and Humans*. Cambridge, MA: Harvard University Press, 2000.

Hill, Brennan. *Christian Faith and the Environment: Making Vital Connections*. Maryknoll, NY: Orbis, 2007.

Hillel, Daniel. *Natural History of the Bible*. New York: Columbia University Press, 2005.

Hobgood-Oster, Laura. *Holy Dogs and Asses: Animals in the Christian Tradition*. Urbana: University of Illinois Press, 2008.

Hope, Marjorie, and James Young. *Voices of Hope in the Struggle to Save the Planet*. New York: Council on International and Public Affairs, 2000.

Hughes, Donald. *American Indian Ecology*. El Paso, TX: Western Press, 1983.

Hull, Fritz, ed. *Earth and Spirit: The Spiritual Dimension of the Environmental Crisis*. New York: Continuum, 1993.

Hultkrantz, Ake. "Ecology." *Encyclopedia of Religion*. New York: Macmillan; London: Collier Macmillan, 1987.

Izzi Dien, Mawil. *The Environmental Dimensions of Islam*. Cambridge, England: Lutterworth, 2000.

James, William. *The Varieties of Religious Experience*. Rockville, MD: Arc Manor, 2008. Originally published in 1902.

Jenkins, Willis. *Ecologies of Grace: Environmental Ethics and Christian Theology*. New York: Oxford University Press, 2008.

Jenkins, Willis, and Whitney Bauman, eds. *Berkshire Encyclopedia of Sustainability*, Vol. 1: *The Spirit of Sustainability*. Great Barrington, MA: Berkshire, 2009.

Johnston, Mark. *Saving God: Religion after Idolatry*. Princeton, NJ: Princeton University Press, 2009.

Jones, Lindsay, ed. *Encyclopedia of Religion*, 2nd ed. New York: Macmillan/Thompson and Gale, 2005.

Joranson, Philip N. *Cry of the Environment: Rebuilding the Christian Creation Tradition*, ed. Ken Butigan. Santa Fe, NM: Bear & Co., 1984.

Kalland, Arne, ed. *Nature across Cultures: Views of Nature and the Environment in Non-Western Cultures*. Boston: Kluwer, 2003.

Kaufman, Gordon D. *In Face of Mystery: A Constructive Theology.* Cambridge, MA: Harvard University Press, 1993.

Kaza, Stephanie, ed. *Hooked!: Buddhist Writing on Greed, Desire, and the Urge to Consume.* Boston: Shambhala, 2005.

Kaza, Stephanie, and Kenneth Kraft, eds. *Dharma Rain: Sources of Buddhist Environmentalism.* Boston: Shambhala, 2000.

Kearns, Laurel, and Catherine Keller, eds. *Eco-Spirit: Religions and Philosophies for the Earth.* New York: Fordham University Press, 2007.

Kellert, Stephen, and Timothy Farnham, eds. *The Good in Nature and Humanity: Connecting Science and Spirituality with the Natural World.* Washington, DC: Island Press, 2002.

Kellert, Stephen, and E. O. Wilson, eds. *The Biophilia Hypothesis.* Washington, DC: Island Press, 1995.

Kinsley, David. *Ecology and Religion: Ecological Spirituality in Cross-Cultural Perspective.* Englewood Cliffs, NJ: Prentice Hall, 1995.

Kleinman, Arthur. *Patients and Healers in the Context of Culture: An Exploration of the Borderland between Anthropology, Medicine and Psychiatry.* Berkeley: University of California Press, 1980.

Knitter, Paul. *One Earth, Many Religions: Multifaith Dialogue and Global Responsibility.* Maryknoll, NY: Orbis, 1995.

Knitter, Paul, and Chandar Muzaffar, eds. *Subverting Greed: Religious Perspectives on the Global Economy.* Maryknoll, NY: Orbis, 2002.

Kraft, Ken, and Stephanie Kaza, eds. *Dharma Rain: Sources of Buddhist Environmentalism.* Boulder, CO: Shambhala, 2000.

Krech, Shepard III. *The Ecological Indian: Myth and History.* New York: W.W. Norton, 2000.

Küng, Hans, and Karl-Josef Kuschel, eds. *A Global Ethic: The Declaration of the Parliament of the World's Religions.* New York: Continuum, 1993.

Lane, Beldon. *Landscapes of the Sacred: Geography and Narrative in American Spirituality.* Baltimore, MD: Johns Hopkins University Press, 2001.

Lansing, J. Stephen. *Priests and Programmers.* Princeton: Princeton University Press, 2007.

Lee, Peter H., Yôngho Ch'oe, and Hugh H. W. Kang, eds. *Sources of Korean Tradition,* Vol. 1. New York: Columbia University Press, 1996.

Leopold, Aldo. *A Sand County Almanac and Sketches Here and There.* New York: Oxford University Press, 1949.

Light, Andrew, John O'Neill, and Alan Holland. *Environmental Values.* New York: Routledge, 2008.

Lincoln, Bruce. *Priests, Warriors and Cattle: A Study in the Ecology of Religions.* Berkeley: University of California Press, 1981.

Linzey, Andrew. *Animal Theology.* Urbana: University of Illinois Press, 1995.

Lodge, David, and Christopher Hamlin. *Religion and the New Ecology: Environmental Responsibility in a World of Flux.* Notre Dame, IN: University of Notre Dame Press, 2006.

Lovejoy, Arthur. *The Great Chain of Being: A Study of the History of an Idea.* Cambridge, MA: Harvard University Press, 1936.

Lowdermilk, Walter. "Lessons from the Old World to the Americas in Land Use," in

Annual Report of the Board of Regents of the Smithsonian Institution. Washington, DC: Government Printing Office, 1944.

MacArthur, Robert H., and E. O. Wilson, *The Theory of Island Biogeography.* Princeton, NJ: Princeton University Press, 1967.

Macy, Johanna. *Mutual Causality in Buddhism and General Systems Theory: The Dharma of Natural System.* Albany: State University of New York Press, 1991.

Macy, Johanna, and Molly Young Brown, eds. *Coming Back to Life: Practices to Reconnect Our Lives, Our World.* Gabriola Island, BC: New Society Publishers, 1998.

Maguire, Daniel. *The Moral Core of Judaism and Christianity: Reclaiming the Revolution.* Philadelphia: Fortress, 1993.

Marsh, George Perkins. *Man and Nature, or Physical Geography as Modified by Human Action.* New York: Charles Scribner, 1865.

Marshall, Peter. *Nature's Web: Rethinking Our Place on Earth.* New York: M.E. Sharpe, 1996.

Martin-Schramm, James, and Robert Stivers. *Christian Environmental Ethics: A Case Method Approach.* Maryknoll, NY: Orbis, 2003.

Masuzawa, Tomoko. *The Invention of World Religions, or, How European Universalism Was Preserved in the Language of Pluralism.* Chicago: University of Chicago Press, 2005.

Matthews, Clifford, Mary Evelyn Tucker, and Philip Hefner, eds. *When Worlds Converge: What Science and Religions Tell Us about the Story of the Universe and Our Place in It.* Chicago: Open Court, 2001.

McCleary, Timothy, and Magdalene Medicine Horse. *The Stars We Know: Crow Indian Astronomy and Lifeways.* Prospect Heights, IL: Waveland, 1997.

McCord, Edward L. *The Value of Species.* New Haven, CT: Yale University Press, 2012.

McDaniel, Jay. *Of Gods and Pelicans: A Theology of Reverence for Life.* Louisville, KY: Westminster/John Knox Press, 1989.

———. *With Roots and Wings: Christianity in an Age of Ecology and Dialogue.* Maryknoll, NY: Orbis, 1995.

McDuff, Mallory. *Natural Saints: How People Are Working to Save God's Earth.* New York: Oxford University Press, 2010.

———. *Sacred Acts: How Churches Are Working to Protect Earth's Climate.* Gabriola Island, BC: New Society Publishers, 2012.

McFague, Sallie. *The Body of God: An Ecological Theology.* Minneapolis, MN: Fortress, 1993.

———. *Life Abundant: Rethinking Theology and Economy for a Planet in Peril.* Minneapolis, MN: Fortress, 2000.

———. *Models of God: Theology for an Ecological Nuclear Age.* Philadelphia: Fortress, 1987.

———. *A New Climate for Theology: God, the World and Global Warming.* Minneapolis, MN: Fortress, 2008.

McGrath, Alister. *The Reenchantment of Nature: The Denial of Religion and the Ecological Crisis.* New York: Doubleday, 2002.

McNeill, J. R. *Something New under the Sun: An Environmental History of the 20th Century World.* New York: W.W. Norton, 2000.

Merchant, Carolyn. *The Death of Nature: Women, Ecology and the Scientific Revolution.* San Francisco, CA: Harper and Row, 1980.

Miller, Char. *Gifford Pinchot and the Making of Modern Environmentalism.* Washington, DC: Island Press, 2001.

Miller, James. *The Way of Highest Clarity: Nature, Vision, and Revelation in Medieval China.* Magdalena, NM: Three Pines Press, 2008. Distributed by University of Hawaii Press.

Mische, Patricia, and Melissa Merklin, eds. *Toward a Global Civilization? The Contributions of Religions.* New York: Peter Lang, 2001.

Moltmann, Jurgen. *God in Creation: A New Theology of Creation and the Spirit of God,* trans. M. Kohl. San Francisco, CA: Harper and Row, 1985.

Murata, Sachiko, and William Chittick. *The Vision of Islam.* London: I.B. Tauris, 2000.

Murphy, Tim. *The Politics of Spirit: Phenomenology, Genealogy, Religion.* Albany: State University of New York Press, 2010.

Nabokov, Peter. *Native American Architecture.* Oxford, England: Oxford University Press, 1990.

Nash, Roderick. *The Rights of Nature: A History of Environmental Ethics.* Madison: University of Wisconsin Press, 1989.

Nasr, Seyyed Hossein. *Man and Nature: The Spiritual Crisis in Modern Man.* Dunstable, England: ABC International Group; Chicago: Distributed by KAZI Publications, 1997.

———. *Religion and the Order of Nature.* New York: Oxford University Press, 1996.

Neidjie, Bill. *Story about Feeling.* Broome, Australia: Magabala Books, 1989.

Nelson, Lance, ed. *Purifying the Earthly Body of God.* Albany: State University of New York Press, 1998.

Nelson, Richard. *Make Prayers to the Raven: A Koyukon View of the Northern Forest.* Chicago: University of Chicago Press, 1983.

Nhat Hanh, Thich. *The Heart of Understanding: Commentaries on the Prajnaparamita Heart Sutra.* Berkeley, CA: Parallax, 1995.

Odum, Eugene. *Ecology and Our Endangered Life-Support Systems.* Stanford, CT: Sinauer, 1989.

Odum, Howard. *Environment, Power and Society.* New York: Wiley-Interscience, 1971.

Oelschlaeger, Max. *Caring for Creation: An Ecumenical Approach to the Environmental Crisis.* New Haven, CT: Yale University Press, 1994.

Osborn, Fairfield. *Our Plundered Planet.* Boston: Little, Brown, 1948.

Otto, Rudolf. *Idea of the Holy.* Oxford, England: Oxford University Press, 1923. Originally published in 1917 as *Das Heilige.*

Palmer, Clare. *Animal Ethics in Context.* New York: Columbia University Press 2010.

Peet, Richard, and Michael Watts. *Liberation Ecologies: Environment, Development and Social Movements.* New York: Routledge, 1996.

Pinchot, Gifford. *Breaking New Ground.* Washington, DC: Island Press, 1998. Originally published in 1947.

Queen, Christopher. *Engaged Buddhism in the West.* Somerville, MA: Wisdom Publications, 2000.

Queen, Sarah. *From Chronicle to Canon: The Hermeneutics of the Spring and Autumn Annals According to Tung Chung-shu.* Cambridge, England: Cambridge University Press, 1996.

Rapport, Roy A. *Pigs for the Ancestors: Ritual in the Ecology of a New Guinea People.* New York: Oxford University Press, 1969.

Rasmussen, Larry. *Earth Community, Earth Ethics.* Maryknoll, NY: Orbis, 1997.

———. *Earth-Honoring Faith: Religious Ethics in a New Key.* New York: Oxford University Press, 2013.

Raymo, Chet. *When God Is Gone, Everything Is Holy: The Making of a Religious Naturalist.* Notre Dame, IN: Sorin Books, 2008.

Reaka-Kudla, Marjorie, Don Wilson, and Edward O. Wilson. *Biodiversity II: Understanding and Protecting Our Biological Resources.* Washington, DC: Joseph Henry Press, 1997.

Robbins, Frank. *The Hexaemeral Literature: A Study of the Greek and Latin Commentaries on Genesis.* Chicago: University of Chicago Press, 1912.

Rockefeller, Steven, and John Elder, eds. *Spirit and Nature: Why the Environment Is a Religious Issue.* Boston: Beacon, 1991.

Rolston, Holmes III. *Conserving Natural Value.* New York: Columbia University Press, 1994.

———. *A New Environmental Ethics: The Next Millennium for Life on Earth.* New York: Routledge, 2012.

Ronnow, Tarjei. *Saving Nature.* New Brunswick, NJ: Transaction Publishers, 2006.

Rowe, John Stanley. *Earth Alive: Essays on Ecology,* ed. Don Kerr. Edmonton, AB: NeWest Press, 2006.

Ruether, Rosemary Radford. *Gaia and God: An Ecofeminist Theology of Earth Healing.* San Francisco, CA: HarperSanFrancisco, 1992.

Santmire, Paul. *The Travail of Nature: The Ambiguous Ecological Promise of Christian Theology.* Philadelphia: Fortress, 1985.

Schielke, Samuli, and Liza Debevec, eds. *Ordinary Lives and Grand Schemes: An Anthropology of Everyday Religion.* New York: Berghahn, 2012.

Schmidt, Oswald. *Ecology and Ecosystem Conservation.* Washington, DC: Island Press, 2007.

Scott, Peter. *A Political Theology of Nature.* Cambridge, England: Cambridge University Press, 2003.

Sears, Paul. *Deserts on the March,* 4th ed. Norman: University of Oklahoma, 1980.

Selin, Helaine, ed. *Nature across Cultures: Views of Nature and the Environment in Non-Western Cultures.* Norwell, MA: Kluwer, 2003.

Shivaraksha, Sulak. *Seeds of Peace: A Buddhist Vision for Renewing Society.* Berkeley: Parallax Press, 1992.

Sideris, Lisa. *Environmental Ethics, Ecological Theology, and the Natural Sciences.* New York: Columbia University Press, 2003.

Singer, Peter. *One World: The Ethics of Globalization.* New Haven, CT: Yale University Press, 2002.

Snyder, Gary. *The Gary Snyder Reader: Prose, Poetry, and Translations, 1952–1998.* Washington, DC: Counterpoint, 1999.

———. *The Practice of the Wild.* San Francisco, CA: North Point Press, 1990.

Soper, David E. *The Geography of Religions.* Englewood Cliffs, NJ: Prentice Hall, 1967.

Spencer, Daniel. *Gay and Gaia: Ethics, Ecology, and the Erotic.* Cleveland: Pilgrim Press, 1996.

Speth, James Gustave. *America the Possible: Manifesto for a New Economy.* New Haven, CT: Yale University Press, 2012.

———. *Bridge at the Edge of the World.* New Haven, CT: Yale University Press, 2008.

Spinoza, Baruck. *Ethics.* Vol. 1 of *The Collected Works of Spinoza,* ed. and trans. Edwin Curley. Princeton, NJ: Princeton University Press, 1985.

Sponsel, Leslie. *Spiritual Ecology: A Quiet Revolution.* Santa Barbara, CA: Praeger, 2012.

Spring, David, and Eileen Spring, eds. *Ecology and Religion in History.* New York: Harper & Row, 1974.

Steward, Julian. *Evolution and Ecology: Essays on Social Transformation.* Urbana: University of Illinois Press, 1977.

Sutter, Paul. *Driven Wild: How the Fight against Automobiles Launched the Modern Wilderness Movement.* Seattle: University of Washington, 2002.

Swidler, Leonard. *Stepping Stones to a Global Ethic,* ed. Marcus Braybrooke. London: SCM Press, 1992.

Swimme, Brian. *The Hidden Heart of the Cosmos: Humanity and the New Story.* Maryknoll, NY: Orbis, 1999.

Swimme, Brian, and Thomas Berry. *The Universe Story: From the Primordial Flaring Forth to the Ecozoic Era—A Celebration of the Unfolding of the Cosmos.* San Francisco, CA: HarperSanFrancisco, 1992.

Swimme, Brian, and Mary Evelyn Tucker. *Journey of the Universe.* New Haven, CT: Yale University Press, 2011.

Szerszynski, Bronislaw. *Nature, Technology and the Sacred.* Oxford, England: Blackwell, 2005.

Taylor, Bron. *Dark Green Religion: Nature Spirituality and the Planetary Future.* Berkeley: University of California Press, 2009.

———, ed. *Encyclopedia of Religion and Nature,* 2 vols. New York: Continuum International, 2005.

Taylor, Charles. *A Secular Age.* Cambridge, MA: Harvard University Press, 2007.

Taylor, Sarah. *Green Sisters: A Spiritual Ecology.* Cambridge, MA: Harvard University Press, 2007.

Teeuwen, Mark, and Fabio Rambelli, eds. *Buddhas and Kami in Japan: Honji Suijaku as a Combinatory Paradigm.* London: RoutledgeCurzon, 2002.

Thomas, William Jr., ed. *Man's Role in Changing the Face of the Earth.* Chicago: University of Chicago Press, 1956.

Thomashow, Mitchell. *Bringing the Biosphere Home: Learning to Perceive Global Environmental Change.* Cambridge, MA: MIT Press, 2002.

Tirosh-Samuelson, Hava, ed. *Judaism and Ecology: Created World and Revealed Word.* Cambridge, MA: Harvard Center for the Study of World Religions, 2003.

Tu Weiming. "Beyond the Enlightenment Mentality," in *Worldviews and Ecology: Religion, Philosophy, and the Environment,* ed. Mary Evelyn Tucker and John Grim. Maryknoll, NY: Orbis, 2006, 19–29.

———. *Centrality and Commonality: An Essay on Confucian Religiousness.* Albany: State University of New York Press, 1989.

———. *Confucian Thought: Selfhood as Creative Transformation.* Albany: State University of New York Press, 1985.

Tu Weiming and Mary Evelyn Tucker, eds. *Confucian Spirituality,* 2 vols. New York: Crossroad, 2003, 2004.

Tuan, Yi-Fu. *Topophilia: A Study of Environmental Perception, Attitudes and Values.* Englewood Cliffs, NJ: Prentice Hall, 1974.

Tucker, Mary Evelyn. "Globalization and the Environment," in *Globalization and Catholic Social Thought,* ed. John Coleman and William Ryan. Maryknoll, NY: Orbis, 2005.

———. *The Philosophy of Qi: The Record of Great Doubts.* New York: Columbia University Press, 2007.

————. *Worldly Wonder: Religions Enter Their Ecological Phase.* Chicago: Open Court, 2003.

Tucker, Mary Evelyn, and John Berthrong, eds. *Confucianism and Ecology: The Interrelation of Heaven, Earth, and Humans.* Cambridge, MA: Harvard Center for the Study of World Religions, 1998.

Tucker, Mary Evelyn, and John Grim, eds. *Religion and Ecology: Can the Climate Change? Daedalus* 130(4), Cambridge, MA: American Academy of Arts and Sciences, Fall 2001, online at http://http://amcad.org/content/publications/publication.aspx?d=845.

————. *Worldviews and Ecology: Religion, Philosophy and the Environment.* Maryknoll, NY: Orbis, 1994.

Tucker, Mary Evelyn, and Duncan Ryukan Williams, eds. *Buddhism and Ecology: The Interconnection of Dharma and Deeds.* Cambridge, MA: Harvard Center for the Study of World Religions, 1997.

Twiss, Sumner, and Bruce Grelle, eds. *Explorations in Global Ethics: Comparative Religious Ethics and Interreligious Dialogue.* Boulder, CO: Westview, 1998.

Uhl, Christopher. *Developing Ecological Consciousness: The End of Separation.* New York: Rowman & Littlefield, 2013.

van Berkel, Klaus, and Arjo Vanderjagt. *The Book of Nature in Antiquity and Middle Ages.* Leuven, the Netherlands: Peeters, 2005.

————. *The Book of Nature in Early Modern and Modern History.* Leuven, the Netherlands: Peeters, 2006.

Vecsey, Christopher, and Robert Venables, eds. *American Indian Environments: Ecological Issues in Native American History.* Syracuse, NY: Syracuse University Press, 1980.

Waldau, Paul, and Kimberley Patton, eds. *Communion of Subjects: Animals in Religion, Science, and Ethics.* New York: Columbia University Press, 2006.

Wallace, Mark. *Finding God in the Singing River.* Minneapolis, MN: Fortress, 2005.

Warren, Julianne. *Aldo Leopold's Odyssey: Rediscovering the Author of* A Sand County Almanac. Washington, DC: Island Press, 2006.

Waskow, Arthur, ed. *Torah of the Earth.* Woodstock, VT: Jewish Lights, 2000.

Webb, Benjamin, ed. *Fugitive Faith: Conversations on Spiritual, Environmental, and Community Renewal.* Maryknoll, NY: Orbis, 1998.

Weeramantry, C. G. *Tread Lightly on the Earth: Religion, the Environment and the Human Future.* Pannipitiya, Sri Lanka: Stamford Lake, 2009.

White, Lynn, Jr. "The Historical Roots of Our Ecologic Crisis." *Science* 155(3767) (March 1967):1203–7.

Wilkinson, Katharine. *Between God & Green: How Evangelicals Are Cultivating a Middle Ground on Climate Change.* Oxford, England: Oxford University Press, 2012.

Wilson, E. O. *The Creation: An Appeal to Save Life on Earth.* New York: W.W. Norton, 2006.

Wirzba, Norman. *The Paradise of God: Renewing Religion in an Ecological Age.* New York: Columbia University Press, 2003.

Worster, Donald. *Nature's Economy: A History of Ecological Ideas.* Cambridge, MA: Cambridge University Press, 1994. Originally published in 1977.

————. *A Passion for Nature: The Life of John Muir.* New York: Oxford University Press, 2008.

Yôngho Ch'oe, Peter H. Lee, and William Theodore de Bary, eds. *Sources of Korean Tradition,* Vol. 2: *From the Sixteenth to the Twentieth Centuries.* New York: Columbia University Press, 2000.

Index

Note: page numbers followed by "f" refer to figures.

Island Press | Board of Directors